Social Welfare, Aging, and Social Theory

Social Welfare, Aging, and Social Theory

Jason L. Powell and John Martyn Chamberlain

LEXINGTON BOOKS
Lanham • Boulder • New York • Toronto • Plymouth, UK

Published by Lexington Books
A wholly owned subsidiary of The Rowman & Littlefield Publishing Group, Inc.
4501 Forbes Boulevard, Suite 200, Lanham, Maryland 20706
http://www.lexingtonbooks.com

Estover Road, Plymouth PL6 7PY, United Kingdom

British Library Cataloguing in Publication Information Available

Library of Congress Cataloging-in-Publication Data
Powell, Jason L., 1971–
  Social welfare, aging, and social theory / Jason L. Powell and John Martyn
Chamberlain.
       p. cm.
Includes index.
  ISBN 978-0-7391-4777-1 (cloth : alk. paper)—ISBN 978-0-7391-4778-8 (pbk. : alk.
paper)
  1. Gerontology—Philosophy. 2. Aging. 3. Postmodernism. I. Chamberlain, John
Martyn, 1972– II. Powell, Jason L., 1971– Social theory and aging. III. Title.
  HQ1061.P684 2012
  305.2601—dc23   2011030971

Printed in the United States of America

Contents

Acknowledgments

I would like to thank family and friends for their unstinting support and for giving me the space to co-author this book with Dr. Chamberlain. I have enjoyed working with Dr. Chamberlain. This book is dedicated to Stella Powell, Elizabeth Hawkins, Rebekah Hawkins, Angela Powell and the late Edward Cropper. I would like to acknowledge Rick Moody, Tim May and the late Charles 'Chuck' Longino. Without doubt, the support they have given me over the years has been amazing.

Jason L. Powell

I would like to say thank you to my fellow triathletes from Merseyside Triathlon Club for reminding me what is really important in life. Thanks also to Irene, Shelly, Gemma and Andy for all the support they have given me over the years.

John Martyn Chamberlain

Chapter 1

The Relationship of Social Theory and Aging:
A Critical Exegesis

INTRODUCTION

This book explores theoretical issues that impinge on understanding aging in modern society. It analyzes how knowledge formation of aging is socially constituted and positioned by powerful taken-for-granted assumptions. These assumptions have provided a power/knowledge base for biomedical disciplines, the legitimacy of political-economic discourses, and the practices of professional experts.

Given this objective, the book explores theoretical issues about the ontological status of knowledge, examining and moving beyond conventional biomedical philosophical dualisms of "aging as decline"/"decline as aging." Indeed, Michel Foucault's (1977) notion that we are governed by means of social processes by which we affirm our freedom is highly pertinent. The informed use of "thinking tools" from social theory shatters those taken-for-granted assumptions about constructions of aging, its biomedical contestations, and theoretical relationships of macro/micro, local/global and object/subject to issues of culture, body, power/knowledge, risk and narrative.

The book is in two parts. The first part introduces "modernist" scientific models and theories of gerontology and questions their importance in mapping out the assumptions of aging and how they impinge on identity performance in society through a disciplinary matrix of biology, psychology, and social conceptualizations of gerontology; the second part focuses upon "postmodern" constructions of aging through the articulation and development of novel epistemologies: postmodernism and aging body; discourse and power/knowledge; and "aging" in the "risk society."

Indeed, the book addresses a key question: Can "meta-theories" provide an effective analysis of aging that is radically different from modernist "grand narratives" as epitomized not only by biomedical models of aging but also by mainstream social theories of gerontology inclusive of modernist epistemes of Functionalist theories of activity and disengagement, feminist gerontology, and the political economy of old age?

The acclaimed sociologist C. Wright Mills, in *The Sociological Imagination* (1959) powerfully illustrates that the sociologist seeks, first, to understand the relationship of personal troubles and public issues and the intersection of biography and history; then, these polarities, and the ways in which sociologists address them, define the central problems of social theory in modernity. Mills further argues that the role of the sociologist is to reveal the connections between what is going on in the world and what may be happening within ourselves—in other words, "to grasp history and biography and the relations between the two within society." Mills believed that sociologists develop a quality of mind that enables them to show individuals how their own private troubles may be linked to features of the "public world" of modernity.

Modernity itself was a "war of liberation" and a "war against mystery and magic" (Bauman 1992, x). It was thought that the world should be despiritualized and instead replaced with "Big Science" (Bauman 1992, x). The "master narrative" of "progress" became the new "God," "rational" replaced "irrational," and truth became the new "mission." In modernity the ultimate goals of progress and the mastery of nature became assumed and unquestioned, just as God had gone unquestioned in religious faith (Bauman 1992, xiv). Zygmunt Bauman has suggested that a distinguishing characteristic of modernity was the desperate search for a structured world. In which a search for social facts, such as the ways in which individuals come together in societies through a "social contract," or the ways in which "social facts" may determine individual behavior, continue to be debated along with newer concerns with levels of analysis, freedom, determinism, and morality. Indeed, in recent years the German philosopher Jürgen Habermas (1992) has presented us with the doctrine of dialogical morality in modernity, which suggests that the identification of freedom must be arrived at collectively by all those agents likely to be affected by its adoption.

As a rival to the modernist preoccupation with macro grand narratives of "progress" and "reason," postmodernism became increasingly fashionable in its epistemological war against grand narratives. It brought with it an "anything goes" social context "which renounces purity, mastery of form and elitism and is more playful, ironic and eclectic in style" (Thompson 1992, 227).

Postmodernism not only affects culture but also impinges on a range of developments in all areas of Western society, such as politics, industry, and the media and the rise of social movements, ultimately leading to the development of a postmodern world characterized by "fragmentation, multiplicity, plurality and indeterminacy" (Thompson 1992, 223). If this characterization is correct, it has had strong implications for the Enlightenment aims and values of modernist approaches of social theory. It is the acceptance that modern aims of universalism are futile and the recognition of "pluralism of cultures, communal traditions, ideologies, 'forms of life' or 'language games'" (Bauman 1992, 102). Whereas for modernists such as Habermas (1992) universalism of collective action is central to determine social change in a social world, for postmodernism (Powell and Longino 2001) microprocesses of individualization, subjectification, and risk are part of fragmented social spaces, through which identities are formed and performed, that will run counter to macro processes.

Henceforth, the interpretation of the positioning of aging as macro- and fixed explanations or micro- and fluid existentialism lies at the heart of modern-postmodern debates within contemporary culture that are plugged into a contestation of "aging": How is aging defined? What constitutes the aging process? How relevant is science in its understanding? This demands interrogation from transparent theoretical perspectives.

Clearly what is striking is that one of the major problems of understanding aging in recent years is that it has evidently not been directed by social theory (Powell and Longino 2002). Indeed, theoretical innovations in gerontology have, according to Vern L. Bengston and colleagues (1997), fallen behind other sociological master narratives of race, class, and gender. Linda George (1995, 77) consolidates this by claiming that gerontological research has been "theoretically sterile." For example, in a study of published refereed articles in eight leading North American gerontology journals (as listed in the Social Science Citation Index) from 1990 to 1995, Bengston and colleagues (1997) claimed that 80 percent of the refereed articles lacked a theoretical framework. Bengston and colleagues (1997) further argue that social gerontology, a dimension of gerontology, has been "itty-bitty" in its development of theoretical frameworks to assist an understanding of an important issue such as aging: "it is intellectually irresponsible for a program of research to proceed without a theory" (Bengston, Burgess, and Parrot 1997, 73).

Ironically part of the problem about lack of social theory in the study of aging relates to the field of gerontology itself. Gerontology as a scientific discipline has been dominated with a preoccupation with biomedical sciences and its constituent elements of "decline" models of biology and psychology (Estes and Binney 1989; Longino and Powell 2004). Gerontology based on social theories of aging sees aging as a socially constructed category with differential epistemological prisms: for example, functionalism and feminist gerontology. However, while both definitions are fundamental to the complexities of aging in the social world, the theoretical interpretations of aging are in their "infancy" (Estes, Biggs, and Phillipson 2003; Alley, Putney, and Rice 2010).

If we take the disciplinary dimensions of gerontology, we can illuminate both the relevance and importance they have for understanding the social construction of aging, as well as raising questions about the development of theorizing from wider social theory. We can suggest that gerontology has two focal points in its broad conceptualization: (1) gerontology as science and (2) gerontology as social theory.

Gerontology as "Science"

One of the cornerstones of modern gerontology has been a belief in "science" and "progress" as constituting "discursive practices that give rise to epistemological figures, sciences and possibly formalised systems" (Foucault 1972, 191). Such powerful discourses systematize networks of ideas about the "nature" of aging, the reasons for particular behaviors, and the ways individuals may be classified, selected, and controlled (Alley, Putney, and Rice 2010). The "project of modernity" has inspired the disciplinary development of gerontology to reconstruct aging on the basis of individual abilities, needs, and functions. The aging subject is constructed as an object of knowledge and as a seeker of that knowledge. This tension gives gerontology its character. On the one hand, it produces the subject as an empirically verifiable entity, and on the other, it produces a critical inquiry into the empirical conditions that justify the existence of subjects. Hence, we get a developmental duality of an empirical and transcendental entity. Indeed, knowledge formation in Western gerontology in particular is modeled and characterized by quantitative, positivist, and scientific discourses (Katz 1996; Powell 2001b; Biggs and Powell 2001; Powell and Biggs 2000; Longino and Powell 2004; Alley, Putney, and Rice 2010). Traditional forms of medical-scientific expertise and knowledge under the rubric of the "biomedical model" have attempted to foster understanding of aging and construct "worldview" "truths" about aging that are perceived as "master narratives" (Powell 2001b). Master narratives are dense forms of discourse containing alleged universal truths, totalizing views and symbols with which to explain and understand almost every aspect of social life. These narratives play a central role in the construction of physical and symbolic boundaries, and it is through them that social groups come to know and understand the social world and constitute the classification of perceived aging identities (Biggs and Powell 2001).

Such scientific narratives construct a particular positioning of aging. For example, Bytheway (1995) suggests the notion of "growth" is a central scientific discourse relating to the true changes to the biological body associated with human aging. Growth is seen as a positive development by biologists (Bytheway

1995) in that a baby grows into a child who grows into an adult, but then, instead of growing into old age, the person declines. This scientific sanctioned perception is that growth slows when a person reaches "old age" and is subsequently interpreted as decline rather than as change, which is taken for granted with earlier life-course transitions. These narratives can be understood as textual formations composed by a complex set of truth codes and conventions through which scientifically grounded and privileged forms of true knowledge strive to present their worldviews as universal and hence valid for the whole of society.

Hence, aging is a site upon which power games are played out mainly through such narratives. As Biggs and Powell point out: ". . . narratives are not simply personal fictions that we choose to live by, but are discourses that are subject to social and historical influence" (2001, 113).Coupled with this, the totalizing views of biomedical science, as Longino and Powell (2004) have pointed out, make a particular representation of the world seem so natural that aging, for example, cannot be imagined as an alternative discourse except as an abnormality that can be understood only through biomedical science.

However, the objectivity and neutrality of scientific knowledge expressed in broad approaches such as the biomedical model can be understood as rhetorical surfaces that obscure subterranean, politically structured orders. Coupled with this, it has become increasingly clear that a "scientific" knowledge formation lacks appropriate language for discussing theoretical and philosophical concerns or appreciating their historical and contemporary cultural contexts (Kastenbaum 1993). Therefore, as Katz (1996) has identified, aging is not just a scientific process, and for this reason it cannot be singularly analyzed via "disciplines" such as "biomedical gerontology." Furthermore, according to Katz (1996, 55), the effects of the "decline" analogy can be seen in the dominance of biomedical arguments about the physiological "problems" of the "aging body." Indeed, the master narrative of biological decline hides the location of a complex web of intersections of negative ideas constituting a culture of aging (Powell 2001c). Foucault suggests that the surveillance of bodies was central to the development of modern regimes of power and knowledge or what Estes (1979) calls "aging enterprises"—which are institutions created to manage the "problems" of aging, from social services to nursing care through to social work with older people (Powell and Biggs 2003 Bengtson et al 2009).

We address this in chapters 2 and 3, with an eliciting of scientific assumptions, but it is a question constantly reflected upon throughout the book. The biomedical model is a powerful discipline and practice, but for Powell and Biggs, it obscures wider understanding of gerontology: "It appears . . . that established and emerging master narratives of biological decline yet linked through the importance of techniques for maintenance . . . via medicalized bodily control. However, this focus on medicalization . . . has tended to obscure another . . . discourse on aging . . . the association between old age and social theory" (2000, 95).

Gerontology as Social Theory

The theoretical concerns of positivist biomedical disciplinarity have significant implications for the social discourses that impinge upon the social construction of aging. How have these social discourses and policy implications been interpreted via theories of social gerontology?

A striking feature of theoretical frameworks of aging is that the majority of studies are relatively small in scale (Moody 1998). Despite Functionalist (Cumming and Henry 1961), Marxist (Phillipson 1982, 1998; Walker 1981), feminist (Arber and Ginn 1995) and postmodern (Featherstone and Wernick 1995; Gilleard and Higgs 2000) forms of gerontological analysis, gerontology has remained "theoretically sterile" in comparison with other social science disciplines such as political science and criminology (George 1995); as an apparently "applied" field of gerontological study it has remained "itty-bitty" (Bengston, Burgess, and Parrot 1997) in theorizing aging. Bengston and Schaie (1999) also claim that theoretical developments in gerontology have at best a limited history (1999, 41). Katz (1996, 42) consolidates this by claiming that the use of aging in ways that are informed by the cultivation of wider social theories of postmodernism and Foucauldian studies, for example, is relatively unknown territory.

In order to add and develop the relationship of aging and contemporary social theory in an area left "uncharted," this book contributes to, and strengthens, the critical interconnection between aging and contemporary social theories of aging body, power/knowledge, discourse, and subjectivity and risk. While, for example, postmodernism, Foucauldian theory, and risk are challenging other disciplinary fields in social science, mainstream social gerontology is impermeable (Estes, Biggs, and Phillipson 2003). Surrounded by its biomedical paradigms, gerontology fails to recognize that its most imaginative developments come from the critical and cutting-edge theories of those scholars who transcend so-called fixed disciplinary boundaries. It is therefore timely that this book is written when serious questions (Phillipson 1998; George 1995; Bengston, Burgess, and Parrot 1997; and Biggs 1999) are being raised about the limited development of wider social theory in social gerontology.

Despite this, the "biomedical" study of aging has dominated the disciplinary development of gerontology which has masked the historical development in theorizing aging (Katz 1996). The biomedical model problematizes aging as a pathological "problem" tied to discourses of "decline," "dependency," "decay," "abnormality," and "deterioration" (Powell 2002). Thus, the problem orientation to aging is historically configured in biomedical sciences and discourses that specialize in the medical reductionism of gerontology (Powell 2001a; Powell and Biggs 2000; Biggs and Powell 2001). As Foucault pointed out: "It [is] a matter of analyzing . . . the problematizations through which being offers itself to be, necessarily, thought—and the practices on the basis of which these prob-lematizations are formed" (Foucault 1977, 11).

The biomedical problematization of aging has secreted wider questions of power, inequality, and culture, and the growth in "social aspects" of aging has developed as a direct challenge to the authority of biomedical power and knowledge. The purpose of this book is not only to challenge such knowledge formation but also to map out the terrain of evocative modern and postmodern theories and their contestations and insights for understanding aging. It has only been in the past few years that social theory has been taken seriously within ger-ontology (Estes, Biggs, and Phillipson 2003; Bengtson et al 2009).

Following comments by Bengston and colleagues (2009) on the lack of social theory in aging studies, the embryonic state of a sociological analysis of aging can be judged from the lack of refinement of the term "age." In Western socie-ties, an individual's age is counted on a chronological foundation, beginning from birth to the current point of age, or when an individual has died. Counting age is a social construction because it is a practice underpinned by conceptions of time in regional, national, and global spaces (Powell 2001b), which came to be of increasing importance with the development of industrial capitalism (Phil-lipson 1982).

Furthermore, age has three main focal points of interest to its theorization. First, age and aging have a biological and physiological dimension, so that over time and space the appearances of physical bodies change (Longino and Powell 2004). Second, the aging of an individual takes place within a particular period of time and space. Third, as individuals, society has a number of culturally and socially defined expectations how people of certain ages are supposed to behave and how they are positioned and classified. "Old age," for instance, is difficult to define, especially for the state and its institutional branches. For example, for the United Kingdom's "Department of Pensions and Work," the legal concept of "pensionable age" has defined "old age" at sixty-five (Biggs 1999). The De-partment of Health's National Service Framework defines "old age" at fifty (Powell 2001c), yet the same U.K. department states that those people requiring intensive health services such as hospitals have been predominantly those older people aged seventy-five and over (Age Concern England 1997; Phillipson 1998). The British state is uncertain what old age can be defined as, but it is clear that biomedical models of aging and their viewpoints do influence societal perceptions of aging that impinge on social processes such as life zones of "health," "work," and "retirement" (Phillipson 1998).

It is particularly apt, then, to attempt to ground developments in a social theory that can be applied to questioning what we understand by "aging." It is also clear that theoretical perspectives need to be documented and analyzed in the light of the triumvirate of social, political, and economic transformations in Western society over the past fifty years. Indeed, the book also reflects on the modern/postmodern duality and how this continual provocative debate in social theory impinges on aging studies, by paying particular attention to examples drawn from biomedicine, social theory, popular culture, power relations, and risk.

MAPPING OUT THE TERRAIN:
MODERN AND POSTMODERN THEORIES OF AGING

What is a theory? A theory asks why a particular analogy is used to explain what is meant by aging and how the assumptions contained within bio-medicine and policy spaces influence our understanding of the position of older people in contemporary society. Theories of aging are important in establishing frameworks for understanding, interpreting, and problematizing aging, how the processes of aging are contested and negotiated, and the interplay between various levels at which social relations take place—including hitherto neglected aspects of aging experience such as inequality, body and identity, technologies of power, and subjectivity of the risk society.

Ironically, the solutions to the "problems of aging" are tractable to disciplines such as gerontology because they seem to promise answers to age prejudice and marginalization (Chudacoff 1989). For example, biomedical "solutions" address fears about mental and physical incapacity (Longino and Powell 2004). Medicine, with its focus on individual organic pathology and interventions, has also become a powerful and pervasive force in the definition and treatment of aging. The resulting "biomedicalization of aging" (Estes and Binney 1989) socially constructs old age as a process of decremental physical decline and places aging under the domain and control of biomedicine. It also encourages certain forms of the politics of aging: a focus on age as a question of social welfare and a particular interpretation of the effects of risk and individualization. Theories of aging, albeit in contrasting ways, see these phenomena as indicating particular sites of resistance in which dominant biomedical conceptualizations of aging are to be contested and alternative explanations can be intimated.

For example, in stark contrast to the biomedical approach, the "political economy of old age" theoretical approach examines the structural inequalities that shape the everyday experience of growing old in modern society (phillipson 1998).

THE ORGANIZATION OF THE BOOK

This book attempts to identify two central areas for the study of aging and the epistemological differences and continuities between them: constructions of aging (modern) and deconstructions of aging (postmodern). The book focuses on three general issues. One is the biomedical model and aging and its conceptual contestation. Another is the emergence of modernist social theories of aging, including the influence and dominance of three particular approaches: functionalist sociology and aging, political economy of old age and State power, and feminist approaches to aging. The book then attempts to move beyond these paradigms, with more of a focus on alternative and novel ways of theorizing aging through postmodernism and the aging body; Foucauldian approaches of power relations, surveillance and old age, risk, and aging identity; and, finally, "new horizons, old questions": rethinking social theory and aging.

Chapter 2 provides a historical grounding to the critique of biological and psychological models of aging found in chapters 3 and 4. The chapter outlines the origins of the Western medical tradition in early Greek natural philosophy and the work of two key founding figures of modern medicine: Hippocrates and Galen. It trances the influence of Galen's humoral medicine on medical practice and the care of the embodied self in Europe during the ecclesiastical middle ages up until the birth of modern biomedicine in the French clinics of the eighteenth and nineteenth centuries. In doing so it highlights how the biomedical model focuses on physical processes—the pathology, the biochemistry and the physiology of the body—when conceptualizing the body and the aging process.

Chapter 3 focuses on modern constructions of aging. Leading on from chapter 2, this chapter identifies aging as a biomedically constructed concept. The medical dimension of aging and the body are to be mapped out in relation to how old age has been categorized in modern society. The chapter allows the reader to understand how aging has been positioned by the dominant assumptions that underpin the biomedical gaze in contemporary society. The chapter locates biological and psychological models of aging and analyzes the prevalent discourses of aging that have helped to shape the perceptions of aging and the alleged limitations of such processes. The chapter also looks at counterexplanations of aging derived from social conceptual examinations, especially through the prism of social construction of aging (in particular on demography as a social category).

Chapter 4 examines the postwar development of social theory and its relationship to the study of adult aging. Theoretical coverage of aging can be located to the early postwar years with Western government concern about the consequences of demographic change and the shortage of younger people in the U.S. and U.K. workforces (Phillipson 1998). In the postwar years, particular social theories surfaced which attempted to act in response to the social, health, and economic policy implications and projections of demographic change.

Alongside this the chapter also traces the rise and consolidation of Functionalist "modernist" sociology that dominated the sociological landscape in the United States from the 1930s until the 1960s. The chapter analyzes the work of "disengagement theorists" of the structural-functionalist school regarding the study of aging and discusses the "political economy of old age" approaches of Carroll L. Estes (1979) and Minkler and Estes (1998). Similarly, in the United Kingdom, the writings of Alan Walker (1981), Peter Townsend (1981), and Chris Phillipson (1982, 1998) has added a critical sociological dimension to understanding age and aging, and it addresses the development of a feminist approach to adult aging and implications for theorizing aging. Finally, the chapter assesses the relevance of race and sexuality as key vehicles used to position the identities of older people but that have been overlooked by modernist theories of aging.

From chapter 5 on, the focus is on deconstructions of aging, moving beyond the earlier chapters by introducing new domains of theorizing aging. In particular, this chapter looks at incorporating "aging body" into postmodern dialogue. Henceforth, the chapter points to the emergence of cultural aspects of aging and the impact they have on postmodern understandings of the construction of the body and self-identity. Indeed, in modernist explanations of the aging body— that people's bodies develop from birth to childhood, to adulthood, then on to old age, and are master narratives of "decay" and "deterioration"—have been used to articulate the aging process and underlie the major claims made by the biomedical model.

However, according to Powell and Biggs (2004), the direct use of new technologies to either modify the appearance or performance of older people is symptomatic of postmodern times. To paraphrase Morris (1998), technologies here hold out the promise of "utopian bodies." Indeed, Haraway's (1991) novel reference to cyborgic interconnection of biological and machine entities has been influential to the emergence of postmodern gerontology. The chapter will examine postmodernism and its impact on social theory and its relevance to aging studies; understanding the aging body; cultural representations of aging; gender, culture, and aging; and biotechnology and aging process.

Chapter 6 reflects on what can be entitled "the Foucault Effect" on gerontological theorizing, with particular reference to aging and social welfare. Michel Foucault has devised concepts relevant to reconstructing an understanding of aging: "discourse," "power/knowledge," "technologies of self," and "governmentality." Whereas the Political Economy of Old Age school (cf. Phillipson 1998) and feminist gerontologists (Arber and Ginn 1995) look for the big picture of societal constructions of aging based on policy and resources, they miss one fundamental base: the "microphysics of power" and the relationship between professional experts and subjects/objects of power, in this case, older people (Foucault 1977).

Throughout his work, Foucault looked at the complex relationships between individuals at the microlevel and developed a concept of power. Indeed, we can explore what Foucault means by this by looking at power relations in every relationship: relations between teacher and pupil, doctor and patient, and social worker and client. The relevance to the social construction of aging is that its disciplinary knowledge base has been dominated by the figure of the "expert." Further, many biomedical researchers have perfected the technique of questionnaires to obtain the most intimate of personal information about "the elderly":they profess their knowledge to be the "truth" because the methods they have used are scientific, and hence an expert is born:

> The judges of normality are everywhere. We are in the society of the teacher-judge, the doctor-judge, the educator-judge, the "social worker"-judge; it is on them that the universal reign of the normative is based; and each individual, wherever he may find himself, subjects to it his body, his gestures, his behaviour, his aptitudes, his achievements. The carceral network, in its compact or disseminated forms, with its systems of insertion, distribution, surveillance, observation, has been the greatest support, in modern society, of the normalizing power. (Foucault 1977, 304)

Clearly, this book distinctly separates Foucault's earlier structuralist work on discourse and later post-structuralist work on power/knowledge, governmentality and technologies of self from postmodernism in chapter 4. The movement of "postmodern gerontology" is seen mainly via work of Featherstone and Wernick (1995), who look at the fluidity of the aging body as a counter to modern classifications but do not make use of Foucault's work in their theorizing. In addition, the work of postmodern gerontology has centered on "positive aging," to which Foucault's work is not specifically bound, which, ironically, is more ontologically flexible in looking at power relations between professional experts and older people.

Chapter 7 looks at risk and individualization and their impingement on the aging process. Exploring the notion of risk puts forward two related arguments: first, that power relations, politics, world belief systems, and ageism shape our exposure, perception, and take-up of specific risks associated with aging; second, that these power relations also construct risk as a necessary and unavoidable discursive and material resource for identity formation. This can be seen in the shaping of aging as a form of risk.

Chapter 8 explores the concept of narrative and its relationship to gerontological theorizing. The chapter uses narrative both as an epistemological and methodological tool that can be used to shed light on older people and their relationships with families and social policies focused on them.

Chapter 9 suggests that as part of a reflexive turn in gerontology this is not just linked to micro developments in aging identity but wider frames of reference points. The chapter interrogates the notion of "global aging" and its impact on understanding gerontology beyond its Eurocentric and Americancentric dominance. The chapter compares and contrasts the main issues affecting populational aging in the Americas, Asia, Europe, and Africa, which is sensitized to cultural diversity.

To conclude, chapter 10 suggests that broader insights from wider social theory are required to fully understand the processes and constructions of aging.

The book is not about biological or psychological aging; rather, it is about the discourses and processes that impinge on social construction of aging through prisms of sociological theories. The emphasis is placed upon the processes of aging rather than aging itself. The epistemological and ontological debates discussed throughout the book will provoke thoughtful questions and potential explanations for the social construction of aging.

PART 1: Modern Constructions of Aging

Chapter 2

From Galen to the Clinic: The Birth of Biomedicine

INTRODUCTION

The focus on the science of "aging" is significant in the construction of powerful discourses of aging in modernity (Phillipson 1998; Powell and Biggs 2000). "Gerontology" itself is a broad discipline which encompasses psychological, biological, and social analyses of aging (Longino and Powell 2004). Since the beginning of the twentieth century, the biomedical study of aging, consisting of biological and psychological explanatory frameworks, has dominated the disciplinary development of gerontology (Katz 1996). Alongside this, Powell (2001b) has claimed that social theories of aging are relatively uncultivated territory. There has also been a small body of knowledge relating to social theories of social gerontology, which can be identified as "functionalist" gerontology, which dominated American sociology after World War II with activity and disengagement theories (Cumming and Henry 1961; Neugarten 1996); the development of structured dependency theory and "political economy of old age" gerontology in 1980s (Estes 1979; Estes and Associates 2001; Minkler and Estes 1998; Phillipson 1982, 1988, 1998); the growth of "feminist" gerontology in 1990s (Arber and Ginn 1995); and the evolution of "postmodern" gerontology toward the millennium (Gilleard and Higgs 2000; Longino and Powell 2004). As one can see, the social study of aging is a relatively new discipline of theoretical approaches, albeit with different interpretations of processes of aging. Nevertheless, while these developments are growing in the construction of gerontological knowledge and are assessed in chapter 4, the biomedical model still eclipses the disciplinary dominance of gerontology (Biggs 1993; Phillipson 1998; Bengston, Burgess, and Parrot 1997; Moody 1998). An important point of clarification: while gerontology is defined as the study of the biological, psychological, and social aspects of aging, social gerontology is concerned especially with the impact of social and cultural conditions on the process of growing old. Social gerontology includes the study of societal attitudes toward aging and how these attitudes influence responses to the perceived needs of older persons, both on an interpersonal and structural level.

There are important implications here, not just for how aging is viewed by biomedical models of aging but for how society and its arrangement of political and economic structures create and sanction social policies grounded in such knowledge bases (cf. Powell 2001b). Such knowledge bases are focused on, (1) "biological aging," which refers to the internal and external physiological changes that occur in the individual body, and (2) psychological aging, understood as the developmental changes in mental functioning (i.e., emotional and cognitive capacities). Biomedical theories of aging can be distinguished from social constructions of aging by focusing (1) on the biopsychological constituent of aging; and (2) on how aging has been socially constructed. One perspective is driven from within and privileges the expression from inner to outer worlds. The other is much more concerned with the power of external structures that shape individuality. In essence, social constructionism poses the problem from the perspective of an observer looking in, while the biomedical model takes the position inside the individual, looking out (Biggs 1999).

Biomedical gerontology is a fundamental domain where medical discourses on aging have become located, and this is very powerful in articulating "truths" about aging (Estes and Binney 1989). Similarly, biomedical models of aging have also been prone to what Harry R. Moody (1998) refers to as an "amalgam of advocacy and science" in a neoliberal attempt to position individualized perceptions of aging. Under the guise of science and its perceived tenets of value-freedom, objectivity, and precision (Biggs 1993), biomedical gerontology has a cloak of legitimacy. However, a fundamental question is how biomedical gerontology has stabilized itself with a positivist discourse that not only reflects history but engages the total preoccupation of science and the "problems" of aging. This chapter sets the scene for outlining the historical conditions in which the biomedical model emerged.

EARLY BEGININGS: THALES, HIPPOCRATES, AND GALEN

To explore the birth of the biomedical model, it is necessary to provide an account of the changing sociocultural conditions out of which it emerged. As will be discussed in more detail shortly, the biomedical model and the modern medical profession are entwined entities—one could not have emerged to dominance without the other—and it is therefore necessary to historically outline their symbiotic relationship if one wishes to fully understand just how biomedicine came to dominate contemporary discourse surrounding health and aging. This task requires we begin with an account of early Greek thought.

Western philosophy typically views ancient Greek civilization as the cradle of rational enquiry and modern science. According to canonical tradition, modern science in the form of natural philosophy is said to have begun when Thales of Miletus predicted an eclipse of the sun in 585 BC. Thales was the first in a succession of thinkers known as the Pre-Socratic philosophers who lived before or during the lifetime of Socrates (470–399 BC). These individuals did not belong to any unified school of thought, but shared a commitment to rational empirical inquiry and the belief that the natural world could be explained in terms that did not refer to anything beyond nature itself. This viewpoint influenced the early teachers of Greek society, the Sophists, as well as Socrates whose pupil Plato established his academy as a learning institution built upon dialectical argument and the cultivation of the mind. It is also what separates early Greek from Egyptian and Babylonian thought. True, the Babylonians and Egyptians made advances in mathematics, astronomy, and medicine that informed the development of early Greek philosophy and science, but unlike the Greeks they did not possess a thorough going commitment to observation, reason, and experiment. For example, the famous Edwin Smith papyrus, which dates from at least 1600 BC, contains an account of forty-eight surgical cases divided into sections pertaining to title, examination, diagnosis, and treatment, illustrating that the Egyptians were committed to recording empirical data in much the same way as later Hippocratic doctors did (Allen 2010). Yet even this text, which is generally free of superstition, turns (in case nine) to supernatural aids when it details a charm that is to be recited to ensure a recommended remedy is effective. Conversely, early Greek medical texts in the Hippocratic tradition, for instance the treatise On the Sacred Disease (400 BC), illustrate a growing refutation of superstitious beliefs. In this case in regards to epilepsy: "I do not believe that the 'Sacred Disease' is any more divine or sacred than any other disease but, on the contrary, has specific characteristics and a definite cause. Nevertheless, because it is completely different from other diseases, it has been regarded as a divine visitation by those who, being only human, view it with ignorance and astonishment" (Chadwick and Mann 1950, 1).

Hippocrates (450–370 BC) is best known for his oath, which combined the practice of medicine with moral values which are still highly relevant todayincluding a duty to help the sick, to refrain from doing harm as well as maintain patient confidentiality. The oath also includes a call for an apprenticeship model of medical learning with masters passing on trade secrets to selected apprentices. This being an early sign of medicine exclusive attitude towards outsiders. Hippocrates believed that medicine should be practiced by a special elite group of people (i.e., natural philosophers) who share knowledge and insights freely with each other but not patients (King 2001). Additionally, the oath precluded practitioners from carrying out surgery,—it being deemed unsuitable for early Greek gentlemen of learning to perform surgical procedures as these were deemed to be manual work—creating early on the distinction which is still with us today between physician and surgeon. While the all-male makeup of ancient Greek medicine somewhat supports the view of authors operating from a Feminist perspective that far from being a gender neutral enterprise, medicine in fact has historically reflected, and indeed in many ways reinforced, the patriarchal nature of society through endorsing social practices which seek to place women firmly within the private sphere of home and family (Riska 2001).

The Hippocratic Oath of the early Greek medical club can be said to have begun the long public relations exercise still present today of viewing doctors as an elite group of individuals providing a disinterested service to the needy with absolute integrity and honesty. Hippocrates' successor and the father of Western learned medicine, Galen (129–200 AD), similarly stressed that a good physician should possess a detailed knowledge of the body, a love of philosophy, and respect for human life. Given that it is Galen's theoretical framework that medieval medicine in Europe drew upon until the rise of modern scientific biomedical model in the eighteenth and nineteenth centuries, it is necessary to outline its main features and historical trajectory. As Siraisis (1990, 70–71) notes, there were "certain basic physiological concepts and associated therapeutic methods. Notably humoral theory and the practice of bloodletting to get rid of bad humors had a continuous life extending from Greek antiquity into the nineteenth century."

Though it was first challenged as early as the sixteenth century by the Swedish physician Paracelsus (1493–1541), it is generally accepted by medical historians (Siraisis 1990; Porter 1995) that the Galenic humoral tradition dominated western medicine throughout the middle ages and was influential until the beginning of the nineteenth century. As Turner (1995, 29) notes, "Galen's work 'On the Conduct of Anatomies' became the definitive source for medical understanding of the structure and function of the human body until it was successfully challenged in the late sixteenth century." The chapter will discuss the challenges to the Galenic tradition in a moment but first it will briefly outline the main features of the Galenic worldview.

The ancient Greek Hippocratic-Galenic medical tradition, along with much of early Greek science and philosophy, was transmitted from Arabic and Latin texts to the West in the twelfth and thirteenth centuries as the first modern centers of academic learning—the Universities—were established in Italy, France, Germany, and England (O'Malley 1970). As would be expected, the Galenic tradition believed in natural causes for disease. Indeed it perceived disease to be an environmental but ultimately an individual humoral phenomena. The world was conceived in terms of consisting of four elements: fire, earth, air, and water. Individuals had four humors: black bile, yellow or red bile, blood, and phlegm; as well as four personality types: sanguine, phlegmatic, choleric, and melancholic (Lindeman 1999). Those individuals with a preponderance for phlegm tended to be heavy and slow; those with too much blood, sanguine; those with too much yellow or red bile, quarrelsome; and those with too much black bile, melancholic (Temkin 1973). Good health rested on the proper balance of a person's four humors in line with their personality type. Illness and disease came about due to their imbalance. A state of affairs that could be influenced by the environment, for instance, having hot summers when ones personality type and humors required a mild one could cause illness. Disease was specific to individuals and any alteration in their humors due to changing environmental conditions could place them in mortal danger. Standard therapies to readjust imbalances included inducing vomiting and, of course, bleeding (a tradition which went back to ancient Greece). Yet humoral medicine was also heavily focused on prevention.

In humoral medicine, prevention was as important as treatment. The best means of maintaining health was to practice moderation in all things, especially in the use of (1) air, (2) sleep and waking, (3) food and drink, (4) rest and exercise, (5) excretion and retention, and (6) the passions or emotions. A healthy regimen was predicted on observing these rules of nature and avoiding exhaustion, overheating, overeating, excessive consumption of spirits, and immoderate desires. Such ideas were prevalent, and informed not only medical theories but more popular versions of health and illness as well (Lindeman 1999, 10).

This focus on balance and prevention as much as cure reflects humoral medicine's origin in ancient Greece and its affiliation with natural philosophy and concern with living the good life. To be sure, as Turner (1995, 20) notes, "there was considerable conflict between the secular assumptions of Greek medicine and the spiritual aims of Christian religious practice." But it equally can be argued that there was considerable congruence between the two, particularly given humoral medicine's focus on moderation and the need for the individual to take responsibility for their humor to ensure healthy living. In short, both operate within a moral discourse which promotes a set of practices for the regulation of the body and the mind (and the Christian concept of the soul) at the level of the individual and the population. Indeed, at this point in time the church had powers to license practitioners due to its control of the early universities. With Henry VIII for example making it an offense in 1511 to practice "physic" without a university degree or license directly obtained from a bishop (Copeman 1960).

GALENISM ON THE DISSECTING TABLE

The decline of the Galenic worldview and the ecclesiastic stranglehold over medical practice started with the Renaissance and ended with the Enlightenment and the rise of hospital medicine (Tenkin 1973). Renaissance artists, such as Michelangelo and da Vinci, familiarized themselves with human anatomy, producing detailed drawings of the body as perhaps only an artist can, and in doing so, highlighted that Galen had actually dissected animals, not humans, when constructing his anatomical principles. This viewpoint was supported by the Flemish physician Vesalius in his anatomical text "On the fabric of the human body" (1543) (Siraisis 1990). For instance, Vesalius showed that the human breastbone actually has seven segments, not three as Galen held. Meanwhile, William Harvey established the circulatory system, demonstrating the attachment of veins and arteries and the movement of blood in a circular motion around the body, a point of view which was at odds with the essentially static conception of blood that existed in the humoral system (Tenkin 1973). Paracelsus broke completely with the Galenic tradition of seeing disease as the result of humoral imbalance and laid the foundations for modern medical practice by conceiving it as an entity: an archeus, which entered the human body (Siraisis 1990).

Though he had what can be said to be a modern view of disease, Paracelsus relied on mystical and magical explanations in some of his teachings. For instance he held that the stars influenced a person's health. Yet his obsession with dissection promoted a scientific basis for medical practice by refocusing it away from the rote learning of ancient texts and towards the gaining of direct experience through conducting anatomical experiments (Siraisis 1990). Inspired by Paracelsus and Harvey, Bichat examined the tissues of organs and searched for disease in decidedly natural origins (Carter 1991). Similarly Morgagni used an early microscope to identify, amongst other things, the clinical features of pneumonia, while Baillie accurately described cirrhosis of the liver. Morgagni, Baillie, and Bichat signify the beginning of medicines focus on abnormality as much as normality and its use of morbid anatomy as a methodology to further medical knowledge and practice. Indeed, Bichat is quoted by Carter (1991, 543) as saying "open up a few corpses [and] you will dissipate at once the darkness that observation alone could not dissipate." For though corpses had been dissected since the thirteenth century, at least humoral medicine's dominance had meant that symptoms expressed in life were until now not directly related to findings made during a dissection.

The decline of humoral medicine was not however a straight forward affair. Biomedicine may have been born on the dissecting table, but its growing dominance cannot be divorced from broader socio-economic changes and the power dynamics at play between the different social groups essential to the organization of medical training and practice. Indeed, it is now necessary to turn to the story of the birth of the modern medical profession in order to provide a full account of how biomedicine came to dominate conceptualizations of health and aging.

Medical historians typically hold that at the beginning of the eighteenth century there were three categories of medical practitioners in England, with a not dissimilar division also being found on the continent. Each reflected an elemental aspect of medicine: as learned profession (the physician), as craft (the surgeon) and as trade (the apothecary) (Parry and Parry 1976). Although they were provincial affiliated societies based in major towns and cities, each aspect had its headquarters in London: the Royal College of Physicians, the Royal College of Surgeons, and the Worshipful Company of Apothecaries. The Royal College of Physicians of London was established in 1518. Surgeons joined the barbers in 1540 to form the Barber-Surgeons Company, but they broke this association in 1745, and subsequently the Royal College of Surgeons of London was established in 1800. Apothecaries were at first medicinal shopkeepers, but they were granted a Royal Charter as the Society of Apothecaries of London in 1617. This was primarily because though Physicians may prescribe medicinal remedies, as gentlemen they certainly were not going to engage in trade and actually sell such items. As Carr-Saunders and Wilson (1933, 421) note: "A gentleman might be rich and might even seek riches. But certain roads to the acquisition of riches were closed to him; in particular he must not seek riches through the avenue of 'trade.'"

Entry to each of these three occupational corporations (which were all male) was different, with each possessing their own tests of competence. Entry into the Royal College of Physicians was available only to men of good social reputation who held a degree from Oxford or Cambridge, though those with Scottish medical degrees could become affiliated members. Surgeons and apothecaries, unlike physicians, learnt their trade by apprenticeship. When a surgeon or apothecary took on an apprentice, they signed a legally binding contractual agreement with them. More often than not, the apprentice was a child; this agreement was made with their parents. The apprenticeship process was designed to teach the trade, the mystery, and the business of surgery or apothecary. For instance, the physician prescribed drugs, and the apothecary sold them. Therefore, as Latin was the preferred language of the learned physician, the apothecaries' apprenticeship typically also included some Latin. The apprenticeship system by and large did produce competent practitioners but there was concern that "at its worst, if the master neglected his duties, or the pupil was idle and cared little to learn, the period of apprenticeship too often represented so much precious time wasted" (Muirhead-Little 1932, 6).

Two factors are immediately apparent about these early arrangements for the organization of medical practice and training. First, although women administered medical care in the domestic and local community, they were excluded from these early formalized arrangements for ensuring the quality of "state licensed" medical training and practice (Porter 1997). Second, the system was centralized in London and largely concerned on a day-to-day basis with a geographical area of roughly seven miles outside of the city. Furthermore, at the time, the three medical corporations possessed little control over countryside areas. The only real control the corporations exercised outside of London was in the main cities through various provincial societies (Porter 1995). In short, the medical marketplace in the countryside was unorganized, largely unregulated and dominated by women and "quacks" (defined by the colleges as individuals who have not passed their exams) who operated in direct competition with a few officially licensed practitioners (typically apothecaries).

It can be said that nationally at this time it was still a buyer's market with the sick actively involved in choosing their treatment. The state of affairs outside of London was about to become even more fluid, as the beginning of the industrial revolution and ascent of enlightenment ideals led to a huge increase in urban populations, the development of new industrial cities, and the application of laissez-faire philosophies to marketplace economics. As Holloway (1966, 114) notes: "administrative difficulties, partly the result of the sudden growth of the new industrial towns, and a doctrinaire belief in the efficacy of free competition to ensure the interests of the consumer, led to the decay of . . . the mediaeval system of local regulation."

THE BIRTH OF THE CLINIC AND
EMERGENCE OF MODERN MEDICINE

The stable system of separate medical streams, centralized in London with associated provincial societies in the countryside, had its origins in the early commercial guilds and was well-suited to the essentially static social order of the medieval era. However the industrial revolution brought with it liberal ideals and marketplace economics, which engendered an upward mobility for medical practitioners that gradually broke down the old compartmentalized view of medical practice. This breakdown happened first between the "trade" and "craft" elements of medicine—the apothecary and the surgeon—creating the surgeon-apothecary. Indeed, by 1783 they were some 2,067 registered surgeon-apothecaries, compared to 89 surgeons and 105 apothecaries (Lane 1985). At the same time, physicians educated in Scotland were clashing with those educated in London. This was mainly over their lack of voting rights in regards to college decision-making machinery, which was monopolized by the medical men of Oxford and Cambridge. In addition, Scottish medical training was heavily influenced by "the birth of the clinic" in Europe, so it therefore rejected the Galenic tradition that had long lain at the heart of the traditional Oxbridge approach to medical training and practice.

In summary, by the middle of the eighteenth century, the continental "medical gaze" of modern medicine was entering England via Scottish medicine and beginning its rise to prominence. It was creating a new type of medical practitioner, the early forerunner of the modern general practitioner, who had been trained in medicine, surgery, midwifery, chemistry, and pharmacy. These well-trained doctors needed to generate an income and began to enter general practice (mainly but not solely in the middle and north of England, treating the middle class) and brought with them the idea of the differential fee: the wealthy paying more than the poor. This practice upset their London based counterparts, just as much as Scottish medicines rejection of the Galenic medical tradition did.

However, this heady mixture of socio-economic and epistemological difference between the various elements of the fledging modern medical profession was not to last. By the mid-nineteenth century a generation of London physicians had been directly influenced by Scottish and French medicine. A large number spent a "gap year" in France as part of their initial clinical education. Consequently "experience, from the dissection table and the hospital wards, flowed through the careers of multitudinous young Englishmen as they made the journey out and back. Additionally, the recent introduction of the stethoscope was beginning to secure modern medicine's future in amongst polite (and not-so-polite) society" (Porter 1995). Physicians were as conscious of the possibility of upward social mobility as their fellow surgeons, apothecaries, and general practitioners. They saw that the growing association of medicine with science was changing the nature of the doctor-patient relationship to their advantage and they realized the utility in promoting a united medical profession whose practitioners were self-governing and equal in the eyes of the law. It is to the changing nature of the doctor-patient relationship to which the chapter will now turn.

The preeminence of the modern medical profession lies in its scientific knowledge base and, in turn, this is linked to the historical development of pathological anatomy and the establishment of the hospital clinic as a site for the application of the biomedical model. Medicine's technological and diagnostic advancements and successes throughout the last hundred and fifty years have led to a biomedical discourse dominating contemporary debate surrounding public health as well as the organization and delivery of health care (Lupton 1995). For biomedicine is a "cultural system comprised of numerous variations, the many medicines, it is a more or less coherent and self-consistent set of values and premises, including an ontology, an epistemology and rules of proper action/interaction, embodied and mediated through significant symbols" (Chamberlain 2009, 22). Although it is a somewhat diverse entity, biomedicine at heart is reductionist and materialistic: it largely seeks to explain the phenomena of health and ill health in terms of cellular and molecular processes and events.

Here it must be remembered that the work of Foucault (1973) highlights that the new mode of medical perception and understanding bound up with the birth of the clinic, and which gradually replaced Galenic humoral medicine, was founded upon the discipline of pathological anatomy. This enabled the doctor to treat disease in the form of lesions and processes located within the organs and systems of the body. Observable signs and symptoms were increasingly matched to the findings of pathological science. Emerging techniques such as palpation, auscultation, and percussion further reinforced the legitimacy of this new approach to medical practice.

These developments led to the individual body being firmly established as a site for social surveillance and inspection as well as the advancement of rational, scientific, medical knowledge (Turner 1995). During the eighteenth and nineteenth centuries the hospital increasingly became a location for medical research and training as the body was sampled, measured, and generally coerced into revealing its secrets by a growing number of specialist medical disciplines, departments, and laboratories. As Armstrong (1983, 2) notes: "[the] medical gaze, in which is encompassed all the techniques, languages and assumptions of modern medicine established by its authority and penetration an observable and analyzable space in which was crystallized that apparently solid figure, which has now become familiar, the discrete human body."

Foucault (1973) notes that in addition to laying the foundation stones of modern medicine's formal scientific knowledge base, the birth of the clinic also placed the emphasis of medical training and practice on gaining direct personal experience of a phenomenon. This paved the way for the development of modern medicine's "craft expertise," as a direct result of a doctor's own direct scrutiny of a patient becoming paramount. Indeed, as Foucault (1973, xvii) notes: "clinical experience was soon taken as a simple, unconceptualised confrontation of a gaze and a face, or a glance and a silent body, a sort of contact prior to all discourse, free of the burdens of language, by which two living individuals are trapped in a common, but non-reciprocal situation."

Although not necessarily influenced by the work of Foucault, this emphasis on tacit clinical knowledge and expertise gained through obtaining direct clinical experience under apprenticeship has been a regular feature of published accounts of medical training. Becker (1961, 225) comments on how personal expertise gained from actual clinical experience is often contrasted by clinical teachers to available scientific knowledge, "[so even] though it substitutes for scientifically verified knowledge, it can be used to legitimate a choice of procedures for a patient's treatment and can even be used to rule out the use of some procedures that have been scientifically established." Similarly, Atkinson (1981, 19) in his ethnographic study of bedside teaching and learning in Edinburgh, comments that students experience a "recurrent reinforcement of the primacy of clinical knowledge." Likewise Sinclair (1997), in his study of medical training in London, highlights that during clinical training students encounter an occupational culture that reinforces the primacy of personal knowledge gained through experience. Students are told "quite explicitly that they must learn how to think in a medical way, that preclinical teaching has stopped them being able to think and so on" (Sinclair 1997, 223).

Foucault (1973) recognized that "hands on" clinical training existed in protoclinics before the establishment of the clinic in 1790s France. For example, Rutherford (1695–1779) was giving bedside clinical teaching to medical students in Edinburgh in 1748. What was different for Foucault was not that clinical teaching at Paris was no longer undertaken on an ad hoc basis. Nor was it because there was potentially a vast number of patients involved (20,000 or so) when compared with the protoclinic numbers of roughly less than 100 patients per annum. This in itself obviously did signify a significant break with the past. What separated the protoclinic from the clinic proper was its application of the medical gaze as a diagnostic and teaching tool. This not only led to new ways of defining, understanding, and classifying disease, but also engendered a change in the doctor-patient relationship. In the clinic, the disease (not the patient) mattered. This was reinforced, as Foucault notes, by the lowly social status and poverty-stricken nature of those treated.

Here we see how the clinic contributed to the formation of the modern medical profession through the separation of medical and lay worlds and the reversal of the doctor-patient power relationship. As both Johnson (1972) and Jewson (1974; 1976) note, whereas traditionally the patient acted as a patron and largely determined the dynamics of the medical encounter as well as the course of treatment, the shift to hospital medicine across Europe in the nineteenth century gradually led to the subordination of the patient to medical authority. In other words, the patients' narratives of their personal experiences of illness and disease became secondary to the doctor's esoteric clinical-anatomical experimental expertise, as grounded in the biomedical model. As Jewson (1976, 235) states "henceforth the medical investigator was accorded respect on the basis of the authority inherent in his occupational role rather than on the basis of his individually proven worth. The public guarantee of the safety and efficacy of theories and therapies no longer rested upon the patients' approval of their contents."

The rise of the clinical biomedical gaze of modern medicine in the eighteenth century changed the nature of the doctor-patient power relationship in favor of the medical profession (Jewson 1974; 1976). Bound up with this was a growing focus upon gaining direct personal experience of clinical phenomena on which to build "craft expertise" and justify clinical decisions. The key strength of the biomedical model was quickly recognized by the fledging modern medical profession—the abstract, scientific, nature of modern expert knowledge meant it was open to a process of rationalization and codification, but at the same time it required the doctor obtain direct personal experience of the phenomena under investigation. Medical control of the space by which this experience was obtained, the hospital clinic, served to further reinforce social prestige and distance between the expert and the client. The age of the medical power had firmly begun.

This chapter has discussed how the growth of biomedicine was entwined with the birth of the clinic and emergence of the modern medical profession across the European continent, in order to provide a practical introduction to the subsequent critique of biological and psychological models of aging. In doing so the chapter has noted how the biomedical model focuses on physical processes; that is the pathology, the biochemistry, and the physiology of the body when conceptualizing the human body, health, and the aging process. This theme will be explored in more detail in the next chapter.

Chapter 3

Occidental Modernity, the Biomedical Gaze, and Aging

THE EMERGENCE OF BIOMEDICAL
SCIENCES OF AGING IN OCCIDENTAL MODERNITY

As the previous chapter reinforced, to explore the birth of the biomedical model it is necessary to historically recall the changing social conditions out of which it came. The biomedical model was born out of the re-emergence of natural philosophy in the form of modern science. The anatomical experiments of Bichat, Paracelsus, and Harvey on which it is grounded are in turn a product of, and so are conditioned by, the Enlightenment (King 2001). Thus the "problem orientation" to aging is historically configured in the biomedical sciences and discourses that specialize in one terminology of gerontology (Powell and Biggs 2000). For biomedicine perceives of aging as a pathological problem tied to discourses of decline and dependency (Achenbaum 1978; Phillipson 1998). The medical science "problem" approach to aging can be related to how human subjectivity was structured as occidental modernity crystallized, when, beginning in the seventeenth and eighteenth centuries, the "social sciences," industrial capitalism, and bureaucratic politics simultaneously developed novel ways of objectifying individuals and populations in Western societies (Biggs and Powell 2001). The emergence of Western rationality was accompanied by a growth of scientific traditions such as positivism, each intellectualizing the nature and extent of individuality. Empirical observation, reason, and science are major themes of the modernist project. This is a set of beliefs about validating knowledge that has consolidated modernism. It arose from the intellectual diagnosis of society during and after the Enlightenment. It was the Age of Reason, in the second half of the eighteenth century, with the idea of progress elaborated by Immanuel Kant, Turgot and Condorcet, which gave rise to modernity (May 1996). The French Revolution in 1789, a revolution based on reason, both expressed and gave momentum to this new consciousness, and the Industrial Revolution provided its material substance (Giddens 1991). This modern world, this new social order, was characterized by a new dynamism, a rejection of earlier traditions, a belief in progress, and the potential of human reason to promote freedom. Increasing rationality would enhance social understanding, order and control, justice, moral progress, and human happiness. Coupled with this was Rene Descartes's metaphysical axiom, "Cogito, ergo sum" (I think, therefore I am), which extolled the capacity of individual reason as the foundation of awareness and the locus of knowledge (May 1996). As a rationalist philosopher and mathematician, Descartes forcefully separated "mind" and "body" and thereby articulated a Cartesian dualism that has long provided a pivotal feature for the hegemony of Western culture.

Central to this Cartesian epistemology is a systematic belief in the supremacy of logical reason over the illogical nature. As such, Enlightenment philosophy assumes that the rational self has an "inner" relationship with the mind and an "outer" relationship with the body. Therefore, the body is conceived of as not a part of "who we are" but part of nature, hence an object to be controlled (Powell 2001e). With the Kantian philosophy of ethics, reason is identified with morality, for it provides the a priori principles for knowledge, certainty, and universal law, whereas the body is identified with feelings and emotions, which are, according to Kant, external forms of determination; they imply a lack of freedom that takes individuals away from the path of pure reason (May 1996). Indeed, this very attitude of inflation toward the mind and deflation toward the body has long set the stage for transcendental ideals in an attempt to articulate the order of the "empirical" world beyond its particularities and peculiarities and beyond its "immanence" (May 1996).

Indeed, the notion of transcendence went on to act as a basis for objective and universal knowledge, reinforcing the Cartesian "method" of existence and cognition and ratifying the need for disembodied experience, yet dialectically espousing a synthesis of mind and body in which the latter became the servant rather than the prison of the former. In fact, this disdain for the body entails a disdain for anything relating to it, such as emotions, feelings, and subjectivity. As such and in the episteme of transcendence, experience is deemed to be "real" only if deeply entrenched within consciousness and entirely detached from the corporeal. Personal subjectivity is thus regarded as a threat to the credibility and validity of experiential knowledge, and it can be transcended only if thawed into the crucible of "unity" into the realm of Kant's unified "transcendental subjectivism" (May 1996). This transcendental idealism becomes the legacy of the androcentric, white, Christian, heterosexual culture (Powell and Longino 2001, 2002), in which reason and rationality are regarded as the source of the taken-for-granted superiority.

The causes and consequences of modernity are cultural, social, and metaphysical, but as Tim May (1996) points out, another driving force was capitalism, with its constant quest for new raw materials, new sources of labor power, new technologies, and new applications that might attract new consumers. From the outset, modernity promised to change the world in the name of reason, and each innovation spawned another. However, alongside this, differentials, in terms of who may have access to and be able to deploy "reason," may also be seen to have served as a sophisticated legitimization function between scientific "experts" and the "subjects" of knowledge. For example, given the dichotomous relationship between repression and freedom, individuals will tend to define themselves via their position or identity within a power relationship, such as those of doctor to patient, judge to judged, or aged-care nurse to elderly patient.

Comparative research on aging in Eastern cultures has highlighted a path rather different from the conceptualization of aging as a scientific process developed by Western rationality. For example Powell and Cook (2001) observe that traditional Chinese society placed older people on a pedestal. They were valued for their accumulated knowledge, their position within the extended family, and the sense of history and identity that they helped the family to develop (Powell and Cook 2001). Respect for elderly people was an integral part of Confucian doctrine, especially for the family patriarch:

> The mixed love, fear and awe of the children for their father was strengthened by the great respect paid to age. An old man's loss of vigour was more than offset by his growth in wisdom. The patriarch possessed every sanction to enable him to dominate the family scene. (Fairbank 1959, in Powell and Cook 2001, 55)

This was a view that was also prevalent in ancient Greece, with notions of respect for older people, especially regarding gendered issues of patriarchy (Bytheway 1995). Prior to industrialization, in India it was understood that older people had responsible leadership roles and powerful decision-making positions because of their vast "experience," "wisdom," and "knowledge" (Katz 1996). It seems that, with the advent of Western science and rationality, aging began to be viewed in a context that was different from and more problematic than the Confucian doctrine of aging epitomized in China and traditions of respect for aging in India. Jacques Derrida (1978) made a similar point when he spoke of the westernization of the world through the principles of Western science and language. Coupled with this, the idea of modernity evokes the development of capitalism and industrialization, as well as the establishment of nation-states and the growth of regional disparities in the world system. The period has witnessed a host of social and cultural transformations. Significantly, age categories emerged during this epoch as two fundamental axes along which people were exploited and societies stratified. A hallmark of modernity is the expansion of

America and Europe and the establishment of Western cultural hegemony throughout the world. Nowhere is this more profound than in the production of - scientific-technological knowledge about human behavior.

Indeed, the technological developments due to industrialization, westernization, and urbanization, under the purview of distorted forms of modernity, have neglected these statuses of aging by downgrading its conceptualization. Part of understanding individuality in Western culture, the birth of "science" gave legitimate credibility to a range of disciplines that were part of its umbrella. In particular, the biomedical model has become one of the most controversial yet powerful of both disciplines and practice with regard to aging (Powell and Longino 2002).

The biomedical model represents the contested terrain of decisions reflecting both normative claims and technological possibilities. Biomedicine refers to medical techniques that privilege a biological and psychological understanding of the human condition and rely upon scientific assumptions that position attitudes to aging in society for their existence and practice. As Arthur Frank (1991, 6) notes, the biomedical model occupies a privileged position in contemporary culture and society:

> Bio-Medicine [occupies] a paramount place among those institutions and practices by which the body is conceptualized, represented and responded to. At present our capacity to experience the body directly, or theorize it indirectly, is inextricably medicalized not sociologized.

The end product of this process in Western society is the biomedical model. Indeed, the mind-body dualism has become the location of regimen and control for emergence of the scientific in a positivist methodological search for objective "truth" (Longino and Powell 2004). By developing an all-encompassing range of biomedical discourses, many forms of social injustice, such as mandatory retirement and allocation of pensions, could be justified as "natural," inevitable, and necessary for the successful equilibrium of the social whole (Phillipson 1998).

The next section of this chapter addresses the question as to how the biological body and psychological mind acquire meaning through the guise of science. If we focus on two models of gerontology, we can see the key assumptions that lie at the heart of biomedical definitional explanations of aging: biological and psychological dimensions. It must be stressed that biological and psychological gerontology has traditionally been articulated as the "biomedical model." While this is analytically useful, there is also a need to probe the similarities between biological and psychological aging and map out some of their main assumptions of human aging. Such a dual biological-psychology typology may have inclusions and omissions which may differ from other commentators, but the broad aim is to provide a view of approaches to aging and the assumptions upon which they are based.

THE BIOMEDICAL MODEL:
BIOLOGICAL AND PSYCHOLOGICAL AGING

There has long been a tendency in matters of aging and old age to reduce the social experience of aging to its biological dimension from which are derived a set of normative stages, which overdetermine the experience of aging. Accordingly, being "old," for example, would primarily be an individualized experience of adaptation to inevitable physical and mental decline and of preparation for death (Biggs 1993). The paradox, of course, is that the homogenizing of the experience of old age compelled by such reliance on the biological dimension of old age is in fact one of the key elements of the dominant discourse on aging and old age.

Biological aging is a major facet of gerontology across and through U.S., European, and Western society as a whole (Katz 1996; Freund 1988). Before we assess the ramifications of biological aging and the way it colors particular discourses that have social implications for aging, it is important to contextualize its main assertions.

Biological approaches to aging have focused on searching for the reasons why and how human beings change over time in terms of physical and physiological characteristics. Bromley (1988, quoted in Hughes 1995, 29) suggests that aging is a degenerative process and contends that "aging can be conveniently defined as a complex, cumulative, time related process of biological and psychological deterioration occupying the post-development phase of life."

Furthermore, according to Biggs (1993) and Kunkel and Morgan (1999) the passage of time for human organisms is related to physical changes in and on the body: "hair loss" or "graying of hair," "decrease in reproductive system," and "cardiovascular functioning" are examples. These processes have been called "physiological changes" that are designed to contribute to the body's ability to function as it traverses the aging process.

Such bodily processes are designed to maintain a balance of internal working conditions called homeostasis (Kunkel and Morgan 1999). A key example of this scientific assumption is the relationship of oxygen to the blood system. Oxygen is transported by hemoglobin in the blood system to the body's 100 trillion cells (Kunkel and Morgan 1999). According to Timiras (1997), the inability of the body to maintain homeostasis compromises "normal functions" and "survival." The key issue here is one of internal body functions; however, there is another, wider question whether changes to the body exemplify "decline."

Kunkel and Morgan (1999) suggest that aging is often associated with a reduced ability to maintain homeostasis. According to Morris (1998), the potential of oxygen to all body cells decreases with age. However, changes outside the body, such as social factors or environmental pollution, may also disturb homeostasis (Phillipson 1998). However, the dominant narrative in the biological explanation of aging is that the ability to perform bodily functions will affect an individual's survival. The causal factors of the breakdown of these functions are essentially contested. Major causes of death at the turn of the twentieth century were infections and diseases, whereas major deaths in Western societies at the turn of the twenty-first century are chronic diseases: cardiovascular disease, cancer, and stroke (Powell 2001b). A posing question is whether these changes to the body are inevitable and natural consequences of aging. Aging, it seems, is linked with increased "risk" of illness and disease (Biggs 1993). The relationship is not necessarily causal: aging does not cause disease and disease does not cause aging.

According to Timiras (1997), biological aging affects every individual, evidencing itself overtly and covertly at different ages and in different organs and systems, depending on a whole series of cascading effects (Timiras 1997). Secondly, Timiras (1997) sees aging as a "deleterious" process, involving the functioning of cells and therefore organs and the organism itself.

> We also know that age-related changes that do occur have a limiting effect on a number of bodily functions. Changes in the lens of the eye lead to presbyopia; changes in the cochlea of the ear lead to presbyacusis; a reduction in the accuracy of maintaining posture increases the amount of sway in the standing positions. (Timiras 1997, 55)

Another prominent example of biological gerontology is a focus on the pathological formation of "impairment in the body" (Bronley 1966, quoted in Hughes 1995, 25). It is partly assumed to be due to the aging process, but it may be made worse by a "dementing process" such as Alzheimer's disease (Hughes 1995). According to Timiras (1997), "postural hypotension" is another of those problems that are age related. In age-related vulnerabilities, physiological systems decline with age, resulting in a shift in the competence of the body to control the chemical and cellular environment, thus leaving individuals more prone to so-called diseases of aging. In other words, the biological facet of aging is related to internal problems of the body as a person grows older. Coupled with this, there are certain biological viewpoints that suggest that older people have many "inevitable medical problems":

> In fact, if one were to look at the presenting medical problems of the elderly, six symptoms would stand out: mental confusion, respiratory problems, incontinence, postural instability and falls, immobility and social breakdown. While they are problems of the elderly, no one has definitively shown robust evidence that they are age-related. It is mainly beyond the age of 75 and more particularly 85 years that frailty and the dependence associated with chronic illness becomes apparent. Yet, generally, these changes were going on for many years, at levels below which we are able to detect and associate conclusively with the age-related deterioration process. Conversations with medical personnel suggest that healthy elderly people quite often have laboratory test results which are slightly abnormal, but are not deemed significant. While there are many chance factors that may account for these "abnormalities," they may be precursors of cell or system age-related changes leading to expression of disease at a much later date. The sooner we identify signs of a disorder, the more likely treatment will be effective. (Timiras 1997, 54)

Despite the question of "inevitable" aging, in the United States the average life expectancy is approaching eighty years (Cook and Powell 2003); the fastest-growing segment of the U.S. population consists of persons aged eighty-five and over (Cook and Powell 2003). A key question for physiological theories is why bodies do not function eternally.

Biggs (1993) has suggested the following assumptions impinge on biological aging: that the human body is a machine, and overworked machines and human bodies "wear out" and "decline"; the human body grows but "decays" with time; "abnormal cells" are formed as a result or damage to DNA from "internal problems," all future cells are marked to be different, "in error" and "inferior" to the original intact parent cell; human skin "wrinkles" over time with passing of pigment cells; aging and death are built-in programmed events that result from genes "turning on" and "turning off" (for example, Timiras 1997) suggests there is gendered evidence for this among females such as menopause events; bodily aging causes problems of vision, hearing, and sensory function and balance. Healthy living and diet are seen as key shields to curtail the problems of biological aging (Gilleard and Higgs 2000). The individualized notion of aging as espoused by biological aging suggests that the body is in decline as an individual ages but declines especially sharply in "old age." The term terminal decline or terminal drop has been defined by Riegel and Riegel (1972, quoted in Kunkel and Morgan 1999, 33) as "a sudden drop in performance occurring within 5 years prior to death." As a phenomenon, terminal decline has been observed in the area of intellectual functioning in old age (Hughes 1995).

An interesting question is whether these physical changes are inevitable and "terminal" consequences of aging. The perceptions of aging through biology not only has postulated perspectives about aging but also there has been the psychological approach that has helped to coalesce particular discourses about aging.

Historically, the study of aging and old age was dominated by a Freudian paradigm that suggested that as individuals age and reach "old age" they are structured and regimented and not amenable to development or change. Psychology as a discipline of study had been much more concerned with childhood development (Hughes 1995). Like its biological counterparts, it saw the aging process as a decline in psychological well-being and adaptive ability as people enter old age. The framing of the psychological argument was that human functioning followed the biological journey of positive development in childhood, reaching a peak in early adulthood that was followed by inevitable decline, senescence, and loss of functions into old age.

Furthermore, according to Hughes (1995), psychological aging processes include changes in personality and mental functioning. According to Kunkel and Morgan (1999, 5): "changes are considered a 'normal' part of adult development, [and] some are the result of physiological changes in the way the brain functions."

However, there are psychologists such as Erik Erikson (1980) who see aging as development rather than as a degenerative process. Erikson (1980) hypothesized that each person's life progresses through a series of psychological stages, each of which is important in determining how an individual is able to meet the challenges of subsequent stages of life: infancy, childhood, adulthood, and old age.

This was also influential to the development of "successful aging" that has dominated psychological views of aging in recent years. Successful aging attempts a strategic understanding of late-life issues, grounded in psychological behavior that arises spontaneously among older people in particular (Baltes and Baltes 1990; Baltes and Carstersen 1996). It sidesteps the issue of prescribing contents by engaging with psychological processes, and thus moving from questioning the "what" of aging to the "how" (Baltes and Carstersen 1996).

This theoretical platform is based upon the observation that older people are in the main content with their lives, in spite of increasing "disability" or "hardship" (Hughes 1995). Baltes and Baltes (1990) suggest a "meta-model" of selective optimization with compensation to explain how older people negotiate both gains and losses that manifest with aging with such "psychological success." It is claimed that older people are satisfied because they have found personal and existential strategies to minimize the losses and maximize the gains encountered as individuals age. Nevertheless, as Baltes and Carstersen claim, we cannot predict any given individual's successful aging using this model unless "we know the domains of functioning and goals that the individual considers important, personally meaningful and in which he or she feels competent" (1996, 399).

According to Baltes and Carstersen (1996), this model has the advantage of acknowledging socioemotional dimensions of aging and multiple possibilities for self-development, and is based on the metapriority of mastering the challenges of aging, while allowing wide variety in the ways mastery can be achieved. Everyday existence is converted into successful activities, which are converted into life-satisfaction through techniques applied to the self. Harry R. Moody (1998) has quipped that the approach divides the population into the "wellderly" and the "illderly" and that successful aging is essentially about "surviving." Fundamentally, successful aging emerges as a normalizing identity approach, masking a decline model of aging. Ian Hacking (1990) claims that the notion of the "normal" identity provides a powerful framework for everyday life and individuals. As he states:

> The normal stands indifferently for what is typical, the unenthusiastic objective average but it also stands for what has been, good health, and for what shall be, our chosen destiny. That is why the benign and sterile sounding word "normal" has become one of the most powerful ideological tools of the twentieth century. (Hacking 1990, 23)

An analysis of successful aging reveals that a distinctive and normalized category of aging has been created out of a psychologically defined "success." The category of aging and its coherence derives primarily from the exclusionary treatment on the basis of their psychological categorization and classification.

THE "DARK SIDE" OF BIOMEDICAL GAZE: THE CONSTRUCTION OF "PROBLEMS" OF AGING

> Old age is shamefully seen like head lice in children and venereal disease in their older siblings.
>
> —Stott 1981, 3

Biological and psychological characteristics associated with aging have been used to construct scientific representations of aging in modern society. The characteristics of biological aging as associated with loss of skin elasticity, wrinkled skin, hair loss, or physical frailty perpetuates powerful assumptions that help facilitate attitudes and perceptions of aging. It may be argued that rather than provide a scientific explanation of aging, such an approach homogenizes the experiences of aging by suggesting these characteristics are universal, natural, and inevitable. These assumptions are powerful in creating a knowledge base for health and social welfare professionals who work with older people in particular medical settings, such as a hospital or general surgery, and also for social workers (Powell and Biggs 2004). These new forms of social regulation were also reflected in the family and the community (Donzelot 1979; Delanty 1999). Hence, modern systems of social control have become increasingly bifurcated (Ignatieff 1978; Cohen 1985; Schrag 1980). Increasingly, modern society regulates the perception of the aging population by sanctioning the knowledge and practices of the new human sciences—particularly psychology and biology.

These are the gerontological "epistemes," "the total set of relations that unite at a given period, the discursive practices that give rise to epistemological figures, sciences and possibly formalised systems" (Foucault 1972, 191). The "psy" complex (or biomedical epistemes) refers to the network of ideas about the "nature" of individuals, their perfectability, the reasons for their behavior, and the way they may be classified, selected, and controlled (Howe 1994, 33–47). It aims to manage and improve individuals by the manipulation of their qualities and attributes and is dependent upon scientific knowledge and professional interventions and expertise. Human qualities are seen as measurable and calculable and thereby can be changed and improved. The new human sciences had as their central aim the prediction of future behavior (Ignatieff 1978). Indeed, the psy complex attempted to explain everything from one theory or viewpoint, that being via "infantile sexualism."

This speculative individualist reductionism was inadequate in explaining the complexities of various local group uprisings within society during the past hundred years. It was particularly weak in explaining the mentalities behind the masses of people who united as one individualized group to revolt gainst existing structures that had been suppressing both the individual's sense of "self" and the distinct groups with which they identified. For example, elderly people can be seen as such a distinct group labeled by the health assessments made of them to classify their existence into care by the state and by the care institutions that regulate and disseminate the authority to care staff to "manage" the elderly people (Powell and Biggs 2003).

Individuals who are subjected to multiple discourses are individuals with neuroses such as "dementia," "schizophrenia," or even "Alzheimer's disease" who are considered incapable of governing themselves and are subjected to the highest levels of control and surveillance.

Biggs (1993) suggests that a prevailing ideology of ageism manifests in the biomedical model by its suggestion that persons with such biological traits have entered a spiral of decay, decline, and deterioration. Along with this goes certain assumptions about the ways in which people with outward signs of aging are likely to think and behave. For example, assumptions that "older people are poor drivers" or that older people have little interest in relationships that involve sexual pleasure are all explained away by the "decline" and "deterioration" master narratives that comprise a culture of aging. The effects of the decline-and-decay assumptions can be most clearly seen in the dominance of medico-technical solutions to the problems that aging and even an "aging population" (discussed below) (Phillipson 1998) is thought to pose. Here, the biomedical model has come both to colonize notions of age and to reinforce ageist social prejudices to the extent that "decline" has come to stand for the process of aging itself (Powell 1999).

The French social historian Michel Foucault has provided a shattering critique of medical sciences that can be used to assess the biomedical models of aging. Foucault (1967) was particularly interested in the limits and possibilities of discourses from "human sciences" (biology, for example) because of their attempts to define human subjectivity. Foucault (1977) shows the extent to which medicine objectifies the "sick" body, once it has been medicalized. For Foucault (1977) the body is thus not "natural" but "created" and reproduced through medical discourse. In *The Birth of the Clinic*, Foucault illustrates how the medical gaze opened "a domain of clear visibility" (1973, 105) for doctors, by allowing them to construct an account of the condition of the patient and to connect signs and symptoms with particular diseases. The space in which the gaze operated moved from the patient's home to the hospital. This, too, became the site for social work with older people, as well as the acquisition of knowledge; the object was the "elderly" body of the client. Similarly, the body of the "madman," according to Foucault, was viewed as "the visible and solid presence of his disease." Hence, the gaze focuses upon the body and "normalization" involved "treatment of the body" (Foucault 1967, 159–72).

Biomedicine became a disciplinary strategy that extended "control over minutiae of the conditions of life and conduct" (Cousins and Hussain 1984, 146) of individuals and understanding of bodies. Biomedical gerontology became an institution in its own right, in which the advice and expertise of biomedical professionals were geared to articulating "truths" about bodies (Armstrong, 1983). Medical domination through observation and scientific discourses objectified bodies appropriated through the aging process as "diagnoses began to be made of normality and abnormality and of the appropriate procedures to achieve the norm" (Smart 1985, 43). In this way examining the body and mind of older people was intrinsic to the development of power relationships in contemporary society: "The examination is at the center of the procedures that constitute the individual as effect and object of power, as effect and object of knowledge. It is the examination which by combining hierarchical surveillance and normalizing judgement, assures the great disciplinary functions of distribution and classification" (Smart 1985, 49).

The technique by which biomedicine has developed knowledge of aging is a slender aspect of disciplinary control and power (Katz 1996). This knowledge formation legitimizes the search within the individual body, for signs, for example, that he or she "requires" forms of surveillance and processes of medicalization (Powell and Biggs 2000). This legitimation permeates an intervention into older people's lives, because professional practices of surveillance are said to be appropriate for older people—because of the discourse of "declining" and pathological aging (Powell and Biggs 2000). Biomedicine, hence, constructs the identities of older people as objects of power and knowledge: "This form of power applies itself to immediate everyday life which categorises the individual, marks him by his own individuality, attaches him to his own identity, imposes a law of truth on him which he must recognise and which others have to recognise in him. It is a form of power which makes individuals subjects" (Foucault 1982, 212).

Thus Foucault (1973) has argued persuasively that the birth of the medical profession brought with it a different way of seeing illness and well-being related to structural and personal spaces. Most notably, the older people who became sick became an object to be modified (Powell and Biggs 2000). Under the "biomedical gaze," people become their bodies, bodies disaggregated into a series of dysfunctional parts. This is useful for the biomedical scientific analysis of function and remedy but severely limits any perspective that takes into account interpersonal and wider social factors.

The dominance of the biomedical model has engendered negative conceptualizations pertaining to aging. It has also sought to reinvent itself as the "savior" of the aging via the biotechnological advancements that foster reconstruction of the body and to prevent the aging process (Wahidin and Powell 2001; Powell and Biggs 2004). It appears that:

> *established and emerging master narratives of biological decline on the one hand and consumer agelessness on the other co-exist, talking to different populations and promoting contradictory, yet interrelated, narratives by which to age. They are contradictory in their relation to notions of autonomy, independence and dependency on others, yet linked through the importance of techniques for maintenance, either via medicalised bodily control or through the adoption of "golden-age" lifestyles.*
> (Biggs and Powell 2001, 97)

Biomedical gerontology has attempted to legitimize its existence by playing "games of truth" (Foucault 1980), claiming aging is a "universal" problem but, on the other hand, aging could be "cured" by biomedical intervention for potential "aging consumers" (Biggs and Powell 2001; Powell 2001b; Gilleard and Higgs 2000). Such intervention could include swapping organs from one body to the next; by paying for expensive forms of surgery and modification: plastic surgery, hip replacements, cyborgic facilitation of bodily parts and functions. Indeed, the anti-aging industry has boomed in recent years with regard to such reconstruction, but the boom is premised on consumerism. Science itself has suggested that secrets of eternal youth can be found in genetic codes and that using stem-cell research could curtail the aging process. Aging becomes governed by regimens of exercise in which individuals become the object of their own gaze in order to maintain their commitment to achieving a particular body project generated through discourses from science. Biomedicine may make people "healthier" and "live longer," but they are still not freer from the structures imposed upon them within their society. Biomedicine may allow older people to live longer and maybe even empower them with new technologies and interventions and an awareness of how to encourage healthy aging (Gilleard and Higgs 2000). However, biomedicine still struggles with the notion that being old is positive, in relation to the ideology of aging, especially old age as "decrepit," from decades of negatively stereotyping senescence. These structures change within biomedicine in order to reconstruct narratives of aging, but their dominant discourse of decline is still their master narrative of legitimacy. In order for individuals to survive within contemporary society, the argument espoused is that they must change their attitudes to enjoy the "benefits" of healthy aging professed by biomedical expert powers; aging needs modification as though it were a medical problem to begin with.

Research by Powell and Biggs (2000) indicates that medical discourses of power play a key interventionist role in societal relations and in the management of social arrangements. That is, medical "experts" pursue a daunting power to classify, which has serious consequences for the reproduction of knowledge. The power to classify also serves to maintain power relations (Powell and Biggs 2000). Likewise, we must "challenge the hermeneutic belief in deep meaning by tracing the emergence of sexual confession and relating it to practices of social domination" (Dreyfus and Rabinow 1983, xxv). The significance of biomedical practices reveals an interesting transition in attitude and inward approach to the psyche in both the personal and professional realm of care for older people. The "subject" of biomedicine becomes an "object" when these "speaking subjects" proliferate discourses or narratives that can be analyzed once again for the power relations embedded in their language. As Dreyfus and Rabinow (1983, xxv) assert, this demonstrates that "deep meaning is a cultural construction" accessible by analysis of the culturally constructed language used by subjects. The individual once again is not a free or liberated individual, but one who is culturally regulated by the social order and under surveillance by biomedical powers that can repress individuals with their diagnostic classifications.

Following Powell and Biggs (2000) a dense form of biomedical discourses, containing alleged universal truths, totalizing views, and master narratives with which to explain and understand almost every aspect of social life, play a central role in the construction of physical and symbolic boundaries, and it is through them that both expert groups and individuals come to know and understand the social world and constitute their social identities. As part of this process, certain powerful voices, such as those of geriatricians, increase their legitimacy, while other, often dissenting, voices of older people become delegitimized (Biggs and Powell 2001).

Embedded is a relationship of power in that the classifier or medical expert doing the diagnosing would have the upper hand over the person being classified or diagnosed. The diagnostic knowledge they possessed placed them in an empowered position of authority, affirmed by their expert titles, to exert claims over their patients and police their welfare.

AGING: A SOCIAL CONTEXT

Estes and Binney (1989) have used the expression "biomedicalization of aging," which has two closely related narratives: (1) the social construction of aging as a medical problem; (2) ageist practices and policies growing out of thinking of aging as a medical problem. They suggest:

> Equating old age with illness has encouraged society to think about aging as pathological or abnormal. The undesirability of conditions labeled as sickness or illness transfer to those who have these conditions, shaping the attitudes of the persons themselves and those of others towards them. Sick role expectations may result in such behaviors as social withdrawal, reduction in activity, increased dependency and the loss of effectiveness and personal control—all of which may result in the social control of the elderly through medical definition, management and treatment. (Estes and Binney 1989, 588)

Estes and Binney (1989) highlight how individual lives and physical and mental capacities which were thought to be determined solely by biological and psychological factors are, in fact, heavily influenced by social environments in which people live. This remains invisible to the biomedical approach because these biological and psychological factors stem from the societal interaction before becoming embedded and recognizable as an "illness" in the aging body of the person. For example, in the "sociology of emotions," the excursion of inquiry has proposed that "stress" is not only rooted in individualistic emotional responses but also regulated, classified, and shaped by social norms of Western culture (Powell and Biggs 2003). This type of research enables the scope of aging to be broadened beyond biomedical individualistic accounts of the body. On this basis alone, sociology has invited us to recognize that aging is not merely a socially constructed problem, as viewed by biomedical sciences, but is also the symptomatic deep manifestation of underlying relations of power and inequality that cuts across and through age, class, gender, disability, and sexuality (Powell and Biggs 2000; Powell 2002). At this level of analysis, sociology addresses biomedicine as one of the elements of social control and domination legitimated through power/knowledge of "experts" (Foucault 1972, 1982; Biggs and Powell 2000; Powell and Biggs 2000; Powell and Biggs 2004). Such expert formation has also been labeled as ageist (Bytheway 1995). Ageism is defined as negative assumptions made about old age that treat older people not as individuals but as a homogenous group that can be discriminated against on the basis of their age (Bytheway 1995).

Every society uses age categories to divide this ongoing process into stages or segments of life. These life stages are socially constructed rather than inevitable. Aging, too, is a production of social categorizing. At any point in the life span, age simultaneously denotes a set of social constructs, defined by the norms specific to a given society at a specific point in history. Thus, a specific period of life—infancy, childhood, adolescence, adulthood, middle age, or old age—is influenced by the structural entities of a given society. Therefore, aging is not to be considered the mere product of biological-psychological function but, rather, a consequence of sociocultural factors and subsequent life-chances.

Modern society has a number of culturally and socially defined notions of what Thomas R. Cole and associates (1992) calls the "stages of life." Historically, the stages of life were presented as a religious discourse that formed the basis for the cultural expectations about behavior and appearance across the life-course into old age. As Andrew Achenbaum (1978, 2) perceptively claims: "[P]eople at the end of the life-cycle continuum have constantly been described as 'old.' Old age is an age-old phenomenon."

Indeed, the life-stage model, still used in taken-for-granted popular usage in our society, influences how our lives are structured, albeit by means of biomedical discourses of "decline" (Jefferys and Thane 1989). As Thomas (1977, quoted in Powell and Biggs 2000, 17) points out succinctly: "Of all divisions in human society, those based on age appear the most natural and the least subject to historical change. The cycle of infancy, youth, maturity and decline seems an inexorable process."

In occidental societies, an individual's "age" is counted on a chronological or numerical foundation, beginning from birth to the current point of age, or when an individual has died. Chronological aging is a habit individuals engage in: "birthdays" and "wedding anniversaries," for example. Counting age can be seen as a social construction because it is a practice underpinned by the development of industrial capitalism (Phillipson 1998). Hence, what is critical about aging, then, is how a society uses it to socially construct people into "categories." As a classificatory tool, age is important in three ways. First, like sex, age is an ascribed status or characteristic, based on attributes over which we have little or no control. Second, unlike sex, a specific age is always transitional—constantly moving from one age to another, beginning life at zero and ending with a certain number at death. These transitions also assume that conformity is rewarded whereas deviance is punished; they are regulated by societal expectations of age-appropriate behavior. Third, although in every society some age groups are more powerful, rich, and respectable than others; the unique aspect of aging is that everyone can expect to occupy various positions throughout life on the basis of his or her age. Coupled with this, ideas that centered on social aging coalesced as a theoretical orientation on aging during the 1960s and 1970s. In 1974, Bernice L. Neugarten wrote an influential essay marking a distinction between what is now referred to as the third and fourth ages, the early years of retirement and the later ones. Neugarten (1974) referred to persons in these stages of later adult development as the "young-old" and the "old-old." The young-old are like late-middle-aged persons. They generally have good health and they are about as active as they want to be. The old-old, however, tend to be widowed and are much more likely to be living dependently. Consequently, the concept of old age, with its attending miseries, was only pushed later into the life-course by this reconceptualization. The first decade after the beginning of Social Security retirement benefits seem like "the second middle age," but the biomedically framed "declining body" remains an issue in the fourth, old-old age (Longino and Powell 2004).

THE DEMOGRAPHIC CONSTRUCTION OF AGING: COMPARING THE UNITED STATES, THE UNITED KINGDOM, AND CHINA

Since the turn of the last century, the life expectancy of people born in the United States has increased by approximately twenty-five years, and the proportion of persons sixty-five years or older has increased from 4 percent to over 13 percent. By the year 2030, one in five individuals in the United States is expected to be sixty-five years or older, and people age eighty-five and older make up the fastest-growing segment of the population. In 2000, there were thirty-four million people aged sixty-five or older, in the United States who represented 13 percent of the overall population. By 2030 there will be seventy million over sixty-five in the United States, more than twice their number in 2000. Distinguished scholar and president of the Gerontological Society of America, Charles F. Longino (1994), believes that, thanks to better health, changing living arrangements, and improved assistive devices, the future may not be as negative as we think when we consider an aging population. Thirty-one million people, or 12 percent of the total population, are aged sixty-five and older. In another thirty-five years, the aging population should double again. The aging population is not only growing rapidly, but it is also getting older: "In 1990, fewer than one in ten elderly persons was age 85 or older. By 2045, the oldest old will be one in five. Increasing longevity and the steady movement of baby boomers into the oldest age group will drive this trend" (Longino 1994, 856).

Comparatively, the population structure of western European countries including the United Kingdom has changed since the turn of the twentieth century. Whereas in 1901, just over 6 percent of the population were at or over current pension age (sixty-five in the U.K. for men and women), this figure rose steadily to reach 18 percent in 2001 (Powell 2001b). At the same time, the population of younger people under age sixteen fell from 35 percent to 20 percent. The United Nations estimates that by the year 2025, the global population of those over sixty years will double, from 542 million in 1995 to around 1.2 billion people (Krug 2002, 125).

Alan Walker (1985) argues that the demographic situation for "the population aged 65 and over is set to increase steadily (by one fifth overall) between 1983 and 2021. However the largest rises are due to the numbers aged 75 and over and 85 and over: 30 percent and 98 percent respectively. By the end of this period women will outnumber men in the 85 and over age group by around 2.5 to 1" (Walker 1985, 4).

Thus, the age structure of the population has changed from one in which younger people predominated to a society in which people in later life constituted a substantial proportion of the total population. While the biological and psychological models of aging describe it as an "inevitable" and "universal" process, such terms cannot apply to the aging of an entire aging population. Transformations in the age profile of a population are a response to political and economic structures.

This has been coined as an "aging population" by governments of left and right persuasion and indicative of Eastern and Western cultures. Earlier, we examined the biomedical model and its theoretical assumptions of "decline." Not only has the aging process been viewed as a medical problem but it has also been viewed as a social problem: a "burden" population group. As we discussed earlier, the central focus of modern social systems of regulation is the classification of the "aging population" based on the scientific claims of different experts in the "psy" complex (Biggs and Powell 2001).

Older people in particular constitute a large section of populations in Western society, but the percentage of pensionable age is projected to remain at 18 percent until 2011, when it becomes 20 percent, and to rise to 24 percent in 2025 (Phillipson 1998). In relation to public services that have to be paid for by younger working people, the burden is expressed in alarming percentages. Nor are only older people seen as dependent; children under school-leaving age and people over the retirement age are similarly classified. Dependency rates, that is, the number of dependents relative to those of working age, have altered little over the twentieth century, and yet the notion of a "burden" group retains its currency. The reason for its persistence is that during a period of rapid growth of aging populations there has been a fall in the total fertility rate (the average number of children that would be born to each woman if the current age-specific birthrates persisted throughout her childbearing life).

Changes in the age structures of societies also affect total levels of labor force participation in society, because the likelihood that an individual will be in the labor force varies systematically by age (Walker 1985; Phillipson 1998). Concurrently, global population aging is projected to lead to lower proportions of the population in the labor force in highly industrialized nations, threatening both productivity and the ability to support an aging population (Krug 2002).

Meanwhile, the young adult population in third world countries has been growing rapidly. The World Bank foresees growing threats to international stability as different demographic-economic regions are pitted against one another. The United Nations recognizes important policy challenges, including the need to reverse recent trends toward decreasing labor force participation of workers in late middle and old age, despite mandatory retirement in certain Western countries such as the U.K. (Powell 2001c). Social welfare provisions and private-sector pension policies influencing retirement income have a major impact on retirement timing.

Hence, a major concern for organization such as the United Nations and World Bank centers on the number of such "dependent" older people. Using evidence from the U.K., the percentage of people of working age, that is, sixteen to sixty-four, will drop from 64 percent in 1994 to 58 percent in 2031 (Powell 2001c). As the number of workers per pensioner decreases, there will be pressure on pension provision. This is evident now, in such areas as pensions and long-term care; the retreat of the state made evident in the erosion of State Earnings Related Pay (SERPS) is forcing people to devise their own strategies for economic survival in old age (Alcock 1996). In the British context that also impinges on Western societies in general, private pensions are slowly being introduced in order to prevent the "burden" of an aging population. These are ways in which the state continues to use "apocalyptic projections" such as a "demographic time bomb" about aging populations in order to justify cuts in public expenditure (Warnes 1996). The British newspaper *The Guardian* has echoed such fears of a moral panic of old age by stating:

> A demographic time bomb to tick into the next century—This year, Britain will be attempting to grapple with the implications of the . . . time bomb—the decline of the British teenager, and the rise . . . in the proportion of old people in the community. (Guardian, 2 January 1989, 17)

This type of moral panic reflects profoundly rooted ambivalence toward older people that can lead to an exaggeration of the size of resources required to meet their needs or of the sacrifice required by the sixteen-to-sixty-four age group via taxation (Harper and Laws 1995). Hence, it is not simply that governments and researchers have belatedly recognized "the greying" of populational constructions and policy implications; it is that they continue to look for knowledge of aging as the power to define old age as a social problem. An aging population, like that of an individual being studied by biomedical models, is seen as a "burden" problem in terms of economic management of Western economies. Is this the case with Eastern societies?

Comparatively with China, Du and Tu (2000) identify four "unique characteristics" of China's aging population:

1. Unprecedented speed: The proportion of aging population is growing faster than that of Japan, the country previously recognized as having the fastest rate, and much faster than nations in Western Europe, for example.
2. Early arrival of an aging population: Before modernization has fully taken place, with its welfare implications. "It is certain that China will face a severely aged population before it has sufficient time and resources to establish an adequate social security and service system for the elderly" (Du and Tu 2000, 79).
3. Fluctuations in the total dependency ratio: The Chinese government estimates are that the country will reach a higher "dependent burden" earlier in the twenty-first century than was previously forecast.

4. Strong influence of the government's fertility policy and its implemen-
    tation on the aging process: The SCFP means fewer children being
    born, but with more elderly people a conflict arises between the objec-
    tives of limiting population increase and maintaining a balanced age
    structure.

The combination of such factors means that the increased aging population is
giving rise to serious concerns among Chinese policy makers. Age embraced by
"respect" in Confucian doctrine has been reconstructed through governmental
populational discourses of "risk," "danger," and "threat."

It could be argued, when looking at the effects of a so-called demographic
time bomb across the United States, Europe, and Asia, that it may have been
grossly exaggerated (Powell and Cook 2001). Such a negative perception of old
age has developed via a process of ageism—stereotyping older people simply
because of their chronological age. Ageist stereotypes such as "aging populations" act to stigmatize and consequently marginalize older people and differen-
tiate them from groups across the life-course who are not labeled "old" (Bytheway 1995).

One of the ways to interpret social aging, whether it be in individual or populational terms, is by theorizing about what it means to age in a society; that is,
what concerns and social issues are associated with aging and how these themes
are influenced by, and at the same time influence, the society in which people
live. Thus, to understand the process of aging, looking through the lens of the
"sociological imagination" (Mills 1959) is not to see it as an individualized
problem but, rather, as a societal issue that is faced by both the developed and
underdeveloped nations as a whole.

We do need to ask: How has age been theorized by social theories of gerontology? Different sociological theories of old age are concerned with the social
significance of age. Some are concerned with the individual's adjustment to
growing older and others are concerned with the relative distribution of the material disadvantage of older people. There is a somewhat heterogeneous bundle
of theoretical disciplines, each with a differentiation of concerns, strengths, and
weaknesses. Modernist social theories in social gerontology have been the major
explanations of what forms of social activity take place in Western society and
in a given historical time. Such modernist theories have shaped perceptions
about aging and the nature of the relationship of the individual to modern society related to function, conflict, and gender. The next chapter focuses on these
concerns.

Chapter 4

Theorizing Aging: Critical Explorations of Modernist Sociological Approaches

INTRODUCTION: AGING AS SOCIALLY CONSTITUTED

The previous chapter highlighted the power of the biomedical gaze regarding the positioning of aging as a problem-based discourse in modernity. There has long been a propensity in matters of aging and old age to engage in the ontological and epistemic reductionism of aging to its biological and psychological dimensions. Indeed, in Western culture, aging came to be understood in terms of biological science to be only material, and the scientific approach to medicine became overwhelmingly objective, reductionistic, and rational. These scientific dimensions primarily are a set of normative "stages" of body and mind process that position the experiences and representations of aging and old age in Western culture (Gilleard and Higgs 2000). As the preceding chapter indicated, for the biomedical model, growing old would primarily be a process of inevitable physical and mental "decline" and of preparation for the ultimate ending: death itself. The paradox, of course, is that the biomedical homogenizing of the experience of old age, which the reliance on the biological and psychological dimensions of aging entails, is in fact one of the key elements of the (public) dominant "commonsense" discourses on aging and old age. A deeper understanding of aging requires, however, that we move beyond commonsense approaches and broaden our view to understand how processes, from the biomedical level of the individual cell to overall society, influence us, and in turn are influenced by us as individuals progressing through the life-course.

We also highlighted how aging was a social category in terms of social constructionism with reference to its definition as both a categorization and populational construct. The biomedical and social conceptualizations of aging demand theoretical interrogation of what Phillipson (1998) calls the "social construction of aging." The social construction of aging is an important process in debunking discourses of "truth" and can be used as an alternative to narrow medical narratives (Powell 2002); it includes how "norms" or pervasive attitudes material-

ize—from basic biomedical functions to sophisticated and complex so-
cial/cultural structures including educational, political, and religious institutions,
the arts, customs, morality, ethics, and law.

Social constructs are enormously powerful in determining individual and collective identity because they answer profound existential questions: Who am I?
Where do I belong? What do I do? How do I do it? Where am I? Why am I?
Who are you? Why are you? Those in power present ontologically arbitrary social constructs as "the way life actually is," that is, as reality. For example, biomedical sciences have been important in this process in shaping reality regarding the aging process. The social constructions of aging assert that aging has no
existence independent of social interaction and power relationships in society;
they are not grounded in "nature" as is biomedical gerontology under the auspi-
ces of biological-psychological gerontological knowledge (the meaning of
which is itself socially determined). Indeed, the constructedness of aging is
made invisible by the normal workings of social life, so that it appears natural
rather than artificial. Social constructionism is therefore about helping individuals to stand outside their own prejudices and see the notion of the "other" in order to explain and understand what may be happening in the social world, given
that reality is increasingly seen as fragile, shifting, and coexisting with different
"realities." Further, embracing the social construction of aging can help individuals blame themselves less for their "problems" and strive to change limiting
biomedical discourses of human behavior.

The promise of a sociology of aging then could transcend narrow biomedical
explanations; it might take a cue from C. Wright Mills's tour de force *The Sociological Imagination* (1959). Mills suggested that the promise and responsibility of the discipline of sociology lie in giving individuals the conceptual tools to
make distinctions between "personal troubles" and "public issues." Social theorists can make this distinction if they have a social context and a sense of history
from which to understand personal experiences.

The ability to shift perspectives, to analyze an experience or an issue from
many levels of analysis and to see the intersection of these levels and mutual
influence, is the heart of the sociological imagination. If we develop a new understanding of our own attitudes about aging because we learn about how societies construct meanings of age, then we will have experienced the "sociological
imagination." As Mills (1959, 5) points out: "No social study that does not come
back to the problem of biography, of history and of their intersections within a
society has completed its intellectual journey."

With these "tools for thinking," Mills focuses our attention on the broad social structures that shape our personal stories. Equipped with this understanding,
we can go on to understand how "by the fact of our living, we contribute, how-

ever minutely, to the shaping of our society and the course of history, even as we are made by society and its historical push" (Mills 1959, 4). In order to understand aging we need to be aware of how our personal knowledge is shaped by ourselves and by society as a whole.

Drawing from this definition and process of the "sociological imagination" and the interplay between social context and individuals; the sociology of aging can be defined as the systematic study of the taken-for-granted assumptions that are socially constructed by society and filter through to shape personal attitudes about aging in everyday life. The sociology of aging is also the study of the relationships between institutions and individuals in society. The sociology of aging provides an analytical framework for understanding the interplay between human lives and changing social structures. Sociologists are interested, therefore, in how society works, the arrangements of its structure and institutions, and the mechanisms of its processes of change.

Hence, the sociology of aging is important in examining the interdependence between aging over the life-course as a social process and societies and groups as classified by age. The field of social gerontology contributes to it through reformulation of traditional emphases on process and change and on the multidimensionality of sociological concerns as they touch on related aspects of other social science disciplines.

The field of social gerontology is concerned with both basic sociological research on age and its implications for social theory as well as policy and professional practice. Nevertheless—and it is almost an embarrassing statement to make—as a field of study, mainstream sociology has not been interested in the sociology of aging. As Powell (2002) point outs, in male-dominated sociology the study of aging has been seen as one of the lowest-status areas of all. Despite the poverty of theory in social gerontology in recent years (Bengston, Burgess, and Parrot 1997), this chapter interrogates and problematizes the ways social theories have arisen in relation to interpretations of aging, with particular focus to American and British social gerontology.

This chapter focuses on highlighting the major theoretical schools in social gerontology by addressing functionalist gerontology, political economy of old age, and feminist gerontology. It is arguable that these three theoretical models of aging are dominant in modernist constructions of knowledge of aging, but they remain important reference points about the nature of aging and its structural, interpersonal, and esoteric constructions. The chapter then introduces two essential identity variables that have been historically omitted as to fully understanding the complexity of aging in modernity: race and sexuality.

THE GAZE OF FUNCTIONALIST GERONTOLOGY

In the postwar years, social gerontology emerged as a multidisciplinary field of study that attempted to respond to the social, health, and economic policy implications and projections of populational change in Western society (Phillipson 1998). The disciplinary subject matter of social gerontology encompassed a wide range of social science approaches (economic, political science, and human geography, as well as sociology) that was shaped by significant external forces: first, by state intervention to achieve specific outcomes in health and social policy for older people; secondly, by a sociopolitical and economic setting that viewed an aging population as creating a "social problem" for Western society in general (Phillipson 1998).

However, it was not until the 1950s that social analysis of aging began to emerge in its own right. In the United States, it is significant that this growth was underpinned by the involvement and interest of notable functionalist sociologists who helped lay the foundations for the rapid growth of the discipline between the 1950s and 1975.

In postwar Great Britain, by contrast, social research on old age was largely subsumed within the wider concerns of the expanding welfare state, and it has only recently emerged as a field of academic study in its own right. Considerable shifts in socioeconomic policy and demographic changes have set the stage for what is an increasingly important debate on the interpretation of aging. Until the 1990s, not only was age subsumed under race, class, and gender, but the dominant explanatory framework concerning aging came, as we discussed earlier, from outside of sociology: the so-called medical model. So it is of central importance that aging came to be looked at in social terms.

The important point to note is that theories often mirror the norms and values of their creators and their social times, reflecting culturally dominant views of what should be the appropriate way to analyze social phenomena (Kalish 1979; Turner 1989). The two functionalist theories that dominated U.S. gerontology in the 1950s and 1960s, the disengagement and activity theories, follow this normative pattern. Both disengagement and activity theories not only postulate how individual behavior changes with aging, but also imply how it should change.

Disengagement Theory

Functionalist sociology dominated the sociological landscape in the United States from the 1930s until the 1960s (Blaikie 1999). In the 1940s, functionalist gerontologists were already obsessed with the consequences of role loss among older people. Old age, characterized as a "roleless role" (Cumming and Henry 1961) was seen as a period of life in which feelings of dissatisfaction and low morale prevailed. However, as Dowd points out, the antidote to these "miseries" became part of standard gerontological wisdom by the early 1950s: remain active and make creative uses of leisure time. To this way of thinking, meaning is imposed from the outside and resides primarily in societal tasks and duties such as work and childrearing. Except for some concern for the socially isolating aspects of physical frailty, the body was not a major concern of these scholars.

This view of aging appeared in the United States in the dominant structural-functionalist school via the work of "disengagement theorists" (Phillipson 1998). Such major protagonists of disengagement theory were Cumming and Henry (1961), who looked at how older people should disengage from work roles and prepare for the ultimate disengagement: death (Powell 2000, 2001a). They also proposed that gradual withdrawal of older people from work roles and social relationships is both an "inevitable" and "natural" process: "withdrawal may be accompanied from the outset by an increased preoccupation with himself: certain institutions may make it easy for him" (Cumming and Henry 1961, 14).

Cumming and Henry (1961) maintained that the process of disengagement (an inevitable, rewarding, and universal process of mutual withdrawal of the individual and society from each other with advancing age) was normal and to be expected. This theory argued that it was beneficial for both the aging individual and society that such disengagement take place in order to minimize the social disruption caused by an aging person's eventual death (Neugarten, 1996). Cumming and Henry's disengagement theory of aging proclaims that the aged individuals must be deposed from their various roles for the proper functioning of the society. According to the proponents of this theory, disengagement is a gradual and an inevitable process. Moreover, disengagement theory confines the area of operation of the aged by restricting their scope for employment and commitments. In essence, though controversial, the theory is normative in claiming that disengagement of older people is functional—it offers psychological well-being to older individuals (Cumming and Henry 1961).

Retirement is an example of the disengagement process, enabling older persons to be freed of the roles of an occupation and to pursue other roles not necessarily aligned with generating income. Through disengagement, Cumming and Henry (1961) argued, society anticipated the loss of aging people through death and brought "new blood" into full participation within the social world.

Bronley (1966, quoted in Bond and Coleman 1993, 43) further asserts that "in old age, the individual is normally disengaged from the main streams of economic and community activity."

Not surprisingly for Bromley (1966, quoted in Bond and Coleman 1993, 44): "The [disengagement] process is graded to suit the declining biological and psychological capacities of the individual and the needs of society."

In order to legitimize its macrogeneralizations, disengagement theory boasted of the objective and value-free rigor of its research, citing its survey and questionnaire methods of gerontological inquiry. In a sense, arguing for disengagement from work roles under the guise of objectivity, based on scientific method, gives governments a very powerful argument for legitimizing the definitions of who can work and who cannot, based on age (Powell 1999).

Activity Theory

The second functionalist theory, activity theory, is a counterpoint to disengagement theory, since it claims that a successful old age can be achieved only by maintaining roles and relationships (Powell 2001). Activity theory actually predates disengagement theory. In the 1950s Havighurst and Albrecht (1953, cited in Katz 1996) insisted aging can be a lively and creative experience. For activity theorists, disengagement is not a natural process, as advocated by Cumming and Henry. For activity theorists, disengagement theory is inherently ageist and does not promote, in any shape or form, "positive aging" (Estes, Biggs, and Phillipson 2003).

The activity theory of aging, developed by Havighurst, B. Neugarten and Tobin (Powell 2000), has developed a different approach for the elderly in modern society. According to Powell (2001c), this theory is regarded as an anti-aging perspective and maintains that, if the roles and activities associated with old age are lost, it is important to develop a new set of roles and activities in order to replace them. Thus, replacement of roles and activities is compulsory for the aged because it enhances their life satisfaction. In fact, the activity theory can best be attributed to the perspective of emancipation.

The point here is that old age was understood to be a uniform process and a uniformly problematic and depressing state. Older persons' only hope for contentment lay in increasing their level of social activity.

Nevertheless, activity theory neglects issues of power, inequality, and conflict between age groups. An apparent "value consensus" may reflect the interests of powerful and dominant groups within society who find it advantageous to have age/power relations organized in such a way. While Phillipson (1998) sees such functionalist schools as important in shaping social theory responses to them, such functionalist theories impose a sense of causality on aging by implying that one will either "disengage" or will be "active" in old age. Such theories of aging are very macro-oriented and fail to resolve tensions within age-group relations that impinge upon the interconnection of race, class, and gender with age (Powell 1999).

POLITICAL ECONOMY OF OLD AGE
AND THE POLITICS OF DISTRIBUTION

"Political economy of old age" was coined (cf. Estes 1979) as a critical response to theoretical dominance of functionalism and the epistemic normative explanatory frameworks: either disengage or be active. Political economy of old age emerged as a critical orthodoxy that focused on how the state and its resources and institutions positioned the experiences and life-chances of older people in capitalist Western society (Phillipson 1998).

Arguably, this critical branch of political economic gerontology grew as a direct response to the hegemonic dominance not only of structural functionalism, in the form of disengagement/activity theories, but also of the biomedical paradigm and the world economic crises of the 1970s. As Phillipson (1998) points out, in the United Kingdom huge blocks of social expenditure were allocated to older people. Consequently, not only were older people viewed in medical terms but in resource terms by governments. This brought a new perception to attitudes to age and aging. In the United Kingdom, the William Beveridge post-World War II vision of universal access to welfare services was under sustained attack. As Phillipson (1998, 17) teases out: "Older people came to be viewed as a burden on western economies, with demographic change seen as creating intolerable pressures on public expenditure."

A major concern of "political economy of old age" thinking was to challenge both the epistemological dominance of functionalist thought and the biomedical models of age and aging. The political economy approach wanted to have "an understanding of the character and significance of variations in the treatment of the aged, and to relate these to polity, economy and society in advanced capitalist society" (Estes 1986, 7).

The major focus is an interpretation of the relationship between aging and the economic structure. In the United States, political economy of old age was pioneered in the work of Caroll L. Estes (1979) and Minkler and Estes (1998), for example. Similarly, in the United Kingdom, the work of Alan Walker (1981, 1985), Peter Townsend (1981), and Chris Phillipson (1982, 1998) added a critical sociological dimension to understanding age and aging in advanced capitalist societies. For Estes (1979) the class structure is targeted as the key determinant of the position of older people in capitalist society. For Minkler and Estes (1998), political economy challenges the ideology of older people as belonging to a homogenous group unaffected by dominant structures in society.

Estes and Associates (2001) claim political economy focuses upon an analysis of the state in contemporary societal formations. Here, we can see how Marxism is interconnected to this theory. Estes and Associates (2001) look to how the state decides and dictates who is allocated resources and who is not. This impinges upon retirement and subsequent pension schemes.

Phillipson (1982, 1998) supplements this by suggesting that the retirement experience, linked to the timing of reduction of wages and enforced withdrawal from work, has put many older people in the U.K. in a financially insecure position. Hence, the state can make and break the fortunes of its populace. Consequently, current governmental discourses about cutting public expenditure on pensions and increasingly calling for private provision of support for the aged legitimizes the ideological mystification stereotypes of "burden" groups and populations. This is a case of the state using its power to transfer responsibility of pension provision from the state and onto individuals. Indeed, blaming people for nonprovision of their own savings obscures and mystifies the fact that real economic problems derive from the capitalist mode of production and political decisions.

We can see that political economy is a "grand" theory drawing from Marxian historiography; it locates the determining explanatory factors in the structure of society and focuses upon welfare and its contribution to the institutional decommodification of retired older people. Ageist attitudes toward older people and their often impoverished position are best explained by their loss of social worth resulting from the loss of their productive roles in a society that puts a premium on production (Estes, Swan, and Gerard 1982).

Townsend (1981) further observes that society creates the social problems of old age through "structured dependency" embedded in institutional ageism: poverty due to lack of material resources, retirement policies, negative consequences of residential care, and passive forms of community care services. Townsend focuses on a "structural" perspective of "rules and resources" governing older people in advanced capitalism and wider social system.

Similarly, Alan Walker (1981) has argued passionately for a political economy of old age in order to understand the marginal position of older people. In particular, Walker (1981, 77) paid attention to the "social creation of dependency" and how social structure and relations espoused by the mode of production helps intensify structural class marginalization. In a similar vein, Phillipson (1982, 1988) considers how capitalism helps socially construct the social marginality of older people in key areas such as welfare delivery. The important argument to be made is that inequalities in the distribution of resources should be understood in relation to the distribution of power within society and social class, rather than in terms of individual variation.

Political economy still retains an influence in gerontological theorizing but has reframed and renamed itself as "critical gerontology" (Phillipson 1998). Critical gerontology is a perspective whereby genuine knowledge is based on the involvement of the "objects" of study in its definition and results in a positive vision of how things might be better, rather than an understanding of how things actually are (Phillipson 1998). As suggested, "critical gerontology" grew out of political economy of old age; political economy was criticized for being overly concerned with "structured dependency" (Walker 1981) brought on by social and economic disadvantage and its implicit determinism that can see older people as passive, even insentient beings. Critical gerontology is still concerned with structural inequalities, but it is interested in moral concepts; it has a commitment not only to understanding marginality but also to challenging it. A reflexive critical gerontology also pays more attention to human agency and social class and the way in which individuals both influence the world around them and modify their behavior in response to information from the world in neoliberal contemporary modernity.

For example, from the 1980s on, the neoliberal dominance in social policy has been very successful because it has identified existential concepts such as self-responsibility, self-governance, and self-care that are said to facilitate social action (Leonard 1997). The regulation of personal conduct has shifted from being presented as "structured dependency" by the state (Walker 1981) to the responsibility of "older people" as "consumers" (Phillipson 1998). Since the 1980s, the nature of society is contested hotly by neoliberalism, with its central belief in the virtue of small government, especially in the economic sphere of life. For Estes, Biggs, and Phillipson (2004) the perception for neoliberals is that governments should intervene in markets only when the intervention is less damaging than the consequences of market failure. Where intervention is needed, it should be the minimum possible. If feasible, neoliberal governments should retain market exchanges in social welfarism. Quasi-market solutions should be favored over command solutions. The direct assumption of responsibility for the production of goods and services by government is almost never accepted except for the few special exemptions such as: national defense and maintaining law and order.

Under neoliberalism, the state reinvents itself and its welfare subjects based upon minimal intervention and regulation via a rolling program of privatization, deregulation, and contraction of welfare services (Estes and Associates 2001). Within the mixed economy of welfare there has been the social construction of a market oriented, consumer based approach to the delivery of care. As Peter Leonard (1997) claims, the neoliberal state is being reorganized to include a retention of a strong center to formulate policy but with the dissemination of responsibility for policy implementation to managerial regimes. As Gordon (1991, 36) points out: "The fulfillment of the liberal idea is a recasting of the interface between the state and society to one of market order. It becomes the ambition of neo-liberalism to implicate individuals as players into the market game administered by managerial actors."

Such a development is framed in the language of the market, as opposed to social scientific discourse, although negative stereotyping can be brought in from time to time to reinforce an individualized or stigmatized notion of structured dependency. New neoliberal policy priorities on consumerism require new technologies if they are to influence both the control of resources and the "hearts and minds" of their objects. But for Chris Phillipson (1998), consumerist ideas in modern society ignore the experiences of older people, especially with regard to poverty and social deprivation. This is an enduring theme. After engaging in a series of qualitative and quantitative observations on older people in preindustrial and industrial societies, Powell (2001c) portrays a sense of the abandonment of the role of older people in neoliberal society. Modernity has failed to give due recognition to older people; the older you become, the more you experience a sense of relative deprivation. Fundamentally, the risk of hardship for the aging in modernity is exacerbated through neoliberal ideas of cutting state finance and enforcing people to use their own funds in the management of their own welfare. Indeed, Powell (2000) claims that neoliberalism at surface level consistently equates self-responsibility with freedom and sees people as active agents in consumer market. However, social class as a structural shaper and mover of society may leave many poorer older people in a vulnerable, "choiceless" position in social welfare, despite the neoliberal menu of rights, self-responsibility and "freedoms" equated with becoming a "responsible consumer." Both the Cameron and to a lesser extent Obamagovernments have spoken about the need for private pensions and has constantly reinforced this point by saying that effects of an "aging population" will mean that public finances could not fund a full pension, and older people and families must be more "responsible" with saving for pensions (Powell and Wahidin 2004). However, we have seen the effect of private pension schemes, especially in the United Kingdom; a report by the Office of Fair Trading (1997) found that up to £4 billion had been lost by pensioners in private pension schemes, according to *The Times* "the greatest financial scandal of the century." Then came the discovery after the death of Robert Maxwell that he had embezzled £400 million from his companies' pension schemes (Powell and Wahidin 2004).

"Critical gerontology" has had an enormous impact on theorizing about aging in recent years (Phillipson 1998). This approach to capitalist societies' treatment of older people has overemphasized class relations (Turner 1989) and neglected the differences between capitalist societies (Boneham and Blakemore 1994). More recently, attention has been paid to ways in which capitalist societies structure age relations in terms of gender (Arber and Ginn 1991, 1995) and race and ethnicity (Boneham and Blakemore 1994). Indeed, this theoretical approach reifies "older age" by discounting the potential for improvements in the social situation of older people (Featherstone and Hepworth 1993). Further, Wahidin and Powell (2003) ask why macrotheory overlooks both ontological and epistemological issues associated with the "aging body." This is an important question that will be addressed in chapter 5.

FEMINIST INTERPRETATIONS OF AGING AND GENDER

In recent years, there has been an acceleration of feminist insights into understanding age and gender as entwined identity variables of analysis (Arber and Ginn 1991, 1995). There are two important issues: first, power imbalances shape theoretical construction; second, a group's place within the social structure influences the theoretical attention that they are afforded. Therefore, because older women tend to have lower class status, especially in terms of economics, than men of all ages and younger women, they are given less theoretical attention (Arber and Ginn 1995). Although in recent years there has been a small but growing body of evidence in mainstream sociological theory the interconnection of age and gender has been undertheorized and overlooked. In recent years, there has been an acceleration of feminist insights into understanding age and gender as identity variables of analysis (Arber and Ginn 1991, 1995). Finch (1986) agrees that the epistemological failure to incorporate women into mainstream theoretical perspectives on aging is a reflection of resistance to incorporating women into society and hence into sociological research.

"Mainstream" here refers to dominant theories in the sociological field, such as functionalist and political economy of old age theories, whose proponents could be accused of being "gender blind." As Arber and Ginn (1995) point out, there exists a tiny handful of feminist writers who take the topic of age seriously in understanding gender.

According to Acker (1988, cited in Arber and Ginn 1991), in all known societies the relations of distribution and production are influenced by gender and thus take on a gendered meaning. Gender relations of distribution in capitalist society are historically rooted and are transformed as the means of production change. Similarly, age relations are linked to the capitalist mode of production and relations of distribution. "Wages" take on a specific meaning depending on age. For example, teenagers work for less money than adults, who in turn work for less money than middle-aged adults. Further, young children rely on person-

al relations with family figures such as parents. Many older people rely on resources distributed by the state.

Older women are viewed as unworthy of respect or consideration (Arber and
Ginn 1991). Catherine Itzin claims the double standard of aging arises from sets
of conventional expectations as to age-pertinent attitudes and roles for each sex,
which apply in patriarchal society. These are defined by Itzin as a male and a
female "chronology," socially defined and sanctioned so that the experience of
prescribed roles is sanctioned by disapproval. Male chronology hinges on employment, but a woman's age status is defined in terms of events in the reproductive cycle (Itzin 1986).

It is perhaps emblematic of contemporary Western society that aging margin-
alizes the experiences of women through an interconnected oppression of gender
and aging. The reason for this, as Arber and Ginn (1991) claim, is that patriarchal society exercises power through the chronologies of employment and reproduction and through the sexualized promotion of a "youthful" appearance in
women. This has been shown to be correct in terms of job segregation, marginalization, powerlessness, and the "double jeopardy" of being a woman and being
old. Arguably, Arber and Ginn (1991, 1995) maintain that, because women's
value is exercised, the awareness of a loss of a youthful appearance brings social
devaluation; vulnerability to pressure is penetrated by cosmeticization. Indeed,
the "beauty industrial complex" makes huge profits by articulating "anti-aging"
creams and other products. It is estimated that L'Oreal has an annual turnover of
$9.4 billion on anti-aging products (Powell 2002). Further, Mary Daly (cited in
Arber and Ginn 1991) draws a mirror image between Western cosmetic surgery
and the genital mutilation carried out in some African societies; both cultured
practices demonstrate the pressure on women to comply with male standards of
desirability and the extent of male domination. For older black women, the ideal
of "beauty" portrayed by white male culture was doubly distant and alienating,
until growing black consciousness subverted disparaging language and argued
"black is beautiful" through resistance to patriarchal and racist power relations.

Gender and Marginality in Old Age

In the United States, women comprise 59 percent of those over sixty-five; they
account for 72 percent of the older poor (Powell 2001b). According to Estes and
Associates (2001), the poverty rate in the United States is 19 percent, of which
older women are the poorest social group. In 1993 older women's average income was 43 percent lower than that of older men. Poorest of all are older black
women, with 82 percent classified as poor or "near poor." Indeed, for many
women, such negative financial conditions would express powerlessness and

economic marginalization. Many older women's adverse financial situations came about because their participation in the labor market was limited and dominated by men, thus generating "dependency" upon men. In terms of social security benefits, 66 percent of older women received benefits below the poverty line. Further, the work of Janet Finch (1986) has problematized the construction of social services in Western society for poorer older women by describing how such services contribute to dominant discursive constructions of older women as "incapable" and "dependent."

While feminist theorizing in gerontology continues to raise important questions relating to aging and gender, there are other identity variables that are still given scant attention, a problem that is replicated across functionalism, critical gerontology, and feminist modern theories. In order to address this, the next section explores two issues—race and sexuality—which are important to consider if the full complexity of the processes surrounding modernist discourses of aging are to be understood and appreciated.

RACE AND AGING

According to Powell and Longino (2002) issues of ethnicity in social gerontology have been scarcely researched. First, social gerontology could highlight the significance of cultural values, ethnic traditions, and a sense of belonging to a group with shared experiences in which older individuals may ground their identities. Second, the experience of older black people of being a minority within a minority is important. An examination of the minority concept raises questions about the validity of supposed majority "white" norms. Third, the experiences of minority ethnic groups in trying to obtain social justice and fairness in terms of health care, for example, expose the ethnocentrist nature of social welfare in Western culture.

Boneham and Blakemore (1994) claim that the dominant theories of age and aging need to be reconsidered with racial diversity in mind. Such views of macrotheories of functionalism, political economy, and feminism have ignored the experiences of older black people (Patel 1990).

Further, the biomedical model has discussed how the aging body has declined and has attempted to discover variations through different explanations of the body in different cultures. For example, Stuart Hall (1992) has considered how scientific definitions of "race" are racist and somehow attempt to explain physical characteristics of people and behaviors. Compounding the decline model with inferior/superior scientific discourses generates what Sim (1990) has called "metaphors of pathology," which seep into Western society to engender what Hall (1992) calls different "historical forms of racisms." According to Hall

(1992), racism in Western culture is linked with colonialism and slavery, legacies of the history of the Enlightenment and industrial capitalism in the U.K., United States, and Europe. Conceptually, the concept of "race" refers to a "category composed of individuals who share biologically transmitted traits that members of a society deem socially significant" (Saraga 1998, 324). A critical perspective goes underneath the surface to raise critical questions about categories or types of people based on classification. "Racism" refers to the idea that one racial category is innately superior or inferior to another. Therefore, the assertion of one specific category of individuals over others has served as a powerful tool for relegating the targets of taunts to a status of social inferiority.

According to Patel (1990) the "economic and social conditions of older black people can be explained away by 'blaming the victim.' The focus on such arguments then shifts from individual pathology to family deficiency to cultural defects."

Indeed, Simon Biggs (1993) claims the myth of "looking after one's own" is replicated by professional and institutional practices and services. Biggs (1993) sees the deficiencies in the system that are at fault but the "passing of the buck" by the system is to pathologize stereotypical views that "it's their fault" if they do not provide for their own.

The assumption that ethnic communities are made up entirely of caring, close-knit, extended families that do not require outside care and support has meant that the state, both local and central, has failed to meet the needs of population groups that run along ethnic lines. For example, despite the growing proportion of older black people, very few attend local day care centers or residential care. They are often put off, partly by the absence of other black service users and by the predominance of Western ideologies and traditions regarding activities and fare (Bond and Coleman 1990). Similarly, Wing Au (1996, cited in Powell 2001b) found that among the older Chinese community in Liverpool, Great Britain, social service departments were very slow to meet their care needs because they thought "they looked after their own." This highlights a restricted view of culture in which the concept of normalization causes the system to overlook the very people whom social services should be treating.

Open racism continues to exist. Hall (1992) claims that black older people are subjected to racist abuse and experienced hostility from white older people. Patel (1990, 39) claims that "sufficient importance may not be attached to instances of racial abuse in a home because staff involved deem it as insignificant or because white elders cannot be expected to change their behavior. Hence black elders must put up with racism or not use the service." Indeed, according to Alcock (1996), there exists institutional racism in the British National Health Service in that older black people are not treated by medical staff, including nurses and doctors, the same as older white people. Indeed, not only are there serious questions about health disadvantages coupled with this, but also the manifestation of "elder abuse" is not detected, and consequently many older black people do not have their concerns, needs, or situations addressed. Furthermore, Boneham and Blakemore (1994) suggest that the problems faced by older men and women from both Asian and Afro-Caribbean communities are posed in terms of the devaluation of old age in Western culture, based on consumer demand and reflecting racial disadvantage by a lack of adequate social facilities.

Culture itself can be silencing for many older black people. Hazan (1980, cited in Boneham and Blakemore 1994) compiled a study of an older Jewish community and found that many older people found it painful to talk about memories of the past such as the Holocaust but were dismissed by white professional health workers who had no comparable experience, which in turn created distrust and anxiety.

SEXUALITY AND AGING

The issue of sexuality has been marginal to modernist theories of aging. The oldest gay men and lesbians have few, if any, positive role models for coupling, aging, or creating alternative family structures (Isay 1996; Fullmer 1995). Fullmer explains that people "coming out" later in life must integrate themselves into a new culture and may be faced with some of the same tasks that typically confront adolescents and young adults, and that the age of coming out could influence family structure and support systems. This indicates that the later in life a person comes out, the more difficult it is to integrate into a gay/lesbian social network or restructure the family system one is in to allow for the gay/lesbian relationship (Isay 1996). Fullmer remarks that now that more gay and lesbian couples have the opportunity to adopt children, they may have children and grandchildren who may be more accepting of them and are there to support them in their old age. Gay men or lesbians who have gone from a heterosexual relationship to a homosexual one might encounter more problems with their biological children accepting their sexuality at a time when they may need them the most (Saraga 1998).

Families of older gay and lesbian people have many of the same strengths and deal with the same issues as other families. But along with getting older, they also have to face the prejudices of being gay or lesbian (Fullmer 1995). "Older gays and lesbians have learned through a lifetime of experience that they will likely be discriminated against if it is known that they are homosexual. It is common in our society to typify older gay men and lesbians as pathetic and lonely 'dirty old men' or 'child molesters,' as 'old maids' or as 'drag queens'"

(Fullmer 1995, 66). Gay and lesbian couples and their families may be alienated from institutions such as churches because many religious organizations have been very vocal in their condemnation of homosexuality (Fullmer 1995).

Public retirement housing does not allow "unrelated adults" to live under the same roof. This includes nursing homes and private retirement centers, which can make assumptions that their residents are heterosexual and structure activities on the basis of these assumptions (Isay 1996). Hospitals often have policies that allow only "immediate" family members to be in the rooms of seriously ill patients and help make decisions for them. It is also not uncommon for biological family members to contest a will that names a homosexual partner as the beneficiary and win, because there is no legally defined relationship between the partners (Dalley 1988).

The major sociological issue and lesson to be learned here is how to overcome the impact of class, race, and gender without merely adding more identity formations, such as race and sexuality, to the task of understanding aging in modernity.

CONCLUSION: DECONSTRUCTING MODERNIST THEORIES OF AGING

Taken together, different yet modernist theories of aging consisting of functionalism, critical gerontology, and feminist gerontology have helped shape important debates about the extent and nature of an "aging" society. Such social theories have been used also to analyze pressing social issues such as the engagement of older people with society, active aging, pension politics, and the gendered nature of aging in modernity. However, the concerns of these theoretical resources have been primarily macro-oriented: for example, the political economy approach overemphasizes structural disadvantage (cf. Walker 1985) or "structured dependency" (Townsend 1981) at the expense of focus to older people's sense of human agency in, for example, fighting for political and economic representation through social organization (Tulle 2004).

Such modernist models of aging, by focusing upon the social problems of older people, may have taken up, promoted, and reinforced the "ageism" which many are arguing against (Bytheway 1995). Consequently, modernist epistemologies of aging can be regarded as over-arching explanations of aging. Thus one finds diversity, subjectivity, and microdimensions of aging in the lifestyles and experiences of older people.

Indeed, a pressing question may be, what makes such theories modernist? They are modernist in the sense that they have afforded "grand narratives" to aging. For example, they supply macrogeneralizations to their area of social concern: "in the interests of capitalism" and "in the interests of patriarchy." For Powell and Longino (2002) an alternative form of theorizing drawn from postmodernism suggests that "grand theories" place too many limits on what is conceptually possible regarding aging and that it is too totalized. The objectification of older people that is implied by the term "social class" and "gender" relegates individuals to socially constructed categories. Likewise, the Marxist notion of "false consciousness" fails to recognize that this can be patronizing to many people who resist social marginalization. For Featherstone and Hepworth (1993), individual experiences are no longer believed to be determined by such social constructs such as "class." A postmodern perspective has tended to take a critical stance relative to Marxist developments. It attempts instead to tease out ontologically flexible depictions of aging, and it questions the truth claims behind ontological and epistemological generalizations based on "concrete" social divisions such as race, class, and gender, which are touchstones of modern gerontological theories (Biggs 1999).

The next chapter focuses on postmodern constructions of aging that alternatively emphasize the cultural interaction between the aging body and social context in shaping the way people experience their lifetimes. Even though lives are seen as embedded in social relationships, popular culture, and history, the notion of the "aging body" is an important narrative in the social construction of aging identity. This view has rich epistemological and ontological implications in terms of understanding the aging self and social reality. It draws upon attempts to overcome the aging body as articulated by biomedical gerontology. In terms of identity, we are talking about the possibilities of reinvention and denial of limits. In many ways this approach also reflects the "outside-looking-in" perspective insofar as, as social theory, aging is bounded by the internal-external duality and the possibilities that the external makes available. The reterritorialization of the aging body by society, and paradigmatically by postmodern social theory, is a strategy that parallels the denial of subjectivity within the main traditions of the biomedical model. It is within this postmodern imaginative space that an understanding of the aging body ma

Chapter 5

Postmodernism, Culture, and the Aging Body

INTRODUCTION

In the previous chapter we interrogated modernist and macro theories of aging comprising functionalism, political economy of old age, and feminist gerontology, which maintained that aging is reduced to disengagement/activity and social roles and affected not only by capitalism and economic forces but also by patriarchy and the exploitation of all women by men. It can be suggested that such modernist theories, by focusing on the bigger picture of life, exclude social relations at the micro texture of everyday life. This is not to deny the important and critical points that have been made by the sociological theories discussed in the previous chapter. Indeed, such approaches are significant to pointing to emergence of social problems of aging as cast through the socioeconomic gaze.

Notwithstanding this, and despite the consolidation of these important theories of aging, there was no specific innovative theoretical development with a specific focus on an understanding of the "body." Although functionalism and political economy have their theoretical differences, they both focused on structures to the exclusion of the body. The contentious point to make here is that, by ignoring the sense of "lived experiences" of older people, all modernist theories provide perceptions of adult aging that are over generalized.

Understanding aging bodies plays a crucial part in the identity formation of older people in the representations of the body. Outside of gerontology, feminism has focused on the ways younger women's bodies were controlled and dominated within patriarchy. According to Twigg (2000), feminism has focused our attention as to how women represent the body itself. The current interest in the body and embodiment in social and human sciences encompasses a range of themes and theoretical traditions (Powell 2001c). Historically, the discipline of sociology ignored the centrality of the body in terms of its prioritized "rational" or scientific analysis of modern social systems (Oberg and Tornstam 1999; Wahidin and Powell 2001). Indeed, the sociological tradition has focused upon the social forces that impinge upon the construction of personal biographies and the society in which sociologists live (Mills 1959). The sociological aspirations of Karl Marx, Emile Durkheim, and Max Weber distanced them from a study of the body in order to generate intellectual respectability to ideas about social order and social change (Turner 1989). Sociology simultaneously distanced itself from biological reductionism, which, as part of the "project of modernity," attempted to talk of the body as an object to be predicted and controlled. Coupled with this, the modernist preoccupation with theorizing and constructing grand narratives in theories of aging has also tended to exclude an analysis of the body. As Powell (2001b) points out, theorizing occupies a commanding position in sociological analysis; with a preoccupation with abstraction, bodies are things to be transcended or ignored.

Moreover, gerontology continues to be in the thrall of a biomedical discourse on aging (Powell and Longino 2001); although concerned with the fixed limitations of the aging body, it restricts an ontologically flexible understanding of aging. Conversely, we can question how the aging body acquires meaning, and also how the meaningful body itself, in its turn, influences and limits signifying processes and social efforts as related to society and culture.

The central focus is not on the body as a natural given, or as the conglomerate of neurons, hormones, and genes, but rather as a concrete social and cultural practice of everyday life. Traditionally, the body in its actual realities has been generally neglected within the social sciences and humanities (Shilling 1993; Katz 1996). The investigation of the body was more or less relegated to biology and the medical sciences. In recent years, however, the body has made a major comeback within all realms of scholarly and scientific research (Shilling 1993). Especially those fields that have traditionally focused on the "inanimate" aspects of reality. For example, literary critics, film theorists, political scientists, historians have shown an upsurge in interest in a variety of "bodily matters." That is, in the concrete, corporeal dimensions which render us all recognizable human beings, the physical aspects of our individual and collective embodied specificity and experiences.

It is by querying the role of the body that one can move away from the modernist biomedical approach, which locates the body within the naturalistic framework (Powell and Longino 2001). The postmodern perspective adds a richness to the literature by examining embodiment and the corporeality of the body in all its social guises (Wahidin and Powell 2001, 2003). It places the body not as a passive materiality that is acted upon but one that negotiates the capillaries of power, enabling itself to be always in the process of becoming through the experiences of embodiment (Longino and Powell 2004). Moreover, in a postmodern culture, the prospect of an endless life has been revived through consumer images of perpetual youth and the blurring of traditional life-course boundaries (Featherstone and Hepworth 1993).

Therefore, this chapter focuses on such themes as conceptualizing postmodernism, theorizing the aging body, popular culture and aging body, gendered bodies, and finally biotechnologies and the reconstruction of aging bodies.

THE DEVELOPMENT OF POSTMODERN SOCIAL THEORY

The theory of postmodernism represents a decisive break with modernity (Delanty 1999; Powell and Longino 2002). Postmodernism emerged from Western social theory; the debate was instigated by Derrida, Baudrillard, and Lyotard in the tradition of the modern and calls for breaks within this tradition. This is clearly illustrated by the work of French postmodern theorist Baudrillard, who adopted an extreme abandonment of Enlightenment values in his devastating critique of modernist approaches in sociology. Baudrillard focuses on the transcendental nature of society through the concept of hyperreality. He argued that in modern society there is no distinction between reality and illusion (Seidman 1994; May 1996) and that individuals live their lives through a simulation of reality. Nothing has any true origin or authenticity, and lived experience is itself a mere construction made of a series of depthless signs and representations (Smart 1993, 52). In this way Baudrillard argues that sociology can no longer serve a political purpose, because power relations have been dispersed through the hyperreal nature of society (Smart 1993, 55). The "neat divisions," "hierarchies," and "foundational premises" of both modernity and sociology (Seidman 1994, 347) are no longer relevant. In particular, Baudrillard rejects the economic determinism of Marxism and states that there are no longer such fundamental systems of exploitation, only superficial simulations and exchanges (May 1996):

> Like the philosopher Nietzsche, Baudrillard criticizes such claims to truth and favours a model based on what he calls seduction. Seduction plays on the surface: it is the surface appearance that is effective in determining action, not some latent or hidden structure as claimed by Marxism or Freudianism. (Thompson 1992, 244)

For Lyotard (1984) the project of modernity has become obsolete and society had entered the "postmodern condition." Lyotard deconstructs the way in which bodies of knowledge are created in order to legitimate hierarchical structures in society. In his influential work *The Postmodern Condition* (1984, first published in French in 1979), Lyotard looked at the changes that have occurred to the nature of "knowledge" throughout history. He pointed to how premodern society was based on narratives that were made up of religion and myth (Seidman 1994,

206). Knowledge was a body of stories that were thought to explain the way society was and determine that which was "good" or "evil." In this way such narratives legitimated the social rules of behavior that determined how society was structured and who had authority (Seidman 1994, 206). In contrast, modernity, Lyotard argued, was thought to be based on "true" knowledge that rejected the "narratives" of premodernity. However, in *The Postmodern Condition*, Lyotard asserts that in actual fact supposedly "pure," "real" scientific knowledge is also self-legitimating, so is itself merely another "narrative" (McLennan 1992, 332). Lyotard argues that scientific thought and knowledge have political and philosophical agendas and are therefore value laden and not totally objective (McLennan 1992, 333). An ideal that underpinned the beginnings of Enlightenment thought was that the attainment of absolute knowledge for all would mean the attainment of absolute freedom for all (May 1996).

It was thought that knowledge was the key to breaking down power structures that had existed during the domination of premodern narratives. But Lyotard pointed to the contradictions within modern scientific bodies of knowledge and argued that they are themselves still made up of hierarchical power structures. Just as in earlier societies narratives served to determine who had the right to speak and who did not, Lyotard states, this is still the case. Hierarchies still operate and serve to give the decision-making elite the power to decide what gets defined as legitimate knowledge.

> Countless scientists have seen their "move" ignored or repressed, sometimes for decades, because it too abruptly destabilized the accepted positions, not only in the university and scientific hierarchy, but also in the problematic. (Lyotard 1984, 63)

Lyotard argues, therefore, that science can no longer be seen as a unified body working toward the emancipation of humanity (Longino and Powell 2004). His ideas can be linked to those of Nietzsche, who believes that "truth" and "knowledge" are merely a matter of conventions that falsify and dissimulate to promote human survival (May 1996). Rather than being a grand quest for universal laws, Lyotard argues, knowledge is sought in order to keep human society functioning efficiently (Steuerman 1992, 108). The assertion by science that it is constantly objectively striving for truth and progress is called into question by the fact that the search for knowledge is inextricably linked to achieving economic growth in society (McLennan 1992, 332). That is not to say that these two things are incompatible, but rather to question if the search for truth and progress can ever be totally objective when there is a financial incentive. Lyotard argues that those involved in striving for progress "allocate our lives for the growth of power. In matters of social justice and of scientific truth alike, the legitimation of that power is based on its optimizing the system's performance—efficiency" (Lyotard 1984, xxiv).

Since, as Lyotard (1984) points out, the legitimation of science can be called into question, knowledge as a unified, overarching metanarrative (such as the Enlightenment narrative that knowledge equals liberation, as was key in modernity) breaks down into a wide range of "micronarratives" (Lyotard 1984, xxiv). Each separate specialism has a different discourse and plays different "language games" in an attempt to gain accreditation from its specific audience (Seidman 1994, 208; Lyotard 1984, 64). This, to Lyotard, is what ultimately characterizes the postmodern condition.

Lyotard's rejection of grand narratives obviously has strong implications for the structure of social gerontology. By rejecting the belief in the ability to universalize, philosophical thought loses its authority to make any suggestions as to what action can be taken in order to make changes in society (Smart 1993, 37). In response to the criticisms of the Enlightenment made by Lyotard, Habermas wishes to consolidate the "project of modernity" and further argues that we should not completely abandon the possibility of a rational pursuit of truth (Steuerman 1992, 107). He defends modernity and argues that what is needed is more philosophical discussion, not less (Steuerman 1992, 113). Habermas states that through the use of communicative action, language, and rational dialogue, the Enlightenment aims of truth, justice, and freedom are still attainable alongside social consensus (Steuerman 1992, 104–7). However, Lyotard argues that Habermas ignores the fact that communication cannot simply take the form of consensual, rational dialogue; it will always take place in the context of power struggles (Powell and Biggs 2000).

Therefore, rather than holding on to the ideals of Enlightenment scientific thought, Lyotard might suggest that we attempt to "restructure" social theory (and social gerontology) in a postmodern vein so that we might find a democratic, pluralistic solution (Seidman 1994, 207). He argued that while grand narratives, such as the Marxian narrative of class conflict, were well intentioned and essential to modernist social theory, to continue to utilize such concepts fails adequately to challenge the hierarchical structures in society and therefore continues to marginalize and repress issues of difference.

"Postmodernism abandons absolute standards, universal categories and grand theories in favour of local, contextualized, and pragmatic conceptual strategies" (Seidman 1994, 207). Seidman outlines the postmodern idea that the splintering of metanarratives has occurred to such an extent that society has become decentered. That is, there is no longer a common unifying culture in existence (Seidman 1994, 206). Individuals experience their lives at constantly shifting intersections of different discourses and language games. Instances of oppression, therefore, occur in many different contexts as individuals constantly construct, deconstruct, and reconstruct themselves in terms of these "fractured identities" (Powell 2000). Indeed, Lyotard argues that a postmodern analysis does offer a way of explaining issues of multiplicity and difference (Lyotard 1984, 81).

Powell and Longino (2002) suggest that there are several themes that are shared in postmodern analysis of aging, which consolidate Baudrillard's, Lyotard's and Seidman's theoretical excursions. First, there is distrust in the concept of absolute and objective truth. "Truth" is viewed as contextual, situational, and conditional (Biggs and Powell 2001). Second, emphasis is placed on fragmentation rather than universalism, again pushing away from the general and toward the particular (Powell 2001b). Third, local power is preferred over the centralized power of the nation-state, and decentralization, or the process of democratization of power, is a pervasive theme of postmodern narratives (Powell and Longino 2001). Fourth, reality is simulated but is otherwise not held to be a very meaningful concept; reality conceived as a general and universal truth is profoundly doubted (Powell and Longino 2002). Fifth, we are seeing the rise and consolidation of consumer culture that tends to put "power" in the hands of the consumers but can also equally manipulate consumers through marketing ploys and interpolating discourses of consumer freedom by dictating costs in the global marketplace (Biggs and Powell 2001). Finally, diversity and difference are emphasized and valued above commonality based on homogeneity (Powell 2001b; May 1996). Postmodern analysis of culture is no longer a fringe perspective inasmuch as it apparently promotes strategies of individualism and diversity, and postmodernism is critical of strategies that devalue individuals because of any characteristic that would control access to knowledge and could thereby assault identity (Biggs and Powell 2001). In ethics, as in epistemology, the final result is a kind of moral relativism (Longino and Powell 2004).

Central to postmodern assertions is that in the twenty-first century there has occurred a radical shift in the constitution of social order, paralleling the significance of the Enlightenment and birth of modernity that led to the emergence of the biomedical sciences and social sciences in general. This new sociocultural formation has been termed "postmodernity" and is seen as to be characterized by increasing diversity and the loosening of structural modernist principles. Postmodern thought may be seen as a revolt against both the structural version of gerontology theory, that is political economy and feminism, and as a break with the rigidity and certainties of the positivist or biomedical strand of gerontology. All forms of meaning and "knowledge" are rendered problematic and no longer to be taken for granted as the myth of the biomedical objectivity is debunked. Hence, the controversial point is that modernist sociological theories claim the same forms of certainty, universalism, and rigidity that are seen as master narratives of positivism. For example, political economy of aging (cf. Estes 1979) emphasizes the importance of economic materiality, applicable to every older person in North America. But this has also been conflated with the biomedical obsession with an objective social world that was to be scientifically knowable. Although the political foundations of these very two different "modernist" explanations are diametrically opposed, they are treated as one in treating aging as an "object" to be predicted or problematized.

THEORIZING THE AGING BODY

Postmodern discussions relating to the aging body in social gerontology are slowly developing (Powell and Longino 2002). While the "body" as a concept implies an objectified and "natural" entity, the body is now beginning to be viewed as increasingly complex. The importance of the body to gerontology is in many ways obvious. For example, illness can limit the "normal" functioning of the body, and this can have profound psychological, political, and social consequences that interest gerontologists of all backgrounds. Moreover, health is often thought of in terms of body maintenance, and such activities form a pivotal feature of consumer societies. However at a personal level the age one appears to be may be different from the age one actually is, as though one is wearing a disguise. Featherstone and Hepworth (1993) maintain that old age is a mask that "conceals the essential identity of the person beneath" (148). That is, while the external appearance is changing with age, the essential identity is not, so that the difference between physical appearance and the unchanging image in his or her head may surprise the aging individual. Bytheway and Johnson (1998) assert that we need a well-constituted image of what "old" looks like before we could recognize the signs in our own images. Thompson (1992) argues that people derive their sense of identity in later life from the achievements of the past and what remains to be accomplished in the future, rather than from a set of stereotypical, usually negative, attributes of old age. Unless they are ill or depressed, old people do not feel old "inside." Furthermore, old people tend to associate old age with the residents of nursing homes, an image from which they want to distance themselves (Biggs 1999).

Simultaneously, the aging body has been exploited by popular consumer culture, which has attempted to colonize narratives afforded to the aging body (Longino and Powell 2004). Morris (1998) agrees, asserting that consumer culture is preoccupied with reconstructing aging bodies, promoted through the glamorized representations of advertising. The visual image is increasingly dominant in Western culture; images can also be used to disseminate alternative constructions of old age. In their analysis of retirement magazines, Featherstone and

Hepworth (1993) argue that the types of images of old people presented in specialist magazines are consonant with attempts at focusing on the positive side of being old. This is usually linked to "young" old age, early retirement, and the continuation of full activities, usually through the engagement in leisure activities funded by careful financial planning. The message here is that there now exist opportunities for consumption (McAdams 1993; Gilleard and Higgs 2000) and enjoyment in old age that act as a counterpoint to traditional images of old people inexorably driven toward death via senility, physical decrepitude, loneliness, and disengagement. Thus, consumer society reinforces negative language and images of later life; in turn, this can produce a slide into "symbolic" death (Powell and Longino 2001).

Indeed, postmodern gerontology would claim that life-course models that associate aging with both decline and universal stages of life are fundamentally flawed (Powell and Longino 2001). To exemplify the fluid and blurred nature of aging identity, a uni-age style, Meyrowitz (1984, cited in Featherstone and Hepworth 1993), argues that in Western society, "children" are becoming more like adults and adults more childlike. There is a growing similarity in modes of presentation of self, gestures and postures, fashions, and leisure-time pursuits adopted by both parents and their children.

For Featherstone and Hepworth (1993) the private sphere of family life is becoming less private, as children are granted access to the larger world through popular media such as television and the Internet. Previously concealed aspects of adult life (such as sex, death, money, and problems besetting adults who are anxious about the roles and selves they present to children) are no longer so easy to keep secret. A uni-age behavioral style is influenced by the advent of media imagery that, as a powerful form of communication, bypasses the controls that adults once established over the kinds of information believed to be suitable for children. (An interesting premodern comparison relative to childhood resides with the work of Aries. He claims that in premodern times the child was allowed to participate as an adult after the age of seven.) One contribution of postmodern ideas is to illuminate the blurring of age identities in terms of "dress" and "work."

Therefore, the importance of the "body" to social gerontology is in many ways apparent. For example, the body in pain: illness can limit functions of the body and have effects that attract the interest of social gerontologists of all backgrounds globally. David B. Morris posits in his engaging study, *The Culture of Pain*: "Pain not only hurts but more often than not frustrates, baffles, and resists us. Yet it seems we cannot simply suffer pain but most always are compelled to make sense of it" (Morris 1991, 18).

Beyond the problem of making sense of pain (for example), the reason why the body is central to the discipline of social gerontology is that the biomedical model in particular has given intellectual respectability to "scientific" ideas concerning aging that raise issues about altering the boundaries of the physical body (Freund 1988). For example, biomedical science can reconstruct bodies through plastic surgery. Further, it can interfere with genetic structures; and it can swap internal organs from one human body to another (Haraway 1991; Powell and Longino 2001). "We," according to Haraway (1991), have become "cyborgs"— not wholly machines and not wholly natural organisms either. She argues: "Twentieth century machines have made thoroughly ambiguous the difference between natural and artificial, mind and body, self-developing and externally designed, and many other distinctions that used to apply to organisms and machines" (10).

However, Shilling (1993) argues that there is a schizophrenic ambivalence about the body: the more we know about bodies, and the more we are able to control, intervene, and restructure them, the more uncertain we become as to what the body really is. The boundaries between the physical body and society are becoming increasingly bifurcated. The body, like parchment, is written upon, inscribed by variables such as gender, age, sexual orientation, and ethnicity and by a series of inscriptions that are dependent on types of spaces and places. However, as Shilling (1993) powerfully argues, the more we know about bodies, the more we are able to govern and modify norms: highlighting how gendered and ageist discourses serve to confine and define aging bodies.

The role of the body has become a discursive site of power to be produced, acted upon, and received. Sandra Bartky, for instance, has argued that "normative femininity is coming more and more to be centred on woman's body. Not its duties and obligations or even its capacity to bear children, but its sexuality, more precisely its presumed heterosexuality and its appearance" (S. Bartky 1988, quoted in Wahidin and Powell 2003, 8).

One cannot argue in relation to body modification that the performance of the body is solely one to counter hegemonic biomedical discourses, or one based purely on aesthetic value, without fully encapsulating the varied and multifaceted technologies of the corporeal and the self. Through these bodily practices, old bodies are transforming their gendered habitus and thus creating identities for themselves that transgress the boundaries of how to manage old bodies (Longino and Powell 2004).

Bryan S. Turner (1995) emphasizes several key processes that work upon and within the body across time and space. Longino and Powell (2004) give as an example, here, how the effort to crack the genetic code of biological aging has directed attention away from socially determined life-chances in later life. Power relations become eclipsed by narratives of technological application subject to manipulation and control by a skilled professional. This is often a concern of medical students as they begin their education, but it is also often lost as part of their induction into a biomedical culture (Longino and Powell 2004).

Powell and Longino (2002) have argued that the disaggregation of the aging body takes a number of forms. First, the experience of aging is broken down into a number of separate age categories, each with its accompanying medical specialism. Second, the dominance of biomedical perspectives on aging has led to an acceptance of the association between adult aging and bodily and mental deterioration. Finally they note that a combination of specialism and a separation of mind from the body has compromised the gendered experience of bodily aging (Powell and Longino 2002). If aging becomes associated with illness, and the avoidance of aging with cure, then an expansion of medical discourse to include ever more aspects of the older person's life-world leaves two alternatives: subsumption of the self under the rubric of a sick body or a continual flight from the "symptoms" of aging (Longino and Powell 2004). Both depend upon biomedical hegemony (Biggs and Powell 2001). It follows from the above analysis that a biomedical approach to aging encourages the evacuation of certain forms of experience through the reclassification of experience into symptoms that can then be addressed separately from wider social impacts (Phillipson 1998).

Frank (1998) argues that the ability to tell one's own story of illness is by no means straightforward. If, as Foucault (1977) claims, the maintenance of existing power relations depends not on the use of force but on the ability to persuade active subjects to reproduce those relations for themselves, then the telling of narratives will always be suspect. Further, Frank (1996) poses the almost unanswerable question, When does self-care turn into a technology for producing a certain sort of self? For example, Estes, Biggs, and Phillipson (2003) suggest that personal narratives, particularly for older people in health settings, remain both a means of taking care of oneself and conformity to a restricted legitimizing discourse of their bodies and physical appearance.

Simultaneously, becoming and being old are about the corporeality of being old, the experience of holding on to physical/mental integrity and reasonable health (Baltes and Carstersen 1996). It is therefore important to focus on the construction of identity that is imposed upon the discourses of exteriority and interiority that impinge upon the body.

The postmodern interest in the body presents paradoxical aspects of the contemporary world. On the one hand, it is obsessed by the body and its materiality, emphasized by the attention given over to it in the media and consumer society in general. On the other hand, it has emptied the body of its symbolic meaning. It is no coincidence that recent artistic performances (e.g., body art) and popular youth culture practices (e.g., body piercing) appear like a desperate and contradictory attempt to recover the ritual significance of the body. To examine historically the various theories about the body is to become aware that Western culture has always, in a Manichean manner, separated the material from the spiritual, the body from the soul (May 1996). Western philosophy, founded on the Platonic dichotomy between body and soul, has considered the body as a prison and tomb for the psyche. Intellect in the Platonic conception becomes an autonomous and independent entity (May 1996). This disjoining operation conceived the soul positively and the body, with its materiality, negatively. As May (1996) stresses, this paradox in Western culture is to be found at the origin of Greek civilization because, if philosophical thought tries to disregard the body because of its corporeality, it nevertheless returns as a metaphor for the representation of the political system. In place of this dichotomy, primitive communities have endowed the body with a polysemic meaning: the body was the center of a symbolic network that ensured that both the natural and social world were modeled on its possibilities. In this way, the body was never an isolated and single entity but always a cosmic one, part of a community. Every individual managed to preserve, by means of a dense circulation of symbols connecting the one with the whole, his/her own individual perception of the body, albeit within a range of multiplicities and differences. At a time when youthfulness is valued, the dislocation felt between the eternality of the body or the surfaces of the body that symbolize the self and the internality of the body leaves many to combat age through "maintaining" their bodies via the commodification of youth.

The performance of the body is indicative of how the body is a discursive site of power to be produced, acted upon, negotiated, and received. These techniques create the space for resistance, enabling power to be positive yet at the same time negative. It is the polysemic nature of the body in all its guises that the performance is not solely one to counter, resist, and subvert hegemonic biomedical discourses. It is rather a relationship encapsulating the multivaried technologies of corporeal and self inscriptions based on what went on before, the present and immediate past (Wahidin and Powell 2003).

In a postmodern culture, the prospect of an endless life has been revived through consumer images of perpetual youth and a blurring of traditional life-course boundaries (Featherstone and Hepworth 1993). Bauman (1992) posits of the "postmodern strategy of survival," compared to "traditional ways of dabbling with timelessness," that "instead of trying (in vain) to colonize the future, it dissolves it in the present. It does not allow the finality of time to worry the living . . . by oscillating time (all of it, exhaustively, without residue) into short lived, evanescent episodes. It rehearses mortality, so to speak, by practicing it day by day" (Bauman 1992, 2).

POPULAR CULTURE AND THE AGING BODY

Throughout particular literary texts and through representations of the celebrated youthful body, the old body is something to be feared and resisted and thus at all costs should be held at bay (Longino and Powell 2004; Powell and Longino 2002).

For example, the motif of the woman's body transposed into a mythical and allegorical dimension returns in an essay on Irish women's literature in which Roberta Gefter Wondrich examines the contradictory relationship that women have with the images related to the myth of Ireland as a nation. On the one hand, Ireland is a great mother, a Marian Catholic image characterized by self-denial, an ever obedient woman who sacrifices herself for her son and is thus essentially passive; on the other hand, Ireland is the "old woman" who symbolizes the nation devastated by its destroyers (Greenblatt 1980).

The sense of isolation marks the works of a writer like Samuel Beckett, who uses the elderly body to express the absurdity of existence (Miller 1993). In several of his plays, Beckett represented old age through the violent divide between body and mind; he dramatized the inevitable physical decay of the body, until the only trace left of it on the stage is the word, the voice. Beckett studied and explored all the possible relations between the elderly body and space, between body and movement and between body and the objects that surround it. Beckett's ideal seems to be that of a man on a bicycle, a sort of a Cartesian centaur who emblematizes the phrase "mens sana in corpore disposito." In this respect the author explodes the dilemma "Cogito ergo sum": he rebels against the definition of man as a thinking machine (Miller 1993). Beckett's characters experience a tension between mind and body: a mind that is subject to continuous changes even if imprisoned in a body that is caught in a process of decaying and decrepitude. It is interesting to compare Beckett's characters with the disconcerting images of painter Francis Bacon, which are characterized by a prevailing sense of the vulnerability of man and, above all, his solitude, in the hell of the modern condition (Miller 1993). At the center of Bacon's representation is a view of man as a contingency, a creature with a disfigured face and body. This can be seen in his *Study after Velazquez's Portrait of Pope Innocent X* (1953), in which the theme of the cage and the imprisonment of the body underlines the horror of old age, emphasized by the screaming mouth of the figure (Greenblatt 1980).

Powell and Longino (2002) deal with some paradoxes implicit in our postmodern society, which is characterized by global information networks that work to project a conformist and consumerist view of the body and, at the same time, testifies to the different perceptions of the body by heterogeneous ethnic groups and peoples. The recent information revolution has forced us once again to question the relationship between the body and the machine. If it is true that the continuous bombardment of television images of mutilated and cut-up bodies has, so to speak, dematerialized them, on the other hand, the corporeality of the body comes obsessively back, as mentioned earlier, in the tribal rites that young people in the big metropolises impress on themselves.

Longino and Powell (2004, 177) further suggest that the aging body has a negative representation by cartoon fiction:

> Cartoonists tend to include deep lines on the face and loose skin beneath the chin, loss of or grey hair, a shorter distance between the nose and chin (if false teeth have been removed), glasses, liver spots on the hands, bowed legs and stooped backs. And, of course, there are the appropriate appendages and related signifiers, such as "walking canes," "walkers" or "wheel chairs." (Powell and Longino 2002)

At the other extreme, there are positive representations of aging via, for example, fictional characters from the J. R. Tolkien's *Lord of the Rings* that epitomize an agelessness, immortality, and wisdom in the role of wizardry. Nevertheless, the issue of gender and the body is crucial to understand the full complexity of aging in contemporary society.

THE GENDERED AGING BODY

Although we have analyzed modernist theoretical movements of functionalism, political economy of old age, and feminist gerontology, they ignore a postmodern understanding of aging identity, the body, cultural representations of aging, and gendered images of aging. The "gendered body" itself is a discursive site in which power is produced, acted upon, engaged with, and received. These aspects of power allow spaces for resistance to emerge, enabling power to be positive and at the same time negative. The experiences and knowledge of life before, in the celebrated young body and in the life threads of familial responsibilities and motherhood or fatherhood, can enable or disable the individual for success on the aging platform.

Theoretical arguments on gender sometimes fall prey to the philosophical error of essentialism: the appeal to metanarratives that claim to capture universal processes underlying essential differences between men and women and are insensitive to local knowledge and diversity (Harper 1997). Rather, the body is like a hinge, a pivot point, between two realities. Grosz (1994) asserts that the body is neither, while being both. Some of these binary categories are inside/outside, subject/object, and active/passive. It is not that older women are one way and older men the opposite. Bodies, whether men or women, are both ways. It is primarily their relationship to power that makes them different.

Women's stories are often about their relationship to their bodies; men's are not. Women "use" their bodies as an asset to accomplish their goals more than men do. Therefore, according to Shilling (1993), they are more likely than men to develop their bodies as objects of perception for others. The downside of this conscious embodiment of women is that as they age, they tend to lose a key asset, and thus come to think of themselves, and to be thought of, as invisible. If beauty and sexual allure are perishable values, men's power is embedded in status and wealth, more enduring values that tend to increase, not diminish, with age. The impact of the diminished assets of female identity is undeniable. Angie Dickenson, a sixty-eight-year-old American actress, reflecting on her experience of female embodiment and aging, put it well in an interview in a popular magazine:

> I'm surprised by every photograph I see of myself, because I don't look like I used to. I am not shocked anymore, just disappointed. I did look pretty good. I was all heart and sexiness, and that came from within. I had beautiful eyes, and unfortunately in trying to help them, I practically destroyed them with plastic surgery. I wish I looked now how I looked before, when I was young. (Life 2000, quoted in Longino and Powell 2004, 112)

Oberg and Tornstam (1999) found no evidence for the notion that women become more discontented with their bodies as they grow older, as compared with men. When asked to agree or disagree with the statement "I am satisfied with my body," about 80 percent of men agreed, regardless of their age. Only about two-thirds of young women agreed. But women in a successively older decade tended to agree more with the statement until there was essentially no difference between men and women after age sixty-five. It is younger women, not the older ones, who are the most dissatisfied.

The "body" within modernist theories of social gerontology pays insufficient attention to the ways in which gendered bodies have always enjoyed varying degrees of absence or presence in old age: in the guise of "female corporeality" and "male embodiment" (Gittens 1997). Indeed, there are discursive strategies whereby "the body" and "the social" are dissociated in the first place. In this framework, woman is saturated with, while man is divested of, corporeality. Older women have higher rates of chronic illnesses than do men, and their bodies outlast those of men. In clinical settings old women outnumber old men in nearly all waiting rooms. Yet the woman is divested while the man is invested with "the social," implying that knowledge is "gendered" and is male. The absent women in social gerontology were the women in the body excluded from the social. It is male bodies that animate the social; they appear for a fleeting moment, only to disappear immediately, in the space between "corporeality" and "sociality." Thus, it is not simply a case of recuperating bodies into the social, but of excavating the gendered discourses whereby gendered bodies were differently inscribed into and out of the social in the first place. The crucial point here is not the more familiar story of her saturation with corporeality but the less familiar one of what happened to his body. As a needed qualification, Harper (1997, 169), reminds us that because women are always embodied and men are not, "men become embodied as they age through the experience of the experiential and constructed body." So the gap between women and men may narrow, in some ways, as they age.

Indeed, feminist social theorists beyond macro-based "feminist gerontology" have underlined the limits of Cartesian thought, which considered the subject as disembodied and, above all, asexual (Braidotti 1994). In the representation of the female body, the dichotomy between body and mind has been used to emphasize sexual difference. On the one hand, we have masculinity, which is defined in relation to the mind and the logos, while the feminine is defined in relation to the body and its procreative functions: an essentialist construction, par excellence (Twigg 2000). As Adrienne Rich reminds us, women have had to deconstruct the patriarchal stereotype that links the female body with its procreative function: "I am really asking whether women cannot begin, at last, to think through the body, to connect what has been so cruelly disorganized" (1976, 184). With this incisive sentence, Rich stresses that women have to overcome the damning dichotomy between soul and body in order to reappropriate their bodies and to create a female subject, in which the two entities are complementary. Women often find themselves defined as "the other" (the residual category) against men, just as black people do against white people and gay people do against heterosexual people (Harper 1997). As Harper (1997) points out, they are the ones in the shadows, not in the positions of power: the defined, not the definers. For example, as we discussed earlier, contemporary cultural representations of aging focus on the body because this provides the clearest evidence of the historical inequality between gender differentiation: that the body of women is inscribed with oppressive ideological mystifications (Friedan 1993; Sontag 1991). Western literature and iconography are full of anthropomorphic discursive representations of old age as a woman with "grey hair," "withered," "faded," "pale and wan face," "foul and obscene" (Friedan 1993).

From this discussion, it would seem that the aging body is yet another mode of embodied subjectivity for gerontologists to unravel. The re-territorialization of the aging body by society, and paradigmatically by social gerontology, is a strategy that parallels the denial of wider social theory within the main traditions of social gerontology (Bengston, Burgess, and Parrot 1997). We have suggested that the concept of the "body" itself may take on particular sets of meanings for older people, both men and women, whose subjectivity of identity formation may conflict or legitimize cultural representations of aging.

The notion of "intertextuality" can be used as it is a mechanism by which the social world is fabricated, and this explains why cultural ideologies continually perpetuate perceptions of aging and gender. Postmodern perspectives can facilitate an understanding of how older people can intertextually reconstruct cultural narratives to explain their representations of identity and self-identity. Such a strategy involves a challenge to the homogeneity of the social category "elderly" as an embodiment of the "time's up" medical narrative. When the issue of social identity in later life is analyzed, Foucault's (1977) contention seems powerful in articulating that there has been a growth in the localities of power and knowledge that seek to inscribe physical and social bodies with discourses of normality and self-government. In the search for a stable identity not dominated by both professional and cultural discourses of power, older people must "achieve" it through "ontological reflexivity" (Giddens 1991). Accordingly, the self-identity needs to be consciously constructed and maintained. The aging self has a new existential pathway to follow, stepping outside dominant discourses of medical and patriarchal reason, to include a process of safety, self-exploration, self-struggle, and self-discovery (Powell and Longino 2002).

Contrary to Eurocentric philosophical traditions, feminist philosophical studies have emphasized that the body is a symbolic construct, located in a specific historical and cultural context: in other words its conceptualization can no longer ignore the close nexus between gender, class, and race (Blaikie 1999; Twigg 2000). Further, a significant issue for the articulation of aging with gender to further understand the "body" is represented by the theories of Foucault (1977) and Sontag (1991), which show the extent to which institutional medicine objectifies the "sick" body, once it has been biomedicalized (Powell 2001f). Foucault (1977) claims that medical practices produce the "soul" of the individual by disciplining the body and corporealizing medical spaces. Indeed, the success of modernity's domination over efficient bodies in industry, docile bodies in prisons, patient bodies in clinical research, and regimented bodies in schools and residential centers attest to Foucault's thesis that the human body is a highly adaptable terminus for the circulation of power relations (Powell and Biggs 2001; Armstrong 1983).

We have illuminated some of the paradoxes implicit in society, characterized by the historical discourses of decline and how they are embedded in popular culture relating to aging body and gendered body. Nevertheless, the next section shows how biotechnology networks work to project a conformist and consumerist view of the body, testifying to a different perception of the aging body by machine modification, a movement away from "expert" discourse to a new language based on "consumer identity" and "subjectivity" (Haraway 1991; Gilleard and Higgs 2000).

BIOTECHNOLOGY AND THE BODY: REINVENTING AGING?

The recent information revolution has forced us once again to question the relationship between the body and the machine. If it is true that the continuous bombardment of television images of mutilated and cut-up bodies has, so to speak, dematerialized them, on the other hand, the corporeality of the body comes obsessively back (Powell and Longino 2002; Longino and Powell 2004). However, computer communication has done away with bodily presence, and the new technologies make us see the machine as an extension of our bodies (Haraway 1991). The questions posed by this revolution in the dissemination of information are difficult to answer. It is no longer a question of emphasizing, in prophetic and apocalyptic tones, the end of humanism but rather of understanding how and to what extent technology and science can help us to change, since technology is ultimately inextricable from our aging body, becoming an apparatus which is at the same time material and symbolic. The cyborg, a fusion between machine and organic body, opens up an immense universe of possibility: nowadays, we no longer speak of organic bodies but of transorganic bodies, post-human bodies and bodies in the net (Haraway 1991; Longino and Powell 2004).

These diverse forms of bodily form hold out the promise of "utopian bodies," a movement away from static medical constrainment and objectification to much more self-subjectification practices (Morris 1998; Powell and Biggs 2004). Indeed, Haraway's (1991) original reference to cyborgic fusion of biological and machine entities has been enthusiastically taken up by postmodern gerontology. The list of biotechnologies available extends beyond traditional prosthesis to include virtual identities created by and reflected in the growing number of "silver surfers" using the Internet as a free-floating form of identity management. Thus Featherstone and Wernick (1995, 3) claim that it is now possible to reconstruct "the body itself" as biomedical and information technologies make available "the capacity to alter not just the meaning, but the very material infrastructure of the body. Bodies can be re-shaped, remade, fused with machines, empowered through technological devices and extensions."

The increasing popularization of such key terms for reinvented bodies as "machine bodies" implies an effect of producing an intrasubjective consciousness and a conspicuousness of behavior, either for bodily change or against it. Moral action, whether it is individual or collective, involves the self knowing the self, a process of self-formation as an ethical aging subject (Powell and Biggs 2004). Self-responsibility, when passed through the notion of the "sick body," becomes a covert form of moral judgment upon which decisions to supply or deny often expensive forms of biotechnology can be made (Powell and Biggs 2004). Indeed, one is unwell because one is unhealthy, and one is unhealthy because the proper steps of self-care had not been taken in the past. So why should others have to provide scarce resources to make good this moral turpitude? Such an attitude to the healthy body presents moral decisions on the supply and demand for services in the "neutral" language of technomedical science (Powell and Biggs 2004). However, the outcome is that the prudent do not need it, while the imprudent do not deserve it. Any allusion here to economic planning and to pension policy is more than passing, for in both cases it is the resource-rich who can afford, but may rarely need, such technology, whereas the resource-poor cannot afford it (Moody 1998; Phillipson 1998). For example, biotechnology can sell as "truth" a dream of "not growing old" to older people (Powell and Biggs 2004). However, it is the self-experience of aging subjects that can refute, deny, and accept the "truth" claims of biotechnology (Rose 1996). In the case of lifestyles of the aging, the active adoption of particular consumer practices such as uses of biotechnology contributes to a narrative that is both compensatory and "ageless" in its construction of self (Biggs and Powell 2001). The aging body culturally represents the best hiding place for internal illnesses that remained inconspicuous until the advent of biotechnologies (Frank 1996). Subjective relations to the self will be affected to the extent that biotechnologies confront older people with the proposition that this subjective truth: the truth of their relation to themselves and to others may be revealed by their "aging bodies." If this is legitimate, we may anticipate through "biology and culture" (Morris 1998) the problematic of illnesses associated with aging rejoining the sphere of bioethics through the back door. "Illness" and "body repair" as problematized by biotechnology will again belong to the strategic margin that older people embody as subjects of purposeful action.

There are obvious tensions between the biotechnological commodification of old age. It is through constructing and transgressing the aging body, by subverting the "stigma" surrounding later life (Powell and Biggs 2000), and thus redefining physical capital (May 1996) that many old bodies resisted the fixed images of old age. Moreover, within this discursive space of biotechnology the construction of the aging body allows elders to become their own significant other, to challenge the gaze of others and to "be for themselves." Their reconstructed bodies, therefore, become sites of empowerment whether they collude or resist ageist stereotypes.

CONCLUSION

This chapter has drawn insights from postmodernism, which provides compelling questions of how we interpret, problematize, and understand the body as dancing in-between subject/object. Hence, the chapter has demonstrated how the body is not separate from the body subject (May 1996) but is intertwined. Arthur Frank (1991, 1996) argues that, simultaneously, the embodied agent becomes a producer of society while at the same time it is society that creates the embodied agent.

It is by reimagining the boundaries of the body that we can begin to understand how the gaze inscribes itself unintelligibly on the aging body. The argument that has been presented here demonstrates an understanding of the body as both lived through and as constructed. The study of the body in gerontological literature needs to engage with the real materiality of bodies and at the same time understand the ways in which bodies are performed, represented, and positioned.

Central to this discussion is how the inscription of aging, popular culture, gender, and biotechnology are placed on and work in tandem with the rhythms of the body. The body is constantly operating within fields of temporality in which mobile networks of relations produce and transmit power/knowledge to the object vis-à-vis subject (Butler 2000). Thus the body operates within fields of power and within the realm of signs. It has been argued that time and identity in society consist of a multiplicity of discursive elements that come into play at various times, thus existing in "different and even contradictory discourses" (Foucault 1982, 100–102). The body is a "visage," a collection of signs to be interpreted. It becomes a façade (cf. Biggs 1993), which at the same time both conceals and expresses the inner being. It is by centralizing the historical development of the body in social theory that one can illustrate and interrogate how the architecture of the ageist discourse recodes their now "profaned" bodies. Constructing some bodies as marginal and excluding them from mainstream representations defines boundaries and gives legitimacy to society's claims of what is a "natural" way for a body to look.

The body is a dynamic, nebulous form and always in the process of becoming. The contours of the body outline a visible but transitional object (Featherstone and Wernick 1995). But, as Powell and Longino (2001) argue, there is no surety of what the body is. What one can argue from discussion of the body is that it becomes the threshold through which the subject's lived experience of the world is incorporated and interpolated and, as such, can never be purely understood. The aging body is a "transitional entity"; power is produced, generated, and negotiated in terms of the inscriptions placed on the aging body in micro and local domains.

Indeed, by taking a localized approach, postmodern gerontology has been more adaptable than any "grand narrative" to address issues of power and oppression (Seidman 1994, 207). By focusing on the aging body and how culture impinges on its subject formation, postmodern gerontology goes beyond fixed classifications of modern ideas deriving from biomedical sciences as well as grand narratives of macrotheories of aging (Longino and Powell 2004; Powell 2001c). This is a view consolidated by Bauman (2001), who points to the way that society has become increasingly individualized. All individual lives are affected by localized conditions and narratives, and what is needed is an analysis of the extent to which the individual is governed by external conditions in terms of their life choices (Bauman 2001, 6–7). Bauman argued that postmodern culture is effectively a competitive market, trading in "life meanings" (Bauman 2001, 4), and this can be linked to Lyotard's suggestion that knowledge has become the product of different "specialisms" to be bought and sold for profit (Lyotard 1984, 5). For example, the fragmentation of the aging body has become a commodifiable social space through which biotechnologies can offer body reconstruction in consumer-led Western society through machine extensions to the body (Powell and Longino 2002).

Similarly, Frederic Jameson (1991) understood postmodernism as an extension of the "logic of late capitalism." Jameson argued that globalization and multinational capitalism had resulted in mass consumerism and the total commodification of culture, in which "images, styles and representations are the products themselves" (Connor 1989, 46). However, Stuart Hall argues that the postmodern idea of cultural homogenization is too simplistic (Hall 1992, 304). He suggests that in a restructuring of social theory we should acknowledge how the global and the local articulate and recognize that globalization is unevenly distributed and is also a Western phenomenon indicative of the unequal power relations between the West and the rest. Estes, Biggs, and Phillipson (2003) consolidate this by suggesting that Occidental globalization affects the poverty status of older people universally.

Nevertheless, the great strength of postmodernism is to dissect fixed discourses of modernity and reveal alternative cultural processes that impinge on both epistemic and ontologically flexible narratives pertaining to the human body. As Seidman states, modernist social theory was focused on neat divisions, hierarchies, and foundational premises, and the aim of sociologists was to find universalisms (Seidman 1994, 347). Postmodernism, on the other hand, was to look at subject formation regarding the body as it has been overlooked by macromodernist theories. Whereas postmodernists would question the notion of truth and focus on intrasubjective dimensions of bodily performance, the conceptual "tool kit" Foucault has added allows wider insights to power relationships between and through subjects/objects of knowledge and professional experts.

Indeed, the critical relationship of aging to society and interaction in power relationships has found expression in writings of Foucault. Foucault is not a postmodernist (Smart 1993) but his work has been bound up with it because of Foucault's (1977) own questioning of the "truth" status of epistemological knowledge through historical medical and criminal discourses. His work shifts to the interplay of self-subjectification practices grounded in power/knowledge (Foucault 1977), technologies of self (1978), and governmentality (1978) at microphysical levels of society that operate between social actors such as doctor and patient, teacher and pupil, prison officer and prisoner, and health professional and older person as "client." The next chapter explores the "Foucault effect" on gerontological theorizing and its relevance to how power relations play out in interactions of professional welfare experts with older people by analysis of "discourse," "power/knowledge," "technologies of self," and "governmentality."

Chapter 6

The "Foucault Effect" and Aging: Relations of Power, Surveillance, and Governmentality

Add Foucault and stir. . . .

—Shumway 1989, 5

The theories Foucault devised are not intended as permanent structures, enduring in virtue of their universal truth. They are temporary scaffoldings, erected for a specific purpose, which Foucault is happy to abandon to [whoever] might find them useful.

—Gutting 1994, 16

INTRODUCTION

The subject matter of this chapter is the development of an understanding of aging and professional power over the past fifty years, using examples drawn from social welfare and old age, through developing the theories and philosophies derived from the French social theorist, Michel Foucault. Whereas chapter 4 focused on postmodernism and the body in Western culture, this chapter consolidates analysis of the aging body to explore the interrelationship between discourse, professional power, and intersubjectivity. Foucault's concepts and ideas have become significantly influential in a variety of social science disciplines. At the same time they can be puzzling for those wishing to understand their implications for analyzing professional power and aging. Foucault was a "masked philosopher" who deliberately sought to avoid being aligned with any particular school of thought: "It is true that I prefer not to identify myself, and that I'm amused by the diversity of the ways I've been judged and classified" (1977, 113). For example, David Garland (1985) claims that Foucault has had a "huge impression" on criminological studies and allowed the discipline to develop a new theoretical language. Foucault is yet to have the same effect on social gerontology. Unfortunately, Foucault said little about aging, and one can only speculate as to the ingenuity of his insights on the subject had he lived into old age himself (Katz 1996).

Michel Foucault's scholarly work has been acclaimed as "the most important event in thought of our century" (Veyne 1980, 44). Throughout his work, Foucault has attempted to develop perspectives on psychiatry, medicine, punishment, and criminology.

Indeed, Foucault's diverse range of theoretical works highlights two significant contexts in the analyses of aging. The first is to assert the relevance of discipline and punishment and madness and medicine to both the representations and experiences of older people. The introduction of the "expert gaze" in health and medical professions allows the space for exploration of discourses and impingement of stereotypical "subjects" of knowledge such as the "mentally ill," "criminals," and also the "elderly" as they are constructed through disciplinary techniques.

Secondly, Foucault's (1980) discursive analytical "tools" enable us to analyze both the authoritative discourses embodied in public policies and professional practices within society, in particular the power relations between professional workers and older people (Powell and Biggs 2000). Foucault's scholarly works (1967, 1976, 1977) have relevance to "old age" in the respect that social practices describe patterns of "normalization" in a political landscape dominated by consumer culture. It will be shown that these practices, which are evaluated by "experts" such as "care managers" who problematize "the elderly" (Powell and Biggs 2000) via a process of "assessment" for social and health services in contemporary society, are the center of Foucault's (1977) analysis of "panoptic technology" in "surveying" and managing "elderly" clients. Before we assess the relevance of these gerontological issues, we need to situate the work of Foucault as a contextual backdrop to understanding old age and professional power.

CONTEXTUAL BACKDROP OF
FOUCAULT'S EARLY STRUCTURALISM

The structuralist approach saw the world from a completely opposing viewpoint, their world being "pre-structured" and we, as humans, structured in it. Structuralists take one step back in looking at how the world is organized to influence peoples' self-understanding, from a sense of cultural relation and personal reference or identity within particular social conformities (Powell and Wahidin 2003). As Dreyfus and Rabinow (1983, 8) have asserted: "structuralism attempts to dispense with both meaning and the subject by finding objective laws which govern all human activity."

In opposition to this position, the general foundation of hermeneutics releases the phenomenologists' attempt to understand man as a "meaning-giving subject," but attempts to preserve meaning by locating it in the social practices and literary texts that authors produce. A product of his time, Foucault during the 1960s argued against an entire philosophical and political structure where two main streams of thought existed in fundamental Marxism and psychoanalysis. The problem with psychoanalysis was that it attempted to explain everything from one theory or viewpoint, that being via "infantile sexualism." This speculative reductionism was inadequate in explaining the complexities of various local group uprisings within society during those times. It was particularly inadequate to explain the mentality of the masses of people who united as one individualized group to revolt against existing structures that had been suppressing both the individual's sense of "self" and the distinct groups that they identified with. Foucault is often seen as a structuralist, along with Barthes, Althusser, and Levi-Strauss (May 1996). In reply to questions that sought to make such parallels, he was consistent: "I am obliged to repeat it continually. I have never used any of the concepts which can be considered characteristic of structuralism" (Foucault, quoted in May 1996, 88). Perhaps the best way to view this is by examining his idea of historical "events." He refuses to see events as symptomatic of deeper social structures and focuses upon what seems to be marginal as indicative of relations of power. Events thereby differ in their capacity to produce effects. The following quote helps us see how this can be applied to gerontological analysis:

> The problem is at once to distinguish among events, to differentiate the networks and levels to which they belong, and to reconstitute the lines along which they are connected and engender one another. From this follows a refusal of analyses couched in terms of the symbolic field or the domain of signifying structures, and a recourse to analyses in terms of the genealogy of relations of force, strategic development, and tactics. Here I believe one's point of reference should not be to the great model of language (langue) and signs, but to that of war and battle. (Foucault 1980, 114)

Structuralism can be seen as an important asset to the development of social research and particularly for social gerontology in terms of the promotion of introspection on their life-course by the elderly "subjects of study" and reflections by researchers, policy makers, and the general public on the problematization of "old age" within society and government. It is also important for its discourses into the radical empowerment of older citizens in therapeutic programs to resist suppressive regulatory norms imposed and induced by institutionalized care. Lastly, structuralism provides historical mapping of the changes in our understandings of concepts over time, or lack thereof, within the systems of health and aged care, through analysis of authoritative writings such as policy documents. For instance, the concept of "health" and how we legislate for health has changed considerably since the Poor Law Reform Act of 1834 in Great Britain (Phillipson 1982). This movement acts as a significant benchmark for the origins of institutionalized aged care, which began with authoritative control in managing the masses of vagrants, homeless, and the poor, many of whom were older people (Katz 1996, 55).

Foucault's early works on *Madness and Civilization* and *The Birth of the Clinic* focused on the analysis of historically situated systems of institutions and discursive practices—which were distinguished from the "speech acts" of everyday life. Foucault did not look at individual's narratives but was interested only in what Dreyfus and Rabinow (1983, xxiv) called "serious speech acts," which were what experts perform when they are speaking as experts about a given issue within a discipline of thought or practice such as law or medicine. Furthermore, Foucault's restriction of these analyses to the human sciences introduced new methods to critique the emergence of pseudoscientific tools of analysis within the study of human beings, such as psychoanalysis and sociology, which, with their speculative, introspective, and retrospective techniques in understanding human behavior, were considered as "dubious" disciplines (Wahidin and Powell 2001, 2003).

In *The Archaeology of Knowledge* (1972) Foucault introduced his "archaeological method" whereby the interrelations between the artifacts of study, that is, the people involved, are analyzed for insights into the "power relationships" existing within the structure of these relationships and how the social institutions in which these particular structures existed influenced the discursive practices.

Like Thomas Kuhn's paradigmatic shifts, the Foucauldian discursive practices appear antistructuralist in that there are structures that explain a discourse, such as the fundamental acceptance of the state as the controller of power, which influences and exerts power upon groups and society in general. Foucault's work is beyond structuralism and hermeneutics and is useful in historically situating gerontology within a context of ordering and systematizing practices characteristic of the disciplinary technologies. His interest in the social effects rather than the implicit meaning of banal practices leaves hermeneutic concerns behind.

Foucault's way of reading history proves powerful in understanding the emergence of gerontology in that he manages to both criticize and utilize "phenomenology, hermeneutics and structuralism" (Smart 1993), thus enabling one to explain how the study of elderly people as subjects and objects has had such centrality in both history and culture. Foucault's refusal to be characterized in particular ways may be interpreted as an intentional political strategy central to his overall philosophy. He rejects any allusion to certainty in social and political life and holds that there is no universal understanding beyond history, placing him at odds with currents in Marxism, as well as rationalist thought in general. That noted, we can find imperatives that receive differing degrees of emphasis throughout his work, one of which is "to discover the relations of specific scientific disciplines and particular social practices" (Rabinow 1984, 4). He has engendered an awareness that disciplines, institutions, and social practices operate according to logics that are at variance with the humanist visions that are assumed to be culturally embedded (Powell and Biggs 2000).

The analytical audaciousness of Foucault's approach can be applied to Foucauldian aspects of aging but such forms of knowledge base remains relatively small in social gerontology (Katz 1996).

FOUCAULDIAN GERONTOLOGY

Only a tiny handful of international gerontologists have used Foucault's work to shatter taken-for-granted assumptions centered on aging. In Canada, Stephen Katz's (1996) *Disciplining Old Age: The Formation of Gerontological Knowledge* is a landmark via Foucauldian analysis of aging. This work is a theoretically rigorous analysis of the emergence of gerontology as a discipline from the study of old age. Katz's explorations into the social, political, organizational, and epistemological frameworks involved in the "gerontological web" had articulately demonstrated their influence in the negative characterizations of the elderly as a distinct kind of population. Katz's adept incorporation of Foucauldian theories into an analysis of gerontology showed how the discipline emerged through discourses from the various authoritative powers or "experts" in the health and academic professions, via their writings or "master narratives," associations, funding organizations, and schools of thought. Katz (1996) has identified that aging is not a static process and for this reason cannot be singularly analyzed via any particular discipline. By use of Foucault's work, Katz (1996) demonstrates that the challenge to "age disciplines" impinges upon the "power/knowledge" axis. Crucially, such an axis permeates all formal and informal discourses, their language, logic, forms of domination and classification, measurement techniques and empiricism as essential elements in the technology of discipline and the process of normalization. "Professionals" such as gerontologists and geriatricians are key interventionists in societal relations and, in the management of social arrangements, wield a daunting power to classify, with consequences for the reproduction of knowledge about aging and simultaneous maintenance of power relations (Powell 1998). According to Powell (1998)

Katz's work demonstrates that the challenges to mainstream "age disciplines" have adopted the agendas of these traditions, taking their historical and contemporary agendas as legitimate points of departure. While starting with "knowledge as it stands," that which is "known," Katz reconstructs such knowledge at the interpersonal level of "agency."

In the United Kingdom, Tulle-Winton (1999) has looked at the notion of the body and its relationship to Foucauldian theories of embodiment. Powell has applied the "Foucauldian gaze" to understanding the "ageing body" (2001) and governmentality and social policy (2001). The works of Powell and Biggs (2000) and Biggs and Powell (2000, 2001) have developed Foucauldian approaches relating to "medical power and social welfare" (Powell and Biggs 2000), "care management and elder abuse" (Biggs and Powell 2000), and genealogies of professional power and aging (Biggs and Powell 2001; Powell and Gilbert, 2010). In addition, Powell and Cook (2000, 2001) have developed perspectives on governmentality and "superaging" in China. Coupled with this, Wahidin and Powell (2001) have used Foucauldian narratives to examine "institutional abuse" in special hospitals (Wahidin and Powell 2001). May (1996) has explored nursing's development of holistic care with older people as contributing to the rise and consolidation of disciplinary power of the nurse over the older patient through "therapeutic surveillance."

Biggs and Powell (2001) have described studies that adopt Foucault's conceptual insights as exploring "the differential ways in which bodies are regulated, understood and constructed." Estes, Biggs, and Phillipson (2003) locate a progressive movement toward the construction of the "whole person" as the object of care "gazes" and through a change toward risk-oriented practice. Powell (2001) in his Foucauldian analysis of aging identified how professional practices used to elicit information and profiles about aging populations came to be linked to biomedical techniques and practices used at the individual level in constructing the object of scientific study. Thus statistical data about the nature of older people's health consolidated the biomedical gaze on visual inspection of older people's bodies and minds. The object of study in the nexus of "microphysics of power" is a capillary form of power reaching to the very minutia of detailed profiling of an individual person and profiles of aging populations. Through history, the knowledge base of biomedical practice has shifted to include survey data about social circumstances and beliefs and their effects on care. Professional power emphasized supporting and negotiating strategies in communication with patients in order to alter and shape behavior. What Powell (2001a) is highlighting is that the object of biomedicine is being reconstructed as both object and subject.

Fundamentally, the use of a "Foucauldian" approach in social gerontology is a novel way of interpreting and problematizing knowledge systems. It provides new questions, objects of inquiry, and flexible epistemological and ontological dimensions of gerontological analysis. While retaining a concern with the dynamics of power and knowledge, embedded within and (re)produced by social policy, a Foucauldian approach shifts attention away from a sole analysis of the state, the logic of capital, or patterns of material inequality. Power remains a concept central to any Foucauldian understanding of the social processes and institutional practices but in novel and varying ways.

The effect of this has been to call into question the categories and assumptions of social gerontology, understood here as both a disciplinary field of knowledge and as a practice that focuses on social policy and aging. In raising the question of "knowledge" as a socially constituted category through which "power" is manifested and deployed, a Foucauldian approach can destabilize the notion of a "universal" human subject whose needs can be known through the application of bureaucratic procedures, that is, the subject who is the target of professional power (Katz 1996). This means that the ontological status of the gerontological "subject" becomes open not only to deconstructive scrutiny but also to epistemological discourses by which this subject is categorized and classified.

It can be argued that it is through "historical investigation" that scholars can understand the present which takes aim at understanding Foucault's potential use of methods to understanding social formations relevant to adult aging. If we use "historical inquiry" we should "use it, to deform it, to make it groan and protest" (Foucault 1980, 54). Historical critique should be used to shatter taken-for-granted biomedical assumptions surrounding aging. But Powell and Biggs (2001, 10) warn that this focus: "on medicalization has tended to obscure another discourse on aging the association between old age and social welfare."

As we discussed earlier, gerontology is also the study of social welfare and social policy focused on aging (Biggs 1999). Social policy for older people in "neoliberal" capitalist societies is complex and multifaceted. Neoliberalism considers that a welfare society must reflect only the interplay of social and political structures forged out of self-responsibility and consumerism (Powell 2001c). Older people derive their "care," individually and collectively, from a range of policies, institutions, and sites, so that the organization of care involves markets, families, and state and care institutions. Responsibility for the organization of "care-based" social policy has historically been the social work profession or the contemporary care management institution (Powell and Gilbert 2010).

Medical discourses and neoliberal norms of the positioning of older people are not only about the therapeutic nature of the "health and care" duality, drawn from medical sciences, but also, if not more, about "management enforcers" (Biggs 1999) of competition, quality, inspection, and customer demand.

These definitions of analytical frameworks on aging have significant implications for how "aging" is understood, both as a discipline of study and as a social process: as a discipline in interrogating how knowledge in modernity has been organized and legitimated and as a social process in terms of complex interactions between recent social policy shifts, professional experts, and older people. In combination, these definitions refer to the discourses, perceptions, sites, and practices that are conditions of possibility for the emergence of gerontological knowledge. Engaging with these possibilities for knowledge construction requires a methodological means and gerontological definitional examples drawn from medical power and their antecedent relationship to the positioning of older people as "declining" subjects/objects.

The effects of the decline analogy can be most clearly seen in the dominance of medico-technical solutions to the problems that aging is thought to pose. This, according to Katz (1996), has led to a significant skewing of gerontological theorizing and research toward geriatric medicine, as well as the relative failure of more broadly based social and life-course approaches to change thinking about old age.

Conversely, a preoccupation with the medical challenges presented by aging, underpinned by privatized and insurance-driven health provisions, has resulted in what Foucault (1973) may have observed as an expansion of the medical "gaze" into wider areas of social policy. The medical gaze refers here to discourses, languages, and ways of seeing that shape the understanding of aging into questions that center on, and increase the power of, the health professions and restrict or delegitimize other possibilities. A consequence is that areas of policy that may at first seem tangential to the medical project come to be reflected in its particular distorting mirror.

The influence of the medical gaze can be seen in the policy debates of the late 1980s and early 1990s concerning disadvantaged groups, over a shrinking public purse and fears of a breakdown of an intergenerational social contract, considered to be a foundation of postwar welfare policy (Phillipson 1998). The impact of medicalized notions of aging and its construction as a threat to other sections of the population can also be seen in Harry R. Moody's (1998) critique of bioethics and aging and the rationing of Medicare coverage in American welfare policy. Medical care has come to colonize notions of old age and reinforce ageist prejudices to the extent that infirmity has come to stand for the process of aging itself and medicine its potential, yet prohibitively expensive, savior.

Foucault's (1967, 1972) early works impinge on how "epistemic" discourses problematized human subjectivity. His later work is much more grounded in the interplay of power and knowledge, governmentality, and technologies of self. If we take summaries of both his early and later works, in turn, we can see the relevance of his overall oeuvre to theorizing professional power and aging. Foucault (1977) was principally interested in how particular forms of knowledge came into existence and the social conditions that made this possible. The next section draws from this and sketches the main developments of expert discourses by digging into the past in order to explain present social practices.

The "Expert" Gaze and Discourse of Dependency

Foucault's concern in his earlier structuralist work (1967, 1972) was to show that the epistemological and "truth" status of medical and scientific knowledge derives from the field in which it, as a discourse, is employed, and not from a hermeneutic interpretation of the discoursing subjects' thoughts. A discourse is a set of ideas, practices, and beliefs that coalesce to produce an overarching picture of society. He deliberately subordinated the individual subjects' will to the construction of medical and scientific discourses, as he set about exploring the relationship between such discourses and human subjectivity.

Coupled with this, the "aging body" became the site of medical and scientific practice and designated experts developed the medical gaze with which they viewed and defined human physical properties (Powell 2001a, 2001b; Powell and Biggs 2000; Biggs and Powell 2001). The construction of subjects as authorities, knowers, and speakers of knowledge, is a controversial linking of professional discourse and its dialectical interplay with the subjectivity of older people.

Indeed, the emergence of professional power in what has since come to be called modernity is also associated with transformations that took place from the nineteenth century onward. In the case of social welfare, these transformations have been associated with a series of moral panics about the family in which the state was expected to intervene (Jones 1983). Professional social work developed in this space between public and private spheres and was produced by sets of relations among the law, administration, medicine, the school, and the family. The rise and consolidation of social work was seen as a "benevolent" solution to a major problem posed to the liberal state, namely, how can the state establish the health and development of family members who are "dependent" while promoting the family as the "natural" sphere for caring for those individuals and thus not intervening in all families (Hirst 1981)? Thus, social work developed as a halfway point between individual families and the state, which would be in danger of taking responsibility for everybody's needs and hence undermining the responsibility and role of the family. This hybrid and somewhat ambivalent positioning of a new discipline meant that from its inception the social work profession has had to negotiate the boundary between public expectation and private conduct.

The traditional identity of professional social work rests on what can be identified as "modernist" foundations (Biggs and Powell 2001). While nursing and medicine have drawn heavily on technical/scientific knowledge to justify their expert status, social work has drawn, with relative degrees of success and in succeeding periods, on psychoanalysis and the social sciences. Both health and welfare have been part of a great movement for "progress" characteristic of the twentieth-century grand narrative.

As the twentieth century proceeded, the growth of social work became dependent upon its interrelationships with the welfare state, which provided its primary rationale and legitimacy. As a consequence, social work mediated not only between potentially socially excluded individuals and the state, but also between those individuals and diverse private and voluntary agencies. Further, social work as an expert profession became closely related to the development of new forms of social regulation associated with the increased complexity of modern society (Garland 1985).

Throughout the 1940s, 1950s, and 1960s, the new human sciences had as their central aim the prediction of future behavior (Ignatieff 1978), which fit well with social work's professional mission and what emerged as its chosen method: psychoanalysis (Biggs 1999). The point here is that this negative stance, coupled with the need for a discourse that both reinforced professional power and the marginal positioning of older people, found each other in the early use of psychodynamic language by social workers on both American and British sides of the Atlantic. Thus, the "caring" profession tended to draw upon psycho-analytic discourse to socially construct an image of older people as "greedy and demanding, always clamoring for material help, always complaining of unfair treatment or deprivation; this attitude shades into paranoid imagining" (Irvine 1954, 27). This psychologized view of failing independence closely parallels an economic discourse that old age constitutes a drain on resources that could be used more "productively."

Such an expert "gaze" constructs older people as both subjects and objects of knowledge and power. As Powell and Biggs (2000, 7) elaborate: "The identities of elderly people and old age have been constructed through expert discourses of 'decay' and 'deterioration' and the 'gaze' helps to intensify regulation over older people in order to normalize and provide treatment for such notions."

Techniques of surveillance are so sophisticated, argues Foucault, that "inspection functions ceaselessly. The gaze is everywhere" (1977, 195). Foucault points here to the means through which power is exercised. He places the processes of discipline, surveillance, individualization, and normalization at the center of his analysis. These processes were key elements in the genesis of public welfare agencies from the inception of the British welfare state in 1945 (Phillipson 1998). For example, social work with older people was part of a strategy that extended "control over minutiae of the conditions of life and conduct" (Cousins and Hussain 1984, 146). Within this discourse, the professional social worker became "the great advisor and expert" (Rabinow 1984, 283–84) in the utilization of medicoscientific insights in constructing services for older people.

Discourses of "dependency" formed the foundations of practice development in modernity in relation to older people. The notion of dependency was articulated in terms of policy through the state provision of care services and via social work through the practice of caregiving to older people (Bowl 1986). The aim of such policy was to deliver security to people moving into later life both through financial provision and care services.

Thus a discourse of dependency came to colonize wider perceptions of aging, and as welfarism became the place in which older people became visible to the rest of society (Powell and Biggs 2000). This position was reinforced as knowledge was collected on older populations throughout such agencies and remedies channeled through their offices. Psychoanalytic thinking, rather than an occasion for psychological liberation, became the language and the technique through which the identities of professionals and their clients were shaped.

Under particular social circumstances, discourses emerged that led to the creation of new professions that, in turn, simultaneously reinforced the discourse itself. In that process, a new type of knowledge about older people emerged, and new sites in which to grow old were created. Foucault (1967) was particularly interested in the limits and possibilities of discourses from "human sciences" because of their attempts to define human subjectivity. His attention shifts to the power of professionals because Foucault found that the conditions of possibility for "true" discourses about human subjects include complex relations between knowledge about people and systems of power. Here Foucault focuses on the techniques of power/knowledge that operate within an institution and that simultaneously create "a whole domain of knowledge and a whole type of power" (1977, 185). These domains effectively destroy the legitimacy of other, competing, discourses, just as a professional medical opinion might delegitimize voices arising from folk medicine (Freund 1988) or even informal care (Dalley 1988). As Biggs and Powell (2001, 111) warn: "If they are not careful, both professionals and users of health and welfare systems become trapped in a dance of mutually maintained positions that serves to sustain a particular view of aging and the remedies, the technologies, that can be brought to bear on it."

Subjectivity, Power/Knowledge, and Professional "Practices" of Discourse

Foucault's later work on the "history of the present," was more interested in "power/knowledge" synthesis and how the subject was formed (Foucault 1977, 1978). Here, Foucault's work is on the "microphysics of power" and the interplay of power relations, dividing practices, and tactics in localistic contexts (Foucault 1977): the doctor and the patient, prison officer and prisoner, teacher, and student, and care manager and older consumer (Biggs and Powell 2000; Powell 2001d).

Foucault's archaeological method is not theoretical but "genealogical." As a technique of isolating discourse objects for study, it serves to separate and defamiliarize the serious discourse of the human sciences, which in turn allows Foucault to raise the genealogical questions: "How are these discourses used? What role do they play in society?" (Dreyfus and Rabinow 1983, xxv). Foucault acquired the concept of "genealogy" from the writings of F. Nietzsche. Genealogy maintains elements of archaeology, including the analysis of statements in the archive (Foucault 1977, 1980, 1982). With genealogy Foucault (1977) added a concern with the analysis of power/knowledge, which manifests itself in the "history of the present." As Rose points out, genealogy concerns itself with disreputable origins and "unpalatable functions." For example, Biggs and Powell's (1999, 2001) genealogy of psycho-casework and care management points to the origins, functions, and practices of social work as a scientific and managerial profession that are less benevolent than official histories of professional practice pretend. As Foucault (1980, 109) found in his exploration of psychiatric power: "Couldn't the interweaving effects of power and knowledge be grasped with greater certainty in the case of a science as 'dubious' as psychiatry?"

Foucault (1977, 1978) focuses on the techniques of power that operate within an institution and which simultaneously create "a whole domain of knowledge and type of power" (Foucault 1977, 185). Biggs and Powell (2001) point out that a genealogical argument, as related to professional power, works to "[uncloak] these power relations [and] is characterised, by Foucault, to set out to examine the 'political regime of the production of truth'" (Davidson 1986, 224).

As institutions of power such as social work, newly redefined as "case management" (Powell 2002; Biggs and Powell 2001), arose, they brought into existence new clientele groups such as "consumers" who could be defined as "different" from wider age-based "population formations" based on discourses of "burden" and "dependency" (Powell 2001d). With the marketization of welfare, social work has been significantly eroded, and with it their traditional role as provider and counsellor of services for older people. Not only do new discourses provide a "swarming" of professional power/knowledge, they can also take away. At the same time, the technique of "panopticism" was incorporated into social work relationships in the twentieth century so that older people could be observed by professional power (Powell and Biggs 2000). Social service provision for older people has elements of this kind of surveillance. Supervision is hierarchical in the sense that many mature adults are accompanied by management discretionary power which embraces monitoring, assessing, and calculating older people (Powell and Biggs 2000). Social service departments need to be kept informed of their clientele's progress in order to communicate this at formal review meetings, to establish resource allocation, to service spending planning. Surveillance of older people does not stop at this point, as a network of reciprocal power relationships has been created (Powell and Biggs 2000): "[T]his network 'holds' the whole together and traverses it in its entirety with effects of power that derive from one another: supervisors, perpetually supervised" (Foucault 1977, 176–77).

Older people who require welfare services are the objects of scrutiny within Western society, but for such clients requiring financial services, the gaze reaches further. This evidences a strategic shift toward the policing of welfare and away from the postwar welfare consensus relationship to old age. Old age then became, in this period, increasingly associated with risk, both personal and structural, and at the same time was subject to a privatization of that risk and a withdrawal or rolling back of supports, previously taken as stable and enduring (Biggs and Powell 2001). It is not by chance that an increased focus on risk in social work has coincided with the decline in trust in social workers' expertise, decision-making through psychoanalytical insights, and a growing reliance on increasingly complex systems of managerialism, with older people themselves as "consumers" of services. Hence, the managerial gaze has come to rival the biomedical gaze. The power of the "case manager" as a gerontological expert has supplemented medical power.

Foucault's (1977) idea that power is a "relationship" expresses the effect that repression and productivity will occur with this control over people. A new structure then enters that promotes the possibility for a revolution in thinking or in existing policies, and also a fundamental shift in the power relations between the controller and those being controlled (Powell 2001). The implications are suitable for a critique of how aged-care institutions can appear as suppressive organizations of authoritative power upon the elderly masses in their care (Powell and Biggs 2000). The trickle-down effect of power from the apex of authority, that of the state and its policies, leaves the individual in this power relationship with very little power or sense of autonomy or individuality after being filtered through a complex hierarchy of professional and direct care staff (Clough and Hadley 1996). Institutionalized care can be seen to portray the elderly as a mass of individuals grouped together by similar socioeconomic and physical characteristics to conjure negative images of the elderly population and that of the aging process (Wahidin and Powell 2001).

At the same time, the voices of professionals become louder and older people's voices become softer in the domain of power/knowledge and the politics of social relations. Clough's (1988) study of abuse at a residential care home in England exemplified this. Many staff had neglected older residents. The abuse included neglecting to bathe residents; punishing those residents who left hot water running in bathrooms or opened windows for air; and removing blankets from residents, leading to pneumonia and subsequently many deaths. Vousden (1987, cited in Hadley and Clough 1995) claimed that professionals destroyed the positive identity of many older people in such a repressive residential regime:

> It is self evident that when elderly, often confused residents are made to eat their own faeces, are left unattended, are physically man-handled or are forced to pay money to care staff and even helped to die, there is something seriously wrong. (Vousden 1987, quoted in Clough and Hadley 1996, 55)

Hence, the power/knowledge twist of professional "carers" was detrimental to policy statements concerning "choice" and "quality of life" in residential care. Such care action was a powerful and repressive mechanism used to indent and strip the identities of residents. Biggs and Powell (2001) claim a Foucauldian approach highlights that such professions retain a powerful position in U.K. care policy, not only in terms of what they do but what they say:

> Foucault identified discourses as historically variable ways of specifying knowledge and truth. They function as sets of rules, and the exercise of these rules and discourses in programmes which specify what is or is not the case—what constitutes "old age," for example. Those who are labelled "old" are in the grip of power. This power would include that operated by professionals through institutions and face to face interactions with their patients and clients. Power is constituted in discourses and it is in discourses such as those of "social work," that power lies. (Biggs and Powell 2001, 97)

Professional power under the guise of "case management" "makes sense" as part of a discourse that displaces and reduces the financial "burden" of age on the state and onto the families of vulnerable older people (Biggs and Powell 2000). Economic privatization is accompanied by a wish to see those same older people as active consumers, making choices between services and changing services or residence if they are found wanting. There has been little consideration, however, of the financial costs, the costs to well-being, or the ability of such vulnerable groups to act in accordance within a discourse based on consumption (Biggs and Powell 2001).

While case management has proved an effective technology for transforming welfare economies, it has made little sense in terms of the preceding social work ethos of counselling and direct care (Leonard 1997). Social workers are now the risk assessors and enforcers of a mixed welfare economy, a discourse that leaves older people who use services on the contradictory and risky ground of being simultaneously consumers and potential victims (Powell 2001c). An unwillingness to increase public finance for older people had led the political administrations of presidents Clinton (1992–2000) and Bush (2000–2008) in the United States and that of Britiish prime minister Blair (1997–2007) to leave the market-welfare systems of both North America and Britain relatively untouched.

The next section introduces notions of "technologies of self" and "governmentality" and assesses their relevance to subjectification practices of older people in post-welfare societies.

RETHINKING AGING: TOWARD "TECHNOLOGIES OF SELF" AND GOVERNMENTALITY?

What has not been delineated sufficiently is Foucault's (1978) later works of "technologies of self" and "governmentality." Foucault contextualized the value of subjectivity as a pivotal mode of analysis. Subjectivity is a core idea that "goes beyond theory" (Dreyfus and Rabinow 1983) and a delineation of its ramifications for gerontological study is a useful way to "problematize" the explanatory value of a Foucauldian analysis based on "technologies of self" and governmentality.

Foucault's final works (1976, 1988) on "technologies of self" and sexuality focus on individual self-subjectification practices that challenge dominant discursive representations of social types. Here, Powell (2001e) develops this by pointing to the interplay of "resistance" and domination.

An effect of the mutually reinforcing relationship between power and knowledge that emerges from the above is to construct individuals simultaneously as subjects and as objects. First, people are seen as objects by someone else, through control and restraint. Second, people are deemed to actively subject their own identity to personal direction through processes such as conscience and mediated self-knowledge. Foucault (1988) refers to this second process as "technologies of self."

Foucault's latter works (1988) on technologies of self and sexuality focus on individual self-subjectification practices which challenge dominant discursive representations of idiographic types. Here, Powell and Biggs (2002) develop this by pointing to interplay of "resistance" with domination.

Examples of how technologies are deployed in managing old age can be found in the work of Frank (1996) on stories of illness, Katz (2000) on active aging and "busy bodies," and in Biggs's (2001) critique of contemporary social policy. In each case, macrosocial practices have become translated into particular ways of growing old that not only shape what it is to age successfully, but are also adopted by older adults, modified to fit their own life circumstances and then fed back into wider narratives of aging well.

For Frank (1996) the personal experience of illness is mediated by biomedical procedures that shape and contribute to how the older patient recognizes his or her own process of ill health and recovery. For Katz (1999) the maxim of "activity for its own sake" as a means of managing later life not only reflects wider social values concerning work and non-work, it also provides personal means of control and acts as grounds for resistance. Biggs (2001) argues that policy interest has changed from seeing old age as a burden to seeing it as an opportunity to promote productive aging. This reflects an attempt to shape acceptable forms of aging while encouraging older adults to self-monitor their own success at conforming to the new paradigm. A common thread throughout relies on the adoption of values and the availability of technologies that facilitate self-scrutiny and self-modification.

Powell (2002) suggests that "technologies of self" and "governmentality" are linked in understanding social relations in society. Indeed, Foucault's work (1978) on "governmentality" challenges Marxist and feminist gerontological perspectives, which claim that "state power" reproduces class differences, of which "elderly" people are "victims" with "low pension provision" (Phillipson 1982), while "gender" differences in care provision epitomize a "patriarchal" state (Arber and Ginn 1995). The existing theoretical literature on governmentality refers to Foucault and his concept of a new style of governance in modernity. It is characterized by the "ensemble formed by the institutions, procedures, analyses and reflections, the calculations and tactics that allow the exercises of this very specific albeit complex form of power" (Foucault 1978, quoted in Burchell et al. 1991, 102). According to Foucault (1978, quoted in Burchell et al. 1991) governmentality comprises three tiers: it is the result of transformations within the modern State; it is a tendency to institutionalize a particular form of power, and it is the "ensemble formed by institutions, procedures, analyses and reflections calculations and tactics" (102–3) that enable the exercise of power directed toward the regulation of an (aging) population using various professional apparatuses of security.

For Foucault (1978) government is concerned with the "conduct of conduct," and neoliberal government is especially concerned with inculcating a new set of values and objectives oriented toward incorporating individual older people as both players and partners in a marketized social system. In such a regime older people are exhorted, indeed expected, to become entrepreneurs in all spheres and to accept responsibility for the management of risk (Beck 1992); older people then govern themselves.

Indeed, on a societal level some authors interpret risk as a new meta-narrative strongly linked to the neoliberal projects of government (Powell 2001a). Coupled with this, Rose and Miller argue, we must investigate political rationalities and technologies of government, "the complex of mundane programmes, calculations, techniques, apparatuses, documents and procedures through which authorities seek to embody and give effect to governmental ambitions" (1992, 175). Technologies of government consist of complex devices and practices through which social groups such as care professionals attempt to operationalize, following Rose and Miller, their program of tailoring knowledge for older people (Powell 2001a). Such technologies, Rose and Miller (1992) suggest, articulate and deploy political rationalities and thereby enable action-at-a-distance.

While there is increasing dependence on professional expertise, there is also a drive to make, for example, older people active participants in their own rule via empowerment (Biggs 1999). One of the ways of facilitating both is the representation of issues as nonpolitical, so that expert knowledge becomes dominant in "rendering the complexities of modern social and economic life knowable, practicable and amenable to governing" (Johnson 1995, 23).

Furthermore, there is a multiplication of sources and types of authority and a proliferation of social actors in social policy spaces, so that "so many of those who are subjects of authority in one field play a part in its exercise in others" (Rose 1993, 287). In neoliberal regimes there is also an apparent dispersal of power (Cousins and Hussain 1984) achieved through establishing structures in which professional experts and older people as consumers are co-opted into or coproduce governance through their own accountable and regulated choices. As Burchell (1993) observes, this is directly connected with the political rationality that assigns primacy to marketization and the autonomization of society in which the paradigm of economic action and enterprise culture comes to dominate all forms of conduct, including those areas formerly regarded as noncommercial.

Contrapolitical economy of old age, the very significance of autonomization is that the state appears to relinquish direct control over the actions of public agencies and social policy through a strategy of privatization and insertion of exchange relationships that commodify and monetarize nonmarket welfare goods and services (Burchell 1993). In other words, there is a strategic aim to diffuse the public sector's monolithic power to encourage diversity and fragmentation of provision from public, private, voluntary, and informal modes that is an embodiment of neoliberal policy of maximizing choice for individuals (Powell 2002). Such a strategy, as Rose and Miller (1992) observe, constitutes a fundamental transformation in the mechanisms for governing social life, as it has resulted not only in a rhetorical but a material outcome in their pervasiveness of market disciplines and their objectives of effectiveness, efficiency, and economy.

Marketization thus entails the simultaneous encouragement of consumerism and dependency, the expansion of budgeting and managerial discourse, and structures of accountability in which professional expertise is problematized in new ways. Such technologies of government displace earlier forms with new rationalities of contracts and competition whereby professionals participate in governmentality yet at the same time are themselves subject to intensified forms of regulation and control (Rose 1993).

As Du Gay (1996) has observed, enterprise is a dominant discourse of Western governments, and it has permeated innumerable policies spanning from social welfare to health from the 1980s to the present. Moreover, it has combined two interlinked developments: a stress on the necessity for enterprising subjects or what Burchell terms "responsibilization" (1993, 276) and the resolution of central state control with individual and organizational autonomy, each of which has redefined previous patterns of social relationships within welfare agencies and between those agencies and their older customers/clients. However, while acknowledging the introduction of neoliberal policies to stimulate market modes of action, it is important to recognize, as Burchell (1993) points out, that the implementation of community care is varied, highly contingent, and uncertain. In addition: "the forms of action constructed for schools, hospitals, general practitioners, housing estates, prisons and other social forms are new, invented, and clearly not a simple extension or reproduction of already existing economic forms of action" (Burchell 1993, 275).

Powell (2001d) claims that neoliberal social policies have configured individuals into substrata discourses of the population. For example, social policies explicate "the elderly" as a "clientele" or "consumer" type of people, while statistical and survey knowledges elaborate their status as a demographic entity as an "aging population" discourse. Thus, the formation of subjects as a population makes possible the government of "subjectification" and the cluster of "power/knowledge" that "swarm" around it (Powell 2001d; Biggs and Powell 2001).

While some commentators claim that Foucault rejected monolithic images of the state (Smart 1985), characterized neoliberal government technologies as pluralizing, and conceptualized discipline and power as forms of domination in which subjects are active, governmentality as an analytical construct remains a highly abstract metaphor for a complex and heterogeneous series of interrelated social practices and institutional structures. Hence, the introduction, awareness, and scrutiny of risk are core features of a shift in welfare policy from communitarian values to neoliberal individualization and choice. The new emphasis reflects social and cultural changes that give top priority to the construction of self-identity and lifestyle, while negating the collectivist vision of a universalistic welfare state (Gilleard and Higgs 2000).

The controversial point is that governmentality is more complex than state power. Flynn (2002) shows by the example of the clinical governance of the National Health Service in Great Britain that it would be too simple to interpret governmentality as a "governing without government." There are no self-organized interorganizational networks with a significant autonomy given by the state or a mixture of different measures that smoothly fit together in a general governmental strategy. Instead, his research on the "clinical governance illustrates the contradictoriness and paradoxes of the management of risk and regulation of professional expertise." On the one hand, the governmentality perspective "allows us to identify the interrelationship of discourses and practices surrounding medical power and state control in the health service and to see them as being contested and negotiated," but Flynn (2002, 66) emphasizes the need of "intermediate concepts which capture the complexity of organizational change and the process of negotiation." Governmentality may be a totalizing discourse but in practice it is complex and differentiated, dynamic and fluid. It needs to be thought of as permanently incomplete and dependent on an enormously diffuse system of action which itself is the aggregate or structural effect of innumerable interpersonal and organizational transactions. Mark Granovetter (1985) has criticized oversocialized political economistic theories and stressed the importance of socially embedded networks as a way of theorizing relations between macrostructures and microlevels of action. Thus:

> Actors do not behave or decide as atoms outside a social context, nor do they adhere slavishly to a script written for them by the intersection of social categories that they happen to occupy. Their attempts at purposive action are instead embedded in concrete, ongoing systems of social relations. (Granovetter 1985, 487)

In Granovetter's social theory, economic institutions or aging enterprises (cf. Estes 1979) do not emerge automatically; instead, they are socially constructed "by individuals whose action is both facilitated and constrained by the structure and resources available" (1992, 7). Hence, the nature of governmentality in welfare provision are practical accomplishments (people managing their own affairs through self-government) but in their very social construction are contingent upon many forms of contradictory power relations, social actions, and negotiated constraints relating to resources.

This chapter has sketched out the implications for the balance of power/knowledge between professional welfare workers and older people and identified the utopian and dystopian implications of such a divided discourse in Western society. The chapter also links technologies of self with policy spaces with changes in consumer lifestyle that relate to practices of discourse within governmentality. Examples include "technologies of self" evidenced in a growing interest in the maintenance of existing good health, the adoption of retirement community lifestyles (Longino 1994) and the use of "bio" and other forms of technology to modify and in some cases enhance bodily and communicative performance (Shilling 1993). In each case, a technology of the self has been employed in order to reshape the aging self in later life, to overcome or destabilize existing welfare discourses on aging and identity.

THE IMPLICATIONS OF FOUCAULDIAN ANALYSES OF AGING

> It may be that the problem about the self does not have to do with discovering what it is, but maybe has to do with discovering that the self is nothing more than a correlate of technology built into our history.
>
> —Foucault 1988, 222

We spoke earlier of how objectifying technologies of control are, for example, those invented in conformity with the facets of discourses provided by criminality, sexuality, medicine, and psychiatry. These are deployed within concrete institutional settings whose architecture testifies to the "truth" of the objects they contain. Thus the possibilities of self-experience on the part of the subject are, in themselves, affected by the presence of someone who has the authority to decide that they are "truly" ill, such as a "doctor" of medicine (Powell and Biggs 2000). However, "subjectifying" technologies of self-control are those through which individuals: "effect by their own means or with the help of others a certain number of operations on their own bodies and souls, thoughts, conduct and way of being, so as to transform themselves in order to attain a certain state of happiness, purity, wisdom, perfection or immortality" (Foucault 1988, 18).

The important issues that Foucault raises via a questioning of the centrality of the subject are associated to "truthful" formulations of the task or the problem that certain domains of experience and activity pose for older people themselves. Although Foucault maintained the distinction between the discourses and technologies of power/domination and the technologies of self and governmentality, these should not be regarded as acting in opposition to or in isolation from one another. Indeed, Foucault frequently spoke of the importance of considering the contingency of both in their interaction and interdependence, by identifying specific examples: "the point where the technologies of domination of individuals over one another have recourse to processes by which the individual acts upon himself and, conversely, the points where the technologies of the self are integrated into structures of coercion" (Foucault 1988, 203). The distinction should therefore be considered as a heuristic device and not the portrayal of two conflicting sets of interests. Overall, we should see Foucault's entire works as providing ways of understanding social relations that require on our part active interpretation, not passive regurgitation.

Further, what about those questions concerned with whose culture, whose identity, and how is this produced? These are the questions that preoccupied Foucault. His refusal to see power as a property of a particular class immediately leaves a question over his politics in terms of the idea of struggle. As he said: "I label political everything that has to do with class struggle, and social everything that derives from and is a consequence of the class struggle, expressed in human relationships and in institutions" (1988, 104).

This leaves us with a question: against whom do we struggle if not those who hold and exercise power without legitimacy? Who creates cultures and how might alternative forms find public expression, and does this change anything? These questions immediately bring forth issues concerning the relationship between Foucault and political economy of old age that was identified in chapter 3. For example, for Foucault, subjectivity is not a fabricated part of a deeper reality but is itself an aspect of the reality systematically formulated by discourse and power relations. Foucault sidesteps the binary relationship set up by political economy theory (cf. Estes 1979; Estes, Biggs, and Phillipson 2003) between true and false realities, ways of knowing, and political consciousness (Foucault 1980). Nevertheless, Walker (1981) asks the question, "Is not the class structure a key determinant of the position of older individuals in capitalist society?" The implication is that Western society makes "resistance" difficult for older people as a result of a loss of productive roles that put a premium on production (Phillipson 1982). In addition, Foucault's notion of governmentality is problematic itself.

Further, Habermas (1992) claims that Foucault's neo-Nietzscheanist critique of the modernist project fails because he loses a sense of direction. In regard to Foucault (1977), Habermas (1992) accuses him of "cryptonormativity" and "irrationality": the former applies because Foucault cannot explain the standards

Habermas thinks must be presupposed in any condemnation of the present; the latter, because of Nietzsche's affirmation of power over against reason.

At the same time, Foucault sees subjectivity not as a fabricated part of a deeper reality waiting to be uncovered through use of reason or communicative rationality (cf. Habermas 1981), but an aspect of the reality systematically formulated by resistances and discourses.

Foucault examined medicine, sexuality, welfare, and selfhood and the law, as well as marginalized social groups, local politics, and the micro-levels of culture. In these studies he found social, discursive, and historical substrata in which relations of domination were apparent that were not simply reducible to modes of economic exploitation. The idea of "governing" then captures the ways in which the "possible fields of action of others" (Foucault 1982, 221) are structured. Yet in inheriting this approach authors have produced panoptic visions in which resistance is subsumed within impersonal forces. This results from overlooking two main aspects in Foucault's work: first, his own question, what are the "limits of appropriation" of discourse? (Without this in place, all does appear quiet on the battleground); second, and relatedly, the agonism that exists between power and freedom (May 1996). This suggests that where there is power, there is also resistance; power thus presupposes a free subject. If there is no choice in actions, there is no power. A slave, therefore, is not in a power relationship, but one of physical constraint (Foucault 1982).

Foucault notes three types of struggle relevant to understanding aging: those against domination, those against exploitation, and those against subjection and submission. The latter, while rising in importance in the contemporary era, do not do so to the exclusion of domination and exploitation as many of his followers have appeared to suggest. To understand why particular actors enjoy more power than others, as opposed to seeing power as a "machine in which everyone is caught" (Foucault 1980, 156), an account of resistance is needed. Because Foucault views freedom as part of the exercise of power, he does not provide for such an account.

What makes Foucault's overall theoretical work inspiring is how he animates and locates problems of knowledge as "pieces" of the larger contest between modernity and its subjects. By looking at the social construction of the individual subject, Foucault has illuminated how "bodies" and "populations" are sites where "human beings are made subjects" by "power/knowledge" practices (Smart 1993, 44). To look for a possible form of trangression in order to change social relation, we must examine within contemporary arrangements the possibility for it to be "otherwise." We thus find, in Foucault's later work, an insistence upon the reversibility of dominant discourses through "resistance." Subjects of power are also "agents" who can strategically mobilize disjunctures in discourses and, in so doing, open up possibilities in a world that seeks order through discipline and surveillance. Now we begin to see how a situation of one-sided domination can give way to a two-way dialogue without assuming an "essence" to the other that relieves us of the need to understand their worldview. In a time where dominance through military power and money is such a routinized feature of post-9/11 global politics, what greater urgency is there?

CONCLUSION

In his essay on Kant's *Was ist Aufklärung?* [*What Is Enlightenment?*] Foucault writes of Kant's work as being a "historical ontology of ourselves" through a critique of what we do, say, and think. He is clear throughout the essay concerning what this form of critique is not: neither a theory, doctrine, nor body of knowledge that accumulates over time. Instead, it is an attitude, "an ethos, a philosophical life in which the critique of what we are is at one and the same time the historical analysis of the limits that are imposed on us and an experiment with the possibility of going beyond them" (Foucault 1982, 50). What is the motivation for this work? "How can the growth of capabilities be disconnected from the intensification of power relations?" (1982, 48).

There is no "gesture of rejection" in this ethos. It moves beyond the "outside-inside alternative" in the name of a critique that "consists of analyzing and reflecting upon limits"—the purpose being "to transform the critique conducted in the form of necessary limitation into a practical critique that takes the form of a possible transgression" (Foucault 1982, 45). Overall, it is genealogical in form: "it will not deduce from the form of what we are what it is impossible for us to do and to know; but it will separate out, from the contingency that has made us what we are, the possibility of no longer being, doing, or thinking what we are, do, or think" (1980, 46).

The ideal lies in the possibility of setting oneself free. To examine the internal modes of the ordering of truth, but not in the name of a truth that lies beyond it, is seen to open up possibilities for its transgression.

Despite criticisms that his work lacked a normative dimension (Fraser 1987), the orientation for Foucault's approach is clear. The issue translates into one of how one-sided states of domination can be avoided in order to promote a two-sided relation of dialogue. Foucault's interventions were practically motivated—the journey for these investigations being from how we are constituted as objects of knowledge, to how we are constituted as subjects of power/knowledge. What we can take from Foucault is the insight that critical approaches to gerontological analysis cannot practice on the presupposition that there is an essence to humanity. The idea of coming to know ourselves differently and viewing the possibilities for transformation is about interpreting ourselves differently. Foucault's legacy to understanding aging can be qualified along three lines.

Firstly, gerontology as a "human science" is an archaeological domain where discourse, knowledge, and subjectivity engender each other. The "apparatuses" used to disperse gerontological knowledge—discourses, theories, and policies, for example—can be seen as disciplinary techniques that constitute knowledge of subjects/objects.

Secondly, by downplaying the individual subject, Foucault's genealogies show how "bodies" and "populations" are sites where "human beings are made subjects" by "power/knowledge" practices (Foucault 1977, 44). The "aging body" and "elderly populations," as the central foci of scientific knowledge, cultural images, political rationalities, and institutional practices, have organized the positioning of later life.

Thirdly, there is an ontological reflexivity within Foucault's later work whereby he insists on the reversibility of discourses by subjects through technologies of self and "resistance." Older people are subjects of power who are also "agents" who could strategically mobilize disjunctures of structural discourses through "technologies of self" (Foucault 1978; Biggs and Powell 2001).

While Foucault has provided us with conceptual insights that enrich understanding of discourses of aging and professional power, the notion of risk is an undeveloped theme in his work. The notion of risk is fundamental to the way experts experience and organize the social world. Risk is crucial to the understanding and control of the future (Beck 1992). The central yet uncertain nature of risk and risk assessment is pivotal to understanding the changing nature and role of power/knowledge and professional experts in contemporary society (Beck 1992). Risks come into being where traditions and assumed values such as social work as a form of expertise have deteriorated (Powell and Biggs 2000). As Beck states: "The concept of risk is like a probe which permits us over and over again to investigate the entire construction plan, as well as every individual speck of cement in the structure of civilization" (1992, 176).

The emergence of a risk society arises because of the undermining and loss of faith concerning power/knowledge and hierarchies of truth and expert systems. It is not by chance, then, that the increased focus on risk in social work coincided with the decline in trust in health and welfare professionals' expertise, decision-making, and scientific-medical insights on aging and the growing reliance on the managerial gaze with older people in post-welfare societies. The next chapter looks at the implications of the "risk society" for understanding aging in contemporary society.

Chapter 7

Aging in the "Risk Society"

INTRODUCTION

This chapter explores the relationship of aging to the concept of "risk" that is both an epistemological tool and major facet of "late modernity" (Delanty 1999; Giddens 1991). During the 1970s, the use of the notion of risk was mainly confined to "natural sciences," where the concept was used to analyze and improve the "security" of technological systems (Giddens 1990). According to Lupton (1999) it was not until the 1980s and 1990s that social-science-based disciplines discovered the importance of risk in relation to changes affecting modern society. In particular, the disciplinary development of sociology, for example, has discovered risk as one of the important aspects of neoliberalism and modernity (Beck 1992; Giddens 1990; Luhmann 1993; Delanty 1999). The best-known approach in recent sociology of risk is the perspective of "risk society" (Beck 1992). This approach had a very large initial impact, but conceptual and empirical critiques have developed subsequently. Sociocultural research suggests the idea of a subject that is itself strongly influenced by its cultural contexts and builds up its own risk-knowledge referring to different, competing, and sometimes contradictory knowledge systems which are available in different life situations and stages. For this reason, expert knowledge is only one point of reference among others (Delanty 1999). People build up such "private" knowledge on the base of their experiences during their life-course and in interaction with their contexts, others, the media, science, and expert knowledge (Wilkinson 2001).

Indeed, in contemporary Western society, risk is a broad concept that extends over a broad range of social practices that impinge on the experiences of older people. Current debates about older people and their relationship to sexuality, crime, national security, food safety, employment, and welfare are all underscored by risk (Phillipson 1998). Moreover, there is an increasing recognition that potential risks of the present and future (global warming, genetic cloning, genetically modified foods, and bio-terrorism) shatter the rigid boundaries of nations and demand global cooperation and control.

Awareness of the transboundary nature of risk has led the United Nations to form its own Commission on Human Security. A recent report by the UN Commission suggests ways in which the security of older people, for example, might be advanced: from humanitarian and military strategies through to economic, health, and educational strategies. While "freedom from want" continues to be the most pressing global imperative, in recent years "freedom from fear" has risen up the global political agenda (Commission on Human Security 2003, 4, cited in Powell and Wahidin 2004). Coupled with this, the U.S. Central Intelligence Agency's 2004 World Fact Book suggests that an "aging population" is a risk to the financial safety of Western nation-states (Powell and Wahidin 2004).

In science, risk has traditionally been approached as an objective material entity, to be mastered by processes of calculation, assessment, and probability. In the twenty-first century, "advances" in science and medicine led to the eradication of many infectious diseases, raised life expectancy in old age, and improved quality of life. Accordingly, it is no surprise that the literature on risk was housed within the confines of specialist expert disciplines, such as biomedical gerontology (Timiras 1997).

The nature of scientific knowledge about risk and its impact on aging has articulated the perspective that, as a person goes through the aging process, there are heightened risks to the human body; in the mind and in the internal organs (Hughes 1995). It has gradually become clear that the very institutions entrusted with regulating risks have themselves transmuted into risk producers. In recent times, multinational corporate business, science, medicine, and government have all been accused of generating various dangers to public health that threaten the safety of older people. The rising cultural profile of risk has brought to the fore deep-rooted ethical concerns about the relationship between individuals, institutions, and society (Lupton 1999, 112). The debate currently taking place about the use of reproductive technologies for human cloning to prolong life in old age stands as a case in point.

It has become commonplace for academics and practitioners to explore, develop, and apply an assortment of social science perspectives on risk. In a post-9/11 world, questions around risk and risk management have become ever more pertinent, leading to reflections on a number of different levels about "ontological security." Moreover, how do older people manage their sense of well-being in a world in which less and less can be taken for granted? To what extent does the specter of global risks interplay with more mundane insecurities that reach to the capillary texture of the day-to-day life of older people?

In a climate of indeterminacy, there is an urgent need to draw out the ways in which wider social theory can elucidate the dynamic relationship between risk and aging in contemporary society. In response to public concerns about un-bounded technoscientific development and the apparent inefficacy of expert systems, interest in risk has gathered momentum within social science disci-plines in recent years (cf. Giddens 1991). However, while the language of risk has become prolific, the concept itself remains cloaked in ambiguity and its rela-tionship to aging scantily researched, making risk and aging an important and significant issue for social theory and social gerontology.

A theoretically informed understanding of risk illustrates the interconnected-ness of an aging population, social policy, and social life. From this perspective, risk is more than an estimation of costs and benefits; it is a theoretical instru-ment for weighing dissimilar sets of values and political orientations that affect the positioning of individuals and populations. As Nikolas Luhmann (1993, ix) points out: "How do we comprehend our society if we turn the concept of risk into a universal problem neither avoidable or evadable? What is now necessary? And accordingly: What is chance? How does society in the normal performance of its operations cope with a future about which nothing certain can be dis-cerned, but only what is more or less probable or improbable?"

The deployment of risk to gerontological contexts has facilitated disruptions of both the metanarratives inscribed within gerontology, as both discipline and policy, and the ontological status of its subjects, that is, older people. The ra-tionale for this argument is not about a normative foundation for articulating agency afforded to older people. Part of an understanding of individual freedom is how human action is plugged into and (de)regulated by a social context (Mills 1959). Such an approach seeks to capture the dimensions of subjectivity within the sociopolitical constraints that shape individual lives. This allows reconstruc-tions of logics of action or structuration behind current neoliberal self-representations of aging identity. It could be supposed that such constructions enable us to reconstruct the complexity of aging in social contexts and the influ-ence of, for example, social welfare on these experiences as a ground for risk perception. Hence, we need to understand the major social forces that impinge on aging itself. Such social forces that create risk associated with aging imply a breakdown in trust as a key modernist principle in contemporary society.

FROM TRUST TO RISK

There are increasing attempts to conceptualize the notion of "trust" in social theory as a pivotal dimension of modernity (Giddens 1991). Trust is incompati-ble, on the one hand, with complete ignorance of the possibility and probability of future events and, on the other hand, with emphatic belief when the anticipation of disappointment is excluded. Someone who trusts has an expectation directed to an event. The expectations are based on the ground of incomplete knowledge about the probability and incomplete control about the occurrence of the event. Trust is of relevance for action and has consequences for the trusting agent if trust is confirmed or disappointed. Thus, trust is connected with risk (Giddens 1991).

Up to now there have been few attempts to work out a systematic scheme of different forms of trust between older people and individuals, institutions, or policies that have bearing on their identity performance. Social trust tends to be high among older people who believe that their public safety is high (Wahidin and Powell 2001). As public trust erodes regarding institutions like the government and the media (Phillipson 1998), trust attracts more and more attention in social sciences.

Mölling (2001) distinguishes between trust in contracts between people and state, such as pension provision; trust in friendships across intergenerational lines; trust in love and relationships; and trust in foreign issues associated with national identity. However, sociological theories that suppose a general change in modernity (cf. Beck 1992) assume that, with the erosion of traditional institutions and scientific knowledge, trust becomes an issue more often produced actively by individuals than institutionally guaranteed.

Independent from the insight that social action in general is dependent more or less on trust, empirical results in the context of risk perception and risk taking indicate:

- Trust is much easier to destroy than to build.
- Once trust is undermined, it is more difficult to restore it.
- Familiarity with a place, a situation, or a person produces trust.
- People will develop trust in other people or situations if those people or situations have positively valued characteristics.

Trust seems to be something that is produced individually by experience and over time and cannot immediately and with purpose be produced by organizations or governments without dialogical interaction with older people on issues affecting their lifestyles and life-chances such as care, pensions, employment, and political representation (Walker and Naegele 1999). However, as Giddens (1991) stresses, risk is a feature of a society shifting its emphasis away from trust in traditional ties and social values. How risks are perceived and formulated as a breakdown in trust reflects the essentially discursive practices of politics and power in modern society. The ability to control and manage perceptions about moral intentions of a pervasive governmental rationality may be part of an understanding of risk.

For this reason, risk is an evocative and compelling focus of theoretical analysis, required for understanding a historical backdrop for the emergence of a risk society in the West that influences the identities of older people.

The Historical Rise and Consolidation of "Risk"

Over history, the word risk has changed its meaning and has become far more common applied to the global and the local (Beck 1992). Most commentators link the emergence of the word and concept of risk with early maritime ventures in the premodern period. Ewald (1993) argues that the notion of risk first appeared in the Middle Ages, related to maritime insurance, and alluded to the perils that could compromise a voyage: "At that time, risk designated the possibility of an objective danger, an act of God, a force, a tempest or other peril of the sea that could not be imputed to wrongful conduct" (Ewald 1993, 226).

Luhmann (1993, 9) claims that the German word for risk appeared in the mid-sixteenth century and the English, in the second half of the seventeenth. He notes that the Latin term riscum had been in use long before in Germany and elsewhere.

Importantly, this premodern concept of risk excluded the idea of human fault and responsibility. Risk was perceived to be a natural event, such as a storm, flood, or epidemic, rather than a human-made one. By the eighteenth century, the concept of risk had begun to be rationalized under the new scientific paradigm, drawing upon new ideas of mathematical probability. The development of statistical calculations of risk and the expansion of the insurance industry in the early modern era meant that: "Consequences that at first affect only the individual became 'risks,' systematically caused, statistically describable and in that sense 'predictable' types of events, which can therefore also be subjected to supraindividual and political rules of recognition, compensation and avoidance" (Beck 1992, 99).

By the late nineteenth century, the notion of risk was extended. It was no longer located exclusively in nature but was "also in human beings, in their conduct, in their liberty, in the relations between them, in the fact of their association, in society" (Ewald 1993, 226). The development of this concept assumes human responsibility and that "something can be done" to prevent misfortune. Feelings of insecurity are common, just as they were in premodern times, but we now harbor somewhat different fears, and different objects are causes for our anxiety.

As in premodern times, we are aware of certain types of risks and possible outcomes, but our responses are more governed by a scientific rationale. The symbolic basis of our uncertainties is fundamentally created by disorder or insecurities, such as the loss of control over our bodies, our relationship with others and self, and the extent to which we can exert autonomy in our everyday lives. This body of governance or strategies can take many forms, from dieting, to fitness regimes, to minimizing potential risk to self by taking out life insurance, installing a burglar alarm, etc. These are just some of the ways by which the heightened awareness of everyday risk is negotiated, contained, and managed. Therefore, rational thinking, systems of prevention, and ways of identifying threats before they take effect are means of managing danger and threats in a risk society. These strategies are the products of late modern ways of thinking about, and reacting to, risk.

Every technology produces, provokes, programmes a specific accident. The invention of the boat was the invention of shipwrecks. The invention of the steam engine and the locomotive was the invention of derailments. The invention of the highway was the invention of three hundred cars colliding in five minutes. The invention of the airplane was the invention of the plane crash. I believe that from now on, if we wish to continue with technology (and I don't think there will be a Neolithic regression), we must think about both the substance and the accident (Virilio 1983, 32).

The modernist concept of risk represented a new way of viewing the world and its chaotic manifestations, its contingencies and uncertainties. It assumed that unanticipated outcomes may be the consequence of human action rather than "expressing the hidden meanings of nature or ineffable intentions of the Deity," largely replacing earlier concepts of fate or fortuna (Giddens 1990, 30). As Reddy argues: "Moderns had eliminated genuine indeterminacy, or 'uncertainty,' by inventing 'risk.' They had learnt to transform a radically indeterminate cosmos into a manageable one, through the myth of calculability" (Reddy 1996, 237). Castel goes even further, arguing that the obsession with the prevention of risk in modernity is built upon: a grandiose technocratic rationalizing dream of absolute control of the accidental, understood as the irruption of the unpredictable. A vast hygienist utopia plays on the alternate registers of fear and security, inducing a delirium of rationality, an absolute reign of calculative reason and a no less absolute prerogative of its agents, planners, and technocrats, administrators of happiness for a life to which nothing happens (Castel 1991, 289).

In modernity, risk, in its purely technical meaning, came to rely upon conditions in which the probability estimates of an event are able to be known or knowable. The use of risk in common discourse litters texts, images, and day-to-day conversation. In contemporary Western societies, the noun risk and the adjective risky have become very commonly used in both popular and expert discourses. Risk and uncertainty tend to be treated as conceptually the same thing.

The term tends to be used to refer almost exclusively to a threat, hazard, danger, or harm: we "risk our life savings" by investing on the stock exchange, or we "put our health at risk." In this sense, risk means somewhat less than a possible danger or a threat and more an unfortunate or annoying event. Risk is therefore a very loose term and, as the above shows, is used in a variety of ways. Issues of calculable probability and economic systems of accountability are not necessarily important to the colloquial use of risk. Risk knowledges are historical and local, in the literature known as glocal. What might be perceived to be "risky" in one era at a certain locale may no longer be so viewed later, or in a different place (Phillipson and Powell 2004). As a result, risk knowledges are constantly contested, subject to disputes and debates over their nature, their control, and who is to blame for their creation.

Over time the constellations of risks have changed. The risks of early industrialization were evident: they could be smelt, touched, tasted, or observed with the naked eye. These hazards "assaulted the nose or the eyes and were thus perceptible to the senses" (Beck 1992, 21). Earlier risks were part of a system of stratification and poverty that was highly visible; in contrast, today's hazards are invisibly everywhere in the everyday. Many of the major risks today largely escape perception "for they are localized in the sphere of physical and chemical formulas (e.g., toxins in foodstuffs, toxins in the environment, [certain pollutants] or nuclear threat)" (Beck 1992, 21). These risks exist in scientific knowledge rather than in everyday experience. Expert knowledges tend to contradict each other, resulting in debates over standpoints, calculation, assessment procedures, and results. This has the effect of paralyzing action and bringing insurance systems that promised to cover eventualities into chaos. In Great Britain, for example, the welfare state, an insurance system that promised to care for people from cradle to the grave, is unable to sustain that promise for future generations. The welfare system as a system of social insurance is beginning to lose its legitimacy with the rise of private health insurance.

Scientists have lost their authority in relation to risk assessments, most evidently seen in the collapse of endowment and certain pension funds. Scientific calculations are challenged more and more by political groups and activists (Beck 1994, 125). The nature of such hazards, therefore, returns the concept of risk to the premodern notion of "incalculable insecurities." In common with such hazards, insecurities "undercut the social logic of risk calculation and provision" (Beck 1994, 77). For Beck, then, risk may be defined as a "systematic way of dealing with hazards and insecurities induced and introduced by modernisation itself" (Beck 1992, 21). Dangers and hazards in modern society are the cause and effect of humanly generated productions and in essence can be avoided, monitored, or altered. Therefore the above debates demonstrate that the essence of risk is not that it is happening, but that it might be happening.

These debates include "reflexive modernisation" (cf. Giddens 1991), or the move toward criticism of the outcomes of neoliberalism, and individualization, or the breaking down of traditional norms and values. Older people living in neoliberal societies have therefore moved toward a greater awareness of risk and are forced to deal with risks on an everyday basis: "Everyone is caught up in defensive battles of various types anticipating the hostile substances in one's manner of living and eating" (Beck 1992, 45). The media, for their part, have taken up warnings of experts about risk and communicate them to their mass publics. They have also reported disputes among these experts that concern risks: how serious they are, who should be blamed for them, what the most appropriate course of action might be. In risk society, therefore, the politics and sub-politics of risk definition become extremely important. They highlight the contested nature of who is defining what is a risk and how. Various specialized fields have developed around "risk." Our understanding of risk derives from pervasive references to risk behavior, risk awareness, risk analysis, risk assessment, risk communication, and risk management at any given time. Such terms allude to major fields of research and practice, developed in an attempt to measure, evaluate, and regulate risk in areas as far-ranging as medicine, law, education, social policy, and health, but they also signify the techniques by which, as social actors, we come to make sense of the everyday. In the last few years, there has been a series of "panics" about welfare resources that has revolved around particular items in the United Kingdom, such as the effects of an "aging population" on public resources and taxation. Thus, perceptions of risk are intimately tied to understandings of what constitutes a danger and for whom. This im/materiality or the invisibility gives risk an air of unreality until the moment at which they materialize as symptoms or as irreversible side effects.

The growing disparities between rich countries and poorer ones lead to growing inequalities in risk distribution, where class positions and risk positions overlap. As we see these disparities develop in the new global order, some risks, such as those caused by hazardous industries, are transferred away from the developed countries to the third world. Thus, while Beck sees risk society as a catastrophic society, what we are seeing is the transference of certain risks through aversion and management, which in turn include a reorganization of power and authority (Beck 1992, 4)

The "Risk Society" Thesis

Beck (1992), in his work *The Risk Society*, acknowledges that some social groups are more affected than others by the distribution and growth of risks, and these differences may be structured through inequalities of class and social position. The disadvantaged have fewer opportunities to avoid risk because of their comparative lack of resources. By contrast, the wealthy to a degree (income, power, or education) can purchase safety and freedom from risk (Beck 1992, 33). However, it is the gestation and the constellations of the risks that are unknown, and thus risk also affects those who have produced or profited from them, breaking down the previous social and geographic boundaries evident in modern societies.

Beck argues that the "former colonies" of the Western nations are soon becoming the waste dumps of the world for toxic and nuclear wastes produced by more privileged countries. Risks have become more and more difficult to calculate and control. Hence it can be argued that risks often affect both the wealthy and poor alike: "poverty is hierarchic and smog is democratic" (1992, 36). At the same time, because of the degree of interdependence of the highly specialized agents of modernization in business, agriculture, the law and politics, there is no single agent responsible for any risk: "[T]here is a general complicity, and the complicity is matched by a general lack of responsibility. Everyone is cause and effect" (33), and so "perpetrator and victim become identical" (38) in a consuming society. It is this im/materiality and in/visibility of the threats that saturate the "risk society," making it harder to identify the offender in global risk. Lupton (1999) argues that this fundamentally poses the second challenge for analyses of these socially constituted industrial phenomena: interpretation becomes inherently a matter of perspective and hence political. Politicians constantly invoke science in their attempts to persuade the public that their policies and products are safe. The inescapability of interpretation makes risks infinitely malleable and, as Beck (1992, 23) insists, "open to social definition and construction." This in turn put those in a position to define (and/or legitimate) risks, the mass media, scientists, politicians, and the legal profession, in key social positions.

"Risk society," argues Beck, "is not an option which could be chosen or rejected in the course of political debate" (1996, 28). Instead, this is an inescapable product and structural condition of advance industrialization in which the produced hazards of that system, in Beck's words (1992, 31), "undermine and/or cancel the established safety systems of the provident state's existing risk calculation." Beck (1992) in his work further emphasizes this point by examining contemporary hazards associated with nuclear power, chemical pollution, and genetic engineering and biotechnology that cannot be limited or contained to particular spaces, and that which cannot be grasped through the rules of causality, and cannot be safeguarded, compensated for, or insured against. They are therefore "glocal": both local and global. Risk society is thus "world risk society," and risks affect a global citizenship. The questioning of the outcomes of modernity in terms of the production of risks is an outcome of reflexive modernization. Our awareness of risk, therefore, is heightened at the level of the everyday.

Both Beck (1992) and Giddens (1991) have a commonality of exploring and assessing risk linked to personal conduct and ontological security. Both claim that modernization helps the self become an agent via processes of individualization which they both see as indicative of neoliberalism; they advocate that the self become less constrained by structures and become a project to be reflexively worked on.

Further studies refer to general discourses and their influence of problem definitions and the constitution of groups "at risk" as older people (Estes, Biggs, and Phillipson 2003). Such studies show how generalized social categories in institutional and media discourses produce homogenous groups in relation to risk. On the one hand, these categories do not do justice to the diverse persons behind the categories, and a new reality is entailed that changes the whole notion of a social group. For example, risk anxiety engendered by the desire to keep older people safe may restrict their autonomy and their opportunities to develop necessary skills to cope with the world.

Notwithstanding this, there is a criticism that "risk" is narrowed to the responses of technical and environmental risks as unforeseen consequences of industrialization. This concept of a danger-consequence society (Massumi 1993) fails to grasp the more general societal development regarding the concept of risk as a specific historical strategy to manage uncertainties. This strategy is strongly linked to the idea of insurance and the statistical methods to calculate uncertainties developed in modernity (Hacking 1990). Many risk theorists share this view (Giddens 1991) but support a more general notion on risk and risk responses in current societies concerning the ways in which uncertainties of aging populations are managed in general. The narrowed view on technical and statistical risk management seems to be insufficient for the given complexity concerning, for example, governmental risk strategies and rationalities (Rose 1996) and emotional spaces. Further critique aims at the assumption that new risks produce a general anxiety that would support a higher public awareness of risk and involve increasing the political commitment of the public. It has been argued that this does not apply to all risks, and neither do all people respond in the same way (Lupton 1999).

The existing literature on risk ignores the role of emotion in theorizing. Often it is assumed without further empirical examination that there is a direct link between social structure and emotion or risk consciousness and societal anxiety of "emotions." One clear example of risk associated with emotions and aging is crime and victimization. As with other characteristics that make older people vulnerable to victimization, it is difficult to disentangle the age factor from other variables that mean that older people figure prominently among those for whom victimization has a high risk. In terms of actual rates of victimization, elder abuse is certainly underreported (Biggs 1993). Many older people may feel vulnerable related to crime and abuse (Wahidin and Powell 2001). Older victims tend to report that crime has a high and long-lasting impact upon them compared to younger victims.

Fattah and Sacco (1989) conclude in their study of crime against older people in North America that, while it may be fashionable to view fear of crime as an irrational response on the part of elderly to a world that does not truly threaten them, such a conceptualization is probably not appropriate. Rather than irrationality, elderly fear of crime may represent the exercise of caution by a group in society that frequently lacks the control necessary to manage the risk of criminal harm or to marshal the resources necessary to offset its consequences. (1989, 226)

Hence, the multilayered results of the link between risk, crime, and emotion show that additional theoretical work in social gerontology is necessary. Wahidin and Powell (2001) refer to the idea of a fundamental change in modernity: that there is also a reinterpretation of the uncontrollable and unforeseeable in something observable such as crime.

Aging in Risk Society: A Case Study Based on Social Welfare

Throughout risk literature there has been a growing gap in the application of risk in gerontology. Notwithstanding this, in order to work on itself, the "self" relates to risk: "risks become the motor of self-politicization of modernity in industrial society." How the conjunction between risk and individual awareness has become politicized provides a perspective on the viability of neoliberalism and conditions of human action. One element of the "motor" of self-politicization is how successful neoliberalism has been in fashioning commonsense discourses around its political rhetoric. Jürgen Habermas (1992) claims that what we are witnessing is a "completely altered relationship between autonomous and self-organized public spheres on the one hand, and sub-systems steered by money and administrative power on the other." Self-autonomization coupled with administrative power is indicative of "risk": neoliberal features of social policy for older people.

There is then an ambivalence at the heart of neoliberalism. On the one hand, older people are to be "managed" by other administrative powers such as professional experts in modernity (Leonard 1997). On the other hand, older people are left to govern themselves, a process that Rose and Miller (1992) call "action at a distance" from the state. Hence, as consumers, older people are distanced further away from the state; rather than a cause for celebration, the dystopian implications are far-reaching in that they generate further risks that the self must negotiate with the withdrawal of the state.

Indeed, constituting risk as a centrally defining motif of "late modernity" offers a new perspective: it allows the interrogation of how older people are made subjects. This inevitably impinges on risk. Neoliberalism gives the impression that older people have the capacity to generate their own "human agency" as indicative of "consumer culture" (Gilleard and Higgs 2000) irrespective of structural constraints. The problematic of self-governance, or what Nikolas Rose (1993) calls "the government of freedom," needs critical reflection. Such reflection is sensitized to mapping out key features of neoliberal political rationalities that impinge on "self-government" within the "risk society." Notably those arising from the shift from welfarism to neoliberalism.

We can draw from neoliberal features of social policy to highlight how old age was socially and politically positioned as an opportunity for processes of government related to self-governance (Rose 1993, 1996). Theoretical normativity lies at the heart of the "structure vs. agency" debate as applied to social gerontology. Social gerontology as discipline and practice can be sensitized to how older people ought to have autonomy and control in their own lives; but this masks critical questions of the what is. As Powell (1998) asks: How do we know where we are going until we know where we are coming from? So, we point out features of the "risk society" and how this impacts on any historical, contemporary, and future questioning of aging. The next section traces a genealogy of aging, risk, and its interrelationship with social welfarism.

Genealogy of Risk and Aging Identities

There has been a change in the structure that has underpinned definitions of aging. The key development here concerned the way in which, in industrial societies, growing old was altered by the social and economic institutions connected with the welfare state. These became crucial in shaping the dominant discourse around which aging was framed. A key theme was the reordering of the lifecourse into life zones associated with education, work, and retirement (Phillipson 1982). A final element concerned the role played by services for older people as a measure of the move to a more civilized society. "Old age" was itself the creation of modernity, reflecting the achievements of industrialism, improved public health, and the growth of social welfare (Biggs 1999). The steady growth in the proportion of older people in the population was, until the beginning of the 1980s, largely contained within the institution of the welfare state.

Indeed, older people have had the most to lose. As Biggs (1993) argues, modern life raises at least two possibilities: the promise of a multiplicity of identities on the one side and the danger of psychological disintegration on the other. This development has served to change the definition of what it means to be an older person. In the conditions of advanced modernity, growing old moves from being a collective to an individual experience and responsibility. This new development may be seen as a characteristic of a society in which the "social production of risk" runs alongside that associated with the "social production of wealth" (Beck 1992). Beck (1992, 21) further defines the nature of risk as a "systematic way of dealing with hazards and insecurities induced and introduced by modernization itself." Such modernization is shaped by neoliberalism which in turn positions the role of what it means to be a consumer in Western society.

Conclusion

The neoliberal surface dominance in social policy has been very successful because it has identified existential concepts such as self-responsibility, self-governance, and self-care which are to be used to facilitate human action and self-government (Powell 2001c, 2001d). The regulation of personal conduct is no longer the responsibility of the state.

Here neoliberal discourse attempts to define the social policy domain to interpret valid human needs and limit rights, indicative of risk. Coupled with this, processes and relationships in the management of old age are decided by governmental rationalities that are tied to questions of self-governance, self-actualization, and autonomy. Further, neoliberalism considers that a welfare society must reflect only the interplay of social and political structures forged out of self-responsibility and consumerism (Leonard 1997; Powell 2001e). As we discussed in a previous chapter regarding analysis of Foucault's (1978) notion of "governmentality," older people as autonomous consumers derive their "care," individually and collectively, from a range of social policies, institutions, and sites, so that the organization of care involves market forces, families, and state and care institutions. In the United States, responsibility for the administration of care-based social policy has been the contemporary case management institution (Powell 2001d).

Case management as an institutional apparatus has been presented as consolidating neoliberalism by adding "choice" and reducing "risks" and "problems" associated with aging. This movement away from "helping relationship" to "care management" is an aspect of governance: that is the mechanism by which clients, as individuals and collectively, are "disciplined" away from "structured dependency" to the governance of "self" in the "risk society" (Powell 2001). Such reforms were about recasting older people as consumers in a marketplace to be managed by administrative powers (Powell 2001; cf. Habermas 1992).

Indeed, Biggs and Powell (2001, 110) raise critical questions about the relationship between old age, neoliberalism, and new sources of oppression associated with the risk society: Those who do not conform to the utopian dream appear to have been shunted into a non-participative discourse, bounded by professional surveillance or the more palatable yet closely related discourse of "monitoring." In both cases, it could be suggested that a discourse on dependency has been supplemented, and in some cases replaced, by a discourse on risk. The risk of giving in to an aging body, the risk of thereby being excluded from one's retirement community, the risk of being too poor to maintain a consumer lifestyle, the risk of being excluded from participation through incapacity that has been externally assessed, the risk of being abused, the risk of control being taken out of one's hands, and the risk of tokenism in partnership.

Risk is then more than a calculation of costs and benefits; it is a theoretical endeavor where a simple question such as "Do we live in a risk society?" is one to which we are incapable of providing a straight answer. As consumers, has our duty of care become onerous or riskier as we journey into the stages of later life? Can anyone escape the miasma of a risk? As Phillipson and Powell (2004) critically suggest that "older people, it might be argued, are affected by two major changes: in respect of access to support on the one side, and the construction of identity on the other. On the one side, there is the creation of what Estes and others describe as 'no care zones' where community supports may disintegrate in the face of inadequate services and benefits. On the other side, there may equally be the emergence of 'no identity zones,' these reflecting the absence of spaces in which to construct a viable identity for older people" (Phillipson and Powell 2004, 55)

The lack of spaces adds to a sense of marginalization that exposes the vulnerable status of older people. But this vulnerability also reaches into the texture of everyday life. For more affluent groups, a temporary solution seems to have been found in the denial of aging and the neoliberal promotion of new consumer lifestyles. The social vacuum that this suggests reinforces the sense of uncertainty about the identity of older people in neoliberal consumer society (Phillipson 1998).

Chapter 8

Narrative and Aging

INTRODUCTION

The previous chapter explored risk and aging identity in gerontology. There has been much research in recent times that has called for a "reflexive gerontology" (Powell 2010). Research on risk as an epistemological tool is important. To add to the reflexive project, is to incorporate concepts and methodologies applicable to understanding aging identity: narrative. "Narrativity" has become established in the social sciences, both as a method of undertaking and interpreting research (cf Kenyon et al. 1999; Holstein and Gubrium 2000; Biggs et al. 2003) and as a technique for modifying the self (McAdams 1993; Mcleod 1997). Both Gubrium (1992) and Katz (1999) suggest that older people construct their own analytical models of personal identity based on lived experience and on narratives already existing in their everyday environments. By using a narrative approach, the meaning of family can be told through stories about the self as well as ones "at large" in public discourse.

"Discourse" is a notion more often used to denote a relatively fixed set of stories that individuals or groups have to conform to in order to take up a recognized and legitimate role. Such an understanding of discourse can be found in the earlier work of Michel Foucault (1977) and others (Powell and Biggs 2001). Self-storying, draws attention to the ways in which family identities are both more open to negotiation and are more likely to be "taken in" in the sense of being owned and worked on by individuals themselves.

At the same time, there has been an increasing interest in aging and family, within sociological developments relating to aging and social policy since the late 1990s (Minkler 1998). This is a trend that has cut across Canadian, American, and European research (Cloke et al 2006; Walker and Naegele 1999; Minkler 1998; Bengtson et al. 2000; Biggs and Powell 2001; Carmel et al. 2007). The reasons for such expansion are as much economic and political as they are academic. U.S. and European governments recognize that the "family" is important for social and economic needs and this should be reflected in our understanding of aging, family processes, and in social policy (Beck 2005). This leads to the question: How can we theoretically contextualize this and what are lessons for family research in sociological theorizing?

Families, of course, are made up of interpersonal relationships within and between generations that are subject to both the formal rhetoric of public discourses, and the self-stories that bind them together in everyday life. The notion of family is, then, an amalgam of policy discourse and everyday negotiation and as such alerts us to the wider social implications of those relationships (cf Powell 2005).

The rhetoric of social policy and the formal representations of adult aging and family life that one finds there, provide a source of raw material for the construction of identity and a series of spaces in which such identities can be legitimately performed. It is perhaps not overstating the case to say that the "success" of a family policy can be judged from the degree to which people live within the stories or narratives of family created by it.

In fact, the relationship between families and older people has been consecutively rewritten in the social policy literature. Each time a different story has been told and different aspects of the relationship have been thrown into high relief. It might even be argued that the family has become a key site upon which expected norms of intergenerational relations and late-life citizenship are being built. This chapter explores the significance of such narratives, using developments in the United Kingdom as a case example that may also shed light on wider contemporary issues associated with old age.

The structure of the chapter is fourfold. Firstly, we start by mapping out the emergence and consolidation of neoliberal family policy and its relationship to emphasis on family obligation, state surveillance, and active citizenship. Secondly, we highlight both the ideological continuities and discontinuities of the subsequent social democratic turn and their effects on older people and the family. Thirdly, research studies are drawn on to highlight how "grand-parenting" has been recognized by governments in recent years, as a particular way of "storying" the relationship between old age and family life. Finally, we explore ramifications for researching family policy and old age by pointing out that narratives of inclusion and exclusion often coexist. It is suggested that in the future, aging and family life will include the need to negotiate multiple policy narratives. At an interpersonal level, sophisticated narrative strategies would be required if a sense of familial continuity and solidarity is to be maintained.

Neoliberalism, Aging, and the Family

Political and social debate since the Reagan/Thatcher years, has been dominated by neoliberalism, which postulates the existence of autonomous, assertive, rational individuals who must be protected and liberated from "big government" and state interference (Gray 1995). Indeed, Walker and Naegele (1999) claim a startling continuity across Europe is the way "the family" has been positioned by governments as these ideas have spread beyond their original "English speaking" base.

Neoliberal policies on the family has almost always started from a position of laissez-faire, except when extreme behavior threatens its members or wider social relations (Beck 2005). It can be seen that that neoliberal policy came to focus on two main issues. And, whilst both only represent the point at which a minimalist approach from the state touches family life, they come to mark the dominant narrative through which aging and family are made visible in the public domain (Cloke et al. 2006).

On the one hand, increasing attention was paid to the role families took in the care of older people who were either mentally or physically infirm. A series of policy initiatives (UKG, 1981, 1989, 1990) recognized that families were a principal source of care and support. "Informal" family care became a key building block of policy toward an aging population. It both increased the salience of traditional family values, and independence from government and enabled a reduction in direct support form the state.

On the other hand, helping professionals, following U.S. experience (Pillemer and Wolf 1986), became increasingly aware of the abuse that older people might suffer and the need to protect vulnerable adults from a variety of forms of abuse and neglect (Biggs et al. 1995). Policy guidance, "No Longer Afraid: The Safeguard of Older People in Domestic Settings," was issued in 1993, shortly after the move to seeing informal care as the mainstay of the welfare of older people. As the title suggests, this was also directed primarily at the family.

It is perhaps a paradox that a policy based ostensibly on the premises of leaving-be combines two narrative streams that result in increased surveillance of the family. This paradox is based largely on these points being the only ones where policy "saw" aging in families, rather than ignoring it. This is not to say that real issues of abuse and neglect fail to exist, even though British politicians have often responded to them as if they were some form of natural disaster unrelated to the wider policy environment. To understand the linking of these narratives, it is important to examine trends tacit in the debate on family and aging, but central to wider public policy.

Wider economic priorities, to "roll back the state" and thereby release resources for individualism and free enterprise, had become translated into a family discourse about caring obligations and the need to enforce them. If families ceased to care, then the state would have to pick up the bill. It was not that families were spoken of as being naturally abusive. Neither was the "discovery" of familial abuse linked to community care policy outside academic debate (Biggs 1996). Discourses on the rise of abuse and on informal care remained separate in the formal policy domain. However, a subtle change of narrative tone had taken place. Families, rather than being seen as "havens against a harsh world," were now easily perceived as potential sites of mistreatment, and the previously idealized role of the unpaid career became that of a potential recalcitrant, attempting to avoid their family obligations. An attempt to protect a minority of abused elders thus took the shape of a tacit threat, hanging above the head of every aging family (Biggs and Powell 2000). It is worth note that these policy developments took little account of research evidence indicating that family solidarity and a willingness to care had decreased in neither the United Kingdom (Wenger 1994; Phillipson 1998) nor the United States (Bengtson and Achenbaum 1993). Further, it appeared that familial caring was actually moving away from relationships based on obligation and toward ones based on negotiation (Finch and Mason, 1993).

Family commitment has, for example, varied depending upon the characteristic care-giving patterns within particular family units. Individualistic families provided less instrumental help and made use of welfare services, whereas a second, collectivist pattern offered greater personal support. Whilst this study focused primarily on upward generational support, Silverstein and Bengtson (1997) observed that "tight-knit" and "detached" family styles were often common across generations. Unfortunately, policy developments have rarely taken differences in care-giving styles into account, preferring a general narrative of often idealized role relationships. It is not unfair to say that during the neoliberal period, the dominant narrative of family became that of a site of care going wrong.

Social Democracy, Aging, and the Family

Social democratic policies toward the family arose from the premise that by the early 1990s, the free-market policies of the Reagan/Thatcher years had seriously damaged the social fabric of the nation state and that its citizens needed to be encouraged to identify again with the national project. A turn to an alternative, sometimes called "the third way," emerging under Clinton, Blair, and Schroeder administrations in the United States and parts of Europe, attempted to find means of mending that social fabric, and as part of it, relations between older people and their families (Beck 2005). The direction that the new policy narrative took is summarized in U.K. Prime Minister Blair's (1996) statement that "the most meaningful stake anyone can have in society is the ability to earn a living and support a family." Work, or failing that, work-like activities, plus an active contribution to family life began slowly to emerge, delineating new narratives within which to grow old (Hardill et al. 2007).

Giddens (1998) in the United Kingdom and Beck (1998) in Germany, both proponents of social democratic politics, have claimed that citizens are faced with the task of piloting themselves and their families through a changing world in which globalization has transformed our relations with each other, now based on avoiding risk. According to Giddens (1998), a new partnership is needed between government and civil society. Government support to the renewal of community through local initiative would give an increasing role to voluntary organizations; encourage social entrepreneurship and significantly; and support the democratic family characterized by equality, mutual respect, autonomy, decision-making through communication and freedom of violence. It is argued that social policy should be less concerned with equality and more with inclusion, with community participation reducing the moral and financial hazard of dependence (cf Walker 2002; Biggs et al. 2003; Powell and Owen 2007; Walker and Aspalter 2008).

Through an increased awareness of the notion of ageism, the influence of European ideas about social inclusion and North American social communitarianism, families and older people found themselves transformed into active citizens who should be encouraged to participate in society, rather than be seen as a potential burden upon it (Biggs 2001). A contemporary U.K. policy document, entitled "Building a Better Britain for Older People" (Department of Social Security 1998) is typical of a new genre of Western policy, re-storying the role of older adults. It suggests that the contribution of older people is vital, both to families and to voluntary organizations and charities. We believe their roles as mentors, providing ongoing support and advice to families, young people and other older people, should be recognized. Older people already show a considerable commitment to volunteering. The Government is working with voluntary groups and those representing older people to see how we can increase the quality and quantity of opportunities for older people who want to volunteer.

What is perhaps striking is that it is one of the few places where families are mentioned in an overview on older people, with the exception of a single mention of carers, many of whom, it is pointed out, "are pensioners themselves." In both cases the identified role for older people constitutes a reversal of the narrative offered in preceding policy initiatives. The older person, like other members of family structure, is portrayed as an active member of the social milieu, offering care and support to others (Hardill et al. 2007).

The dominant preoccupation of this policy initiative is not, however, concerned with families. Rather, there is a change of emphasis toward the notion of aging as an issue of lifestyle, and as such draws on contemporary gerontological observations of the "blurring" of age-based identities (Featherstone and Hepworth 1995) and the growth of the grey consumer (Katz 1999).

Whilst such a narrative is attractive to pressure groups, voluntary agencies and, indeed, social gerontologists; there is, just as with the policies of the neoliberals, an underlying economic motive which may or may not be to the long term advantage to older people and their families. Again, as policies develop, the force driving the story of elders as active citizens was to be found in policies of a fiscal nature. The most likely place to discover how the new story of aging, fits the bigger picture is in government-wide policy. In this case the document has been entitled "Winning the Generation Game" (UKG 2000a). This begins well: "One of the most important tasks for twenty-first century Britain is to unlock the talents and potential of all its citizens. Everyone has a valuable contribution to make; throughout their lives." However, the reasoning behind this statement becomes clearer when policy is explained in terms of a changing demographic profile: "With present employment rates" it is argued, "one million more over-50s would not be working by 2020 because of growth in the older population. There will be 2 million fewer working-age people under 50 and 2 million more over 50: a shift equivalent to nearly 10 percent of the total working population."

The solution, then, is to engage older people not only in part of family life but also in work, volunteering, or mentoring. Older workers become a reserve labor pool, filling the spaces left by falling numbers of younger workers. They thus contribute to the economy as producers as well as consumers and make fewer demands on pensions and other forms of support. Those older people who are not thereby socially included can engage in the work-like activity of volunteering.

Most of these policy narratives only indirectly affect the aging family. Families only have a peripheral part to play in the story and do not appear to be central to the lives of older people. However, it is possible to detect the same logic at work when attention shifts from the public to the private sphere. Here the narrative stream develops the notion of "grand-parenting" as a means of social inclusion. This trend can be found in the United Kingdom, France (Girard and Ogg 1998), Germany (Scharf and Wenger 1995), as well as the United States (Minkler 1999).

In the British context the most detailed reference to grand-parenting can be found in an otherwise rather peculiar place, namely from the Home Office, which is an arm of British Government primarily concerned with law and order. In a document entitled *"Supporting Families"* (2000b), "family life," we are told, "is the foundation on which our communities, our society and our country are built." "Business people, people from the community, students and grand-parents" are encouraged to join a school's mentoring network. Further, "the interests of grandparents, and the contribution they make, can be marginalized by service providers who, quite naturally, concentrate on dealing with parents. We want to change all this and encourage grandparents and other relatives to play a positive role in their families," by which it is meant: "home, school links or as a source of social and cultural history" and support when "nuclear families are under stress." Even older people who are not themselves grandparents can join projects "in which volunteers act as 'grandparents' to contribute their experience to a local family."

In the narratives of social democracy, the aging family is seen as a reservoir of potential social inclusion. Older people are portrayed as holding a key role in the stability of both the public sphere, through work and volunteering, and in the private sphere, primarily through grandparental support and advice (Cloke et al. 2006). Grandparents, in particular, are storied as mentors and counselors across the public and private spheres.

Whilst the grandparental title has been used as a catch-all within the dominant policy narrative—bringing with it associations of security, stability, and an easier form of relationship than direct parenting—it exists as much in public as in private space. It is impossible to interpret this construction of grandparenthood without placing it in the broader project of social inclusion, itself a response to increased social fragmentation and economic competition. Indeed it may not be an exaggeration to refer this construal of grand-parenting as neofamilial. In other words, the grandparent has out-grown the family as part of a policy search to include older adults in wider society. The grandparent becomes a mentor to both parental and grandparental generations as advice is not restricted to schools and support in times of stress, but also through participation in the planning of amenities and public services (BGOP 2000).

This is a very different narrative of older people and their relationship to families, from that of the dependent and burdensome elder. In the land of policy conjuring, previously conceived problems of growing economic expense and social uselessness have been miraculously reversed. Older people are now positioned as the solution to problems of demographic change, rather than their cause. They are a source of guidance to ailing families, rather than their victims.

Both narratives increase the social inclusion of a potentially marginal social group: Formerly known as the elderly.

"Grand-Parenting" Policy

There is much to be welcomed in this story of the active citizen elder, especially if policy-inspired discourse and lived self-narratives are taken to be one and the same. There are also certain problems, however, if the two are unzipped, particularly when the former is viewed through the lens of what we know about families from other sources.

First, each of the roles identified in the policy domain, volunteering, mentorship and grand-parenting, have a rather secondhand quality. By this it is meant that each is supportive to another player who is central to the task at hand. Rather like within Erikson's psycho-social model of the lifecycle, the role allocated to older people approximates grand-generativity and is thereby contingent upon the earlier, core life task of generativity itself (Kivnick 1988). In other words it is contingent upon an earlier part of life and the narratives woven around it and fails to distinguish an authentic element of the experience of aging.

When the roles are examined in this light, a tacit secondary status begins to emerge. Volunteering becomes unpaid work: mentoring, support to helping professionals in their eroded pastoral capacities, and grand-parenting, in its familial guise, a sort of peripheral parent without the hassle. This peripherality may be in many ways desirable, so long as there is an alternative pole of authentic attraction that ties the older adult into the social milieux. Either that or the narrative should allow space for legitimized withdrawal from socially inclusive activities. Unfortunately the dominant policy narrative has little to say on either count.

Second, there is a shift of attention away from the most frail and oldest old to a third age of active or positive aging, which, incidentally, may or may not take place in families. It is striking that a majority of policy documents of what might be called the "new aging" start counting from age fifty, an observation that is true for formal government rhetoric and pressure from agencies and initiatives lead by elders (Biggs 2001). This interpretation of the life-course has been justified in terms of its potential for forming intergenerational alliances (BGOP 2000) and fits well with the economic priority of drawing on older people as a reserve labor force (UKG 2000b).

Third, there is a striking absence of analysis of family relations at that age. Possibilities of intergenerational conflict as described in other literature (De Beauvoir 1979), not least in research into three-generation family therapy (Hargrave and Anderson 1992; Qualls 1999), plus the everyday need for tact in negotiating childcare roles (Bornat et al. 1999; Waldrop et al. 1999), appear not to have been taken into account. This period in the aging life-course is often marked by midlife tension and multi-generational transitions, such as those experienced by late adolescent children and by an increasingly frail top generation (Ryff and Seltzer, 1996). Research has indicated that solidarity between family generations is not uniform, and will involve a variety of types and degrees of intimacy and reciprocity (Silverstein and Bengtson 1997).

Finally, little consideration has been given to the potential conflict between the tacit hedonism of aging lifestyles based on consumption and those more socially inclusive roles of productive contribution, of which the "new grandparenting" has become an important part. Whilst there are few figures on grandparental activity it does, for example, appear that community volunteering amongst older people is embraced with much less enthusiasm than policymakers would wish (Boaz et al., 1999). Chambre (1993) claims volunteering in the US diminishes in old age. Her findings indicate the highest rates of volunteering occur in mid-life, where nearly two thirds volunteer. This rate declines to 47 percent for persons aged between 65 and 74 and to 32 percent among persons 75 and over. A U.K. Guardian-ICM (2000) poll of older adults indicated that, amongst grandfathers, but not grandmothers, there was a degree of suspicion of child care to support their own children's family arrangements. More than a quarter of men expressed this concern, compared with only 19 percent of women interviewed. The U.K. charity, Age Concern, stated: "One in ten grandparents are under the age of 56. They have 10 more years of work and are still leading full lives."

One might speculate, immersed in this narrative stream, that problematic family roles and relationships cease to exist for the work-returning, volunteering and community enhancing fifty-plus "elder." Indeed, the major protagonists of social democracy seem blissfully unaware of several decades of research, particularly feminist research, demonstrating the mythical status of the "happy family" (cf e.g. Land 1999).

What emerges from research literature on grand-parenting as it is included in people's everyday experience and narratives of self indicates two trends: (1) there appears to be a general acceptance of the positive value of relatively loose and undemanding exchange between first and third generations and (2) that deep commitments become active largely in situations of extreme family stress or breakdown of the middle generation.

First, grandparents have potential to influence and develop children through the transmission of values. Subsequently, grandparents serve as arbiters of knowledge and transmit knowledge that is unique to their identity, life experience, and history. In addition, grandparents can become mentors, performing the function of a generic life guide for younger children. This "transmission" role is confirmed by Mills' (1999) study of mixed gender relations and by Waldrop et al.'s (1999) report on grandfathering. According to Roberto (1990) early research on grand-parenting in the United States has attempted to identify the roles played by grandparents within the family system and towards grandchildren. Indeed, much US work on grand-parenting has focused on how older adults view and structure their relationships with younger people.

African American grandparents, for example, take a more active role, correcting the behavior of grandchildren and acting like "protectors" of the family. Accordingly, such behaviors are related to effects of divorce and under/unemployment. Research by Kennedy (1990) indicates, however, that there is a cultural void when it comes to grand-parenting roles for many white families with few guidelines on how they should act as grandparents.

Girard and Ogg (1998) report that grand-parenting is a rising political issue in French family policy. They note that most grandmothers welcome the new role they have in child care of their grandchildren, but there is a threshold beyond which support interferes with their other commitments. Contact between older parents and their grandchildren is less frequent that with youngsters, with financial support becoming more prominent.

Two reports, explicitly commissioned to inform U.K. policy (Hayden et al. 1999; Boaz et al. 1999) classify grand-parenting under the general rubric of intergenerational relationships. Research evidence is cited that "when thinking about the future, older people looked forward to their role as grandparents" and that grandparents looked after their grandchildren and provided them with "love, support and a listening ear," providing childcare support to their busy children and were enthusiastic about these roles.

Hayden et al. (1999) used focus groups and qualitative interviewing and report that "grand-parenting included spending time with grandchildren both in active and sedentary hobbies and pursuits, with many participants commenting on the mental and physical stimulation they gained from sharing activities with the younger generation." Coupled with this, the Beth Johnson Foundation (1998) found that older people as mentors had increased levels of participation with more friends and engendered more social activity. With the exception of the last study, each has relied on exclusive self-report data or views on what grand-parenting might be like at some future point.

In research from the tradition of examining social networks, and thus not overtly concerned with the centrality of grand-parenting or grandparent-like roles as such, it is rarely identified as a key relationship and could not be called a strong theme. Studies on the United Kingdom, (Phillipson et al. 2000), Japan (Izuhara 2000), the United States (Schreck 2000; Minkler, 1999), Hispanic Americans (Freidenberg 2000), and Germany, (Chamberlayne and King 2000) provide little evidence that grand-children, as distinct from adult children, are prominent members of older peoples reported social networks.

Grandparental responsibility becomes more visible if the middle generation is for some reason absent. Thompson (1999) reports from the United Kingdom, that when parents part or die, it is often grandparents who take up supporting, caring and mediating roles on behalf of their grandchildren. The degree of involvement was contingent however on the quality of emotional closeness and communication within the family group. Minkler (1999) has indicated that in the United States, one in ten grandparents has primary responsibility for raising a grandchild at some point, with care often lasting for several years.

This trend varies between ethnic groups, with 4.1 percent White, 6.55 percent Hispanic, and 13.55 African American children living with their grandparents or other relatives. It is argued that a 44 percent increase in such responsibilities is connected to the devastating effects of wider social issues, including AIDS/HIV, drug abuse, parental homelessness and prison policy. Thomson and Minkler (2001) note that there is an increasing divergency in the meaning of grandparenting between different socioeconomic groups, with extensive care-givers (7 percent of the sampled population) having increasingly fewer characteristics in common with the 14.9 percent who did not provide child care. In the United Kingdom, a similar split has been identified with 1 percent of British grandparents becoming extensive caregivers against a background pattern of occasional or minimal direct care (Duckworth 2001).

It would appear that grand-parenting is not then, a uniform phenomenon, and extensive grand-parenting or grandparent-like activities are rarely an integral part of social inclusion. Rather, whilst it is seen as providing some intergenerational benefit, it may be a phenomenon that requires an element of unintrusiveness and negotiation in its non-extensive form. When extensively relied on it is more likely to be a response to severely eroded inclusive environments and the self-protective reactions of families living with them. Minkler's analysis draws attention to race as a feature of social exclusion that is poorly handled by policy narratives afforded to the family and old age. There is a failure to recognize structural forms of inequality, and action seeking to socially include older people as a category appears to draw heavily on the occasional helper and social volunteer as a dominant narrative.

Towards Diverse Narrative Streams?

Each phase of social policy, be it the Reagan/Thatcher neoliberalism of the 1980s and early 1990s, the Clinton/Blair interpretation of social democracy in the late 1990s, or the millennial Bush or current Obama administrations leaves a legacy. Moreover, policy development is uneven and subject to local emphasis and elision, which means that it is quite possible for different, even conflicting narratives of family and later life to coexist in different parts of the policy system. Each period generates a discourse that can legitimate the lives of older people and family relations in particular ways and as their influence accrues, create the potential of entering into multiple narrative streams.

A striking feature of recent policy history has been that not only have the formal policies been quite different in their tenor and tacit objectives, one from another, they have also addressed different areas of the lives of aging families. Where there is little narrative overlap there is the possibility of both policies existing, however opposed they may be ideologically or in terms of practical outcome. Different narratives may colonize different parts of policy, drawing on bureaucratic inertia, political inattention, and convenience to maintain their influence. They have a living presence, not least when they impinge on personal aging.

Also, both policy discourses share a deep coherence, which may help to explain their coexistence. Each offers a partial view of aging and family life whilst downloading risk and responsibility onto aging families and aging identities. Neither recognizes aging which is not secondary to an independent policy objective. Both mask the possibility of authentic tasks of aging.

If the analysis outlined above is accepted, then it is possible to see contemporary social policy addressing diverse aspects of the family life of older people in differing and contradictory ways. Contradictory narratives for the aging family exist in a landscape that is both increasingly blurred in terms of roles and relationships and split-off in terms of narrative coherence and consequences for identity. Indeed in a future of complex and multiple policy agendas, it would appear that a narrative of social inclusion through active aging can coexist with one emphasizing career obligation and surveillance. Such a coexistence may occasionally become inconvenient at the level of public rhetoric. However, at an experiential and ontological level. That is to say at the level of the daily lives of older adults and their families, the implications may become particularly acute. Multiple coexisting policy narratives may become a significant source of risk to identity maintenance within the aging family.

One has to imagine a situation in which later lives are lived, skating on a surface of legitimizing discourse. For everyday intents and purposes this surface supplies the ground on which one can build an aging identity and relate to other family members and immediate community. However, there is always the possibility of slipping, of being subject to trauma or transition. Serious slippage will provoke being thrown onto a terrain that had previously been hidden, an alternative narrative of aging with entirely different premises, relationship expectations and possibilities for personal expression. Policy narratives, however, are also continually breaking down and fail to achieve hegemony as they encounter lived experience. Indeed, it could be argued that a continuous process of reconstitution takes place via the play of competing narratives. When we are addressing the issue of older people's identity in later life we can usefully note Foucault's (1977) contention that there has been a growth in attempts to control national populations through discourses of normality, but at the same time this has entailed increasing possibilities for self-government.

Part of the attractiveness of thinking in terms of narrative, that policies tell us stories that we don't have necessarily to believe, is the opening of a critical distance between description and intention. Policy narratives describe certain, often idealized, states of affairs. Depicting them as stories, rather than realities, allows the interrogation of the space between that description and experience (Powell 2005). This chapter explores the term narrative as an epistemological and methodological tool that sheds light on understanding aging identity. The next chapter reviews the impact on aging at a different level of analysis: global. By exploring global aging gives us fuller comparative insights to aging in the aging society from Europe, Asia, the Americas, and Africa.

Chapter 9

Reconstructions of Aging: The Case of Global Aging

INTRODUCTION

Throughout this book we have critically questioned taken-for-granted assumptions about aging and old age. The book aimed to provide a critical reflection to ideas and concepts of social theory and relevance to aging studies so as to facilitate understanding of modernist perspectives through to postmodern dimensions of human aging. The aim of this chapter is to analyze the rapid expansion in the proportion of older people across the globe, and to highlight the main social and economic forces causing this. Specific areas of the globe such as Americas, Europe, Asia, and Africa will be focused on in detail before we discuss some of the key challenges and consequences of global aging for global society. The chapter further highlights how globalization and global aging are colossal driving forces that raise critical questions about the power of the individual nation state to deal with a global problem: an aging population. Globalization as both an analytical tool and social practice throws into flux the policies and practices of individual nation states to address social, economic, and political issues for older people focusing on pensions and health and social care. It highlights how research needs to move from being state centered to one of which acknowledges global forces and the impact on populational aging.

There is no doubt that the rapid increase in population aging across the globe is signaling the most astonishing demographic changes in the history of humankind (Gruber and Wise 2004). In every society in the world, there is concern about population aging and its consequences for nation states, for sovereign governments and for individuals. The United Nations estimates that by the year 2025, the global population of those over sixty years will double, from 542 million in 1995 to around 1.2 billion people (Krug, 2002:125). The global population age sixty-five or older was estimated at 461 million in 2004, an increase of 10.3 million just since 2003. Projections suggest that the annual net gain will continue to exceed 10 million over the next decade: more than 850,000 each month. In 1990, twenty-six nations had older populations of at least 2 million, and by 2000, older populations in thirty-one countries had reached the 2 million mark (Cook and Powell, 2007). UN projections to 2030 indicate that more than sixty countries will have at least 2 million people age sixty-five or older.

While today's proportions of older people typically are highest in more developed countries, the most rapid increases in older populations are actually occurring in the less-developed world (Krug 2002). Between 2006 and 2030, the increasing number of older people in less developed countries is projected to escalate by 140 percent as compared to an increase of 51 percent in more developed countries (Krug, 2002). A key feature of population aging is the progressive aging of the older population itself. Over time, more older people survive to even more advanced ages. The forecast rise in the number of older people aged over seventy-five over the next twenty years will lead to an expansion of demand for health, housing accommodation and pensions for aging populations and is thus of crucial importance for governments, policy makers, planners, and researchers in all nation states. On a global level, the 85-and-over population is projected to increase 151 percent between 2005 and 2030, compared to a 104 percent increase for the population age sixty-five and over and a 21 percent increase for the population under age sixty-five (Bengston and Lowenstein 2004). The most striking increase will occur in Japan: by 2030, nearly 24 percent of all older Japanese are expected to be at least eighty-five years old. As life expectancy increases and people aged eighty-five and over increase in number, four-generation families may become more common.

The age structure of the population has changed from one in which younger people predominated to a global society in which people in later life constituted a substantial proportion of the total population (Powell 2005). Transformations in the age profile of a population are a response to political and economic structures. Older people in particular constitute a large section of populations in western society in particular but the percentage of pensionable age is projected to remain at 18 percent until 2011 when it becomes 20 percent and rising to 24 percent in 2025.

At the same time, there is a stigmatization of such increasing populational numbers by ageist stereotypes. In relation to public services that have to be paid for by younger working people, the percentage of the population has been used to signify such burdensome numbers by the State (Estes, Biggs and Phillipson 2003). Dependency rates, that is the number of dependants related to those of working age, have in fact altered little over the past one hundred years. The reason there has been so little change during a period of so-called rapid aging populations is that there has been a fall in the total fertility rate (the average number of children that would be born to each woman if the current age-specific birth rates persisted throughout her child-bearing life).

In advanced capitalist or first-world countries, declines in fertility that began in the early 1900s have resulted in current fertility levels below the population replacement rate of two live births per woman. Perhaps the most surprising demographic development of the past twenty years has been the pace of fertility decline in many less developed countries (Giddens 1993). In 2006, for example, the total fertility rate was at or below the replacement rate in forty-four less-developed countries (Cook and Powell 2007). Most of the more developed nations have had decades to adjust to this change in age structure. For example, it took more than a century for France's population aged sixty-five and over to increase from 7 percent to 14 percent of the total population. In contrast, many less-developed or third world countries are experiencing rapid increases in the number and percentage of older people, often within a single generation. The same demographic aging process that unfolded over more than a century in France will occur in two decades in Brazil (OECD 2007). In response to this compression of aging, institutions must adapt quickly to accommodate a new age structure. Some less-developed nations will be forced to confront issues, such as social support and the allocation of resources across generations, without the accompanying economic growth that characterized the experience of aging societies in the West. In other words, some countries may grow old before they grow rich (Cook and Powell 2010).

Globalization has also produced a distinctive stage in the social history of populational aging, with a growing tension between nation-state-based solutions (and anxieties) about growing old and those formulated by global institutions (Powell 2005). Globalization, defined here as the process whereby nation-states are influenced (and sometimes undermined) by trans-national actors (Powell 2005), has become an influential force in shaping responses to population aging. Growing old has, itself, become relocated within a trans-national context, with international organizations (such as the World Bank and International Monetary Fund) and cross-border migrations, creating new conditions and environments for older people.

Aging can no longer just be viewed as a national problem but one that affects transnational agencies and communities. Local or national interpretations of aging had some meaning in a world where states were in control of their own destiny (Estes, Biggs and Phillipson 2003). They also carried force where social policies were being designed with the aim or aspiration of levelling inequalities and where citizenship was still largely a national affair (and where there was some degree of confidence over what constituted "national borders"). The crisis affecting each of these areas, largely set in motion by different aspects of globalisation, is now posing acute challenges for understanding global aging in the twenty-first century.

GLOBAL AGING IN PERSPECTIVE

If these examples illustrate the complexity and impact of global aging – then it may be pertinent to highlight how populational aging is impacting more specifically across different continents across the globe. The following section looks at aging in four key areas across the globe: (i) the Americas, (ii) Asia, (iii) Europe, and (iv) Africa. These areas illustrate how population growth is impacting and creating social implications concerning health and disease as well as economic concerns relating to the labour market and pensions.

(i)   *The Americas*

Since the turn of the last century, the life expectancy of people born in North America has increased by approximately twenty-five years and the proportion of persons sixty-five years or older has increased from 4 percent to over 13 percent percent (Estes and Associates 2001). By the year 2030, one in five individuals in the United States is expected to be sixty-five years or older and people age eighty-five and older make up the fastest growing segment of the population. In 2000, there were 34 million people aged sixty-five or older in the United States represented 13 percent of the overall population (Estes and Associates 2001). By 2030 there will be 70 million over sixty-five in the United States, more than twice their number in 2000. 31 million people, or 12 percent of the total population, are aged sixty-five and older. In another thirty-five years, the elderly population should double again. The aging population is not only growing rapidly, but it is also getting older: "In 1990, fewer than one in ten elderly persons was age 85 or older. By 2045, the oldest old will be one in five. Increasing longevity and the steady movement of baby boomers into the oldest age group will drive this trend" (Longino 1994, 856).

The percentage of oldest old will vary considerably from country to country. In the United States, for example, the oldest old accounted for 14 percent of all older people in 2005. By 2030, this percentage is unlikely to change because the aging baby boom generation will continue to enter the ranks of the sixty-five-and-over population (Bengston and Lowenstein 2004). This is obviously causing much concern among policymakers but Longino (1994), for instance, believes that thanks to better health, changing living arrangements, and improved assistive devices, the future may not be as negative as we think when we consider an aging population.

It will be different, however, not least because people currently divorced constitute a small proportion of older populations. This will soon change in many countries as younger populations with higher rates of divorce and separation, age. In the United States, for example, 9 percent of the sixty-five-and-over population is divorced or separated compared to 17 percent of people age fifty-five to sixty-four and 18 percent of people age forty-five to fifty four (Cook and Powell 2010). This trend has gender-specific implications: In all probability nonmarried women are less likely than nonmarried men to have accumulated assets and pension wealth for use in older age, while older men are less likely to form and maintain supportive social networks.

Shoring up public pensions is hardly the only avenue nations in North and South America are exploring. In many countries, privately managed savings accounts have been strongly advocated (Estes and Associates 2001). Two decades ago, nearly every South American nation had pay-as-you-go systems similar to the U.S. Social Security system. Some granted civil servants retiring in their fifties full salaries for life. Widening budget deficits changed that. In 1981, Chile replaced its public system with retirement accounts funded by worker contributions and managed by private firms. The World Bank encouraged eleven other Latin nations to introduce similar features. For example, in Chile the government addressed its fiscal budget deficit by mobilizing a $49 billion of pension-fund assets that make it easier for companies and corporations to fund investments in the local currency with bond offerings, and most workers have some retirement benefits from this (OECD 2007). At the same time, the downside has been those people who cannot afford a private pension have been left to a low state pension which has intensified poverty (Estes and Associates 2001) an enduring feature of all nation states in America. For the future, there is no safety guarantee that private pension schemes are protected and pay out for people who invest their savings in such provision. In a deregulated United States pension system, the issue of corporate crime has highlighted the continuing problem of private pension provision. In one example, this was seen clearly with the energy corporation of Enron's embezzlement of billions of dollars of employees private pension schemes (Powell, 2005). This debate amounts to a significant global discourse about pension provision and retirement ages, but one which has largely excluded perspectives which might suggest an enlarged role for the state and those which might question the stability and cost effectiveness of private schemes. The International Labour Organisation (ILO) concluded that investing in financial markets is an uncertain and volatile business: that under present pension plans people may save up to 30 percent more than they need, which would reduce their spending during their working life; or they may save thirty percent too little-which would severely cut their spending in retirement (Phillipson 1998; Estes, Biggs, and Phillipson 2003).

Holtzman (1997), in a paper outlining a World Bank perspective on pension reform, has argued for reducing state pay-as-you-go (PAYG) schemes to a minimal role of basic pension provision. This position has influenced both national governments and transnational bodies, such as the International Labour Organisation (ILO), with the latter now conceding to the World Bank's position with their advocacy of a mean-tested first pension, the promotion of an extended role for individualized and capitalized private pensions, and the call for Organisation for Economic Cooperation and Development (OECD) member countries to raise the age of retirement.

There is also the impact of Intergovernmental Organizations (IGOs) on the pensions debate in South America. The function of such arguments is to create a climate of fear, of inevitability, and scientific certainty that public pension provision will fail. Insofar as this strategy succeeds it creates a self-fulfilling prophecy. If people believe the experts who say publicly sponsored PAYG systems cannot be sustained, they are more likely to act in ways that mean they are unsustainable in practice. Certainly, in Europe and elsewhere, the state pension is an extremely popular institution. To have it removed or curtailed creates massive opposition. Only by demoralizing the population with the belief that it is demographically unsustainable has room for the private financiers been created and a mass pensions market formed.

Increasingly, the social infrastructure of welfare states is being targeted as a major area of opportunity for global investors. The World Bank has expressed the belief that the public sector is less efficient in managing new infrastructure activities and that the time has come for private actors to provide what were once assumed to be public services. This view has been strongly endorsed by a variety of multinational companies, especially in their work with the World Trade Organisation (WTO). The WTO enforces more than twenty separate international agreements, using international trade tribunals that adjudicate disputes. Such agreements include the General Agreement on Trade in Services (GATS), the first multilateral legally enforceable agreement covering banking, insurance, financial services and related areas (Estes, Biggs, and Phillipson 2003).

(ii)   *Asia*

Asia has the fastest increase in the aging population in the world. As we have cited in previous work, China in particular has been identified as having four "unique characteristics" of populational aging (Du and Tu 2000).

1. *Unprecedented speed*: The proportion of aging population is growing faster than Japan, the country previously recognized as having the fastest rate, and much faster than nations in Western Europe for example.

2. *Early arrival of an aging population*: Before modernization has fully taken place, with its welfare implications, "it is certain that China will face a severely aged population before it has sufficient time and resources to establish an adequate social security and service system for the elderly" (Du and Tu 2000, 79).

3. *Fluctuations in the total dependency ratio*: The Chinese government estimates are that the country will reach a higher dependent burden earlier in the twenty-first century than was previously forecast.

4. *Strong influence of the government's fertility policy and its implementation on the aging process*: The SCFP means fewer children being born, but with more elderly people a conflict arises between the objectives to limit population increase and yet maintain a balanced age structure.

The combination of such factors means that the increased aging population is giving rise to serious concerns among Chinese policy-makers. Kim and Lee (2007) claim the growing elderly population is beginning to exert pressure on the East Asian countries' economies. Three decades ago, major industrialized countries have begun to grapple with a similar problem. With increasing drop in fertility rates, more East Asian economies such as Japan, Hong Kong, South Korea, Singapore and Taiwan are expected to turn into "super-aging societies" by 2025 (Kim and Lee 2007). However, the magnitude of the future impact depends on the (in)ability of individual economies to resolve the demographic changes problem through increased privatization, pension reforms, a migration on more productive countries and extension of retirement age. Like Western countries, Asia will ultimately have to tackle issues related to pension reform and the provision of long-term healthcare services (Cook and Powell 2007).

For Japan, the basic statistical reality of its demographic profile is escalating. Already, seventeen of every one hundred of its people are over sixty-five, and this ratio will near thirty in fifteen years. From 2005 to 2012, Japan's workforce is projected to shrink by around 1 percent each year—a pace that will accelerate after that. Economists fear that, besides blowing an even bigger hole in Japan's underfunded pension system (Cook and Powell, 2007), the decline of workers and young families will make it harder for Japan to generate new wealth.

The future challenge of providing for the elderly is especially urgent in the world's two biggest nations: India and China. Only 11 percent of Indians have pensions, and they tend to be civil servants and the affluent. With a young population and relatively big families, many of the elderly population still count on their children for support. This is not the case in China. By 2030, there will be only two working-age people to support every retiree. Yet only 20 percent of workers have government- or company-funded pensions or medical coverage (Cook and Powell 2007). However, as a counterbalance to such a gloomy perspective, Chindia (China and India taken together) is currently accumulating vast wealth as a result of global change, wealth that could potentially be redirected for the support of their elderly populations.

(iii) *Europe*

The population structure of Western European countries has changed since the turn of the twentieth century. Whereas in 1901, just over 6 percent of the population were at or over current pension age (sixty-five in the United Kingdom for men and women), this figure rose steadily to reach eighteen percent in 2001 (Powell 2005). At the same time, the population of younger people under age sixteen fell from 35 percent to 20 percent. As European countries reach a relatively high level of population aging, the proportion of workers tends to decline. European countries, including France, Germany, Greece, Italy, Russia, and Ukraine have already have seen an absolute decline in the size of their workforce. And in countries where tax increases are needed to pay for transfers to growing older populations, the tax burden may discourage future workforce participation. The impact on a nation state's gross domestic product will depend on increases in labor productivity and that state's ability to substitute capital for labor. Less-developed countries can shift their economies from labor-intensive to capital-intensive sectors as population aging advances. Options for more European nation states may be more constrained. The "rolling back" of pensions promises is just one symptom of a shift in European history: the "graying of the baby-boom generation" (Phillipson 1998). The percentage of sixty-year-olds and older are growing 1.9 percent a year. This is 60 percent faster than the overall global population. In 1950 there were twelve people aged fifteen to sixty-four to support each one of retirement age. Currently, the global average is nine. It will be only four-to-one by 2050 (Powell 2005). By then numbers of older people will outnumber children for the first time. Some economists fear this will lead to bankrupt pensions and lower living standards. It is interesting that in Germany this fear is becoming a battleground for political electioneering. For example, Germany has the highest population in Europe and the third oldest population in the world, which presents both critical questions on public finances to provide pensions and healthcare and an opportunity for innovations in the marketplace. Currently, aging has started to figure prominently in political discussions prior to 2009 elections, as political parties vie for the elderly vote. The current Merkel administration (2011) has been criticized for increasing pensions while opponents talk about a "war of generations" requiring young people to pay for taxation for elder care.

The trend has drawn further attention across Europe, where the working-age population will decline by 0.6 percent this in 2011 (Powell 2005). By 2025 the number of people aged fifteen to sixty-four is projected to dwindle by 10.4 percent in Spain, 10.7 percent in Germany and 14.8 percent in Italy. But aging is just as dramatic in such emerging markets as China—which is expected to have 265 million sixty-five-year-olds by 2020—and Russia and Ukraine (Cook and Powell 2007).

Using evidence from the United Kingdom, the percentage of people of working age, that is sixteen to sixty-four, will drop from 64 percent in 1994 to 58 percent in 2031 (Powell, 2005). As the number of workers per pensioner decreases there will be pressure on pension provision. This is evident now in such areas of pensions and long term care, the retreat of the state made evident in the erosion of State Earnings Related Pay are forcing people to devise their own strategies for economic survival in old age (Phillipson 1998). In the British context that also impinges on global societies in general, private pensions are slowly being introduced in order to prevent the "burden" of an aging population. These are ways in which the state continues to rely on apocalyptic projections such as "demographic time bomb" about aging populations in order to justify cuts in public expenditure (Powell 2005). Hence, the population of Great Britain, like that of other European countries, is aging rapidly. There are only enough young people to fill one in three of the new and replacement jobs that will need to be taken up over the next decade. Older people take much of the responsibility for our social and civic life and for the care of children, the sick, and the very old in the community. Yet the gap between wealth and poverty, choice and the absence of choice for older people is stark and growing wider (Phillipson 1998). The U.K. government is at the time of writing seeking to promote a debate over what they envisage as a multi-billion-pound deficit that will be found in care for the elderly in future.

(iv) *Africa*

Economic security, health and disability, and living conditions in old age are policy concerns throughout the world, but the nature of the problem differs considerably from continent to continent and between and within countries, especially within Africa.

In Africa older people make up a relatively small fraction of the total population, and traditionally their main source of support has been the household and family, supplemented in many cases by other informal mechanisms, such as kinship networks and mutual aid societies. In 2005, Nigeria ranked among the top thirty countries in the world on the basis of the size of its population age sixty and over. Nigeria had the largest older population in sub-Saharan Africa, with over 6 million people age sixty and over; South Africa had just over 3.4 million. Congo and South Africa are projected to have nearly 5 million older people in 2030. Burkina Faso, Cameroon, Cote d'Ivoire, Madagascar, Mozambique, Niger, Senegal, and Uganda are all projected to have their older populations grow to over one million people by 2030 (Building Blocks 2004). Very little careful empirical research has been undertaken on long-term trends in the welfare of older people, but there are a number of reasons to believe that traditional caring and social support mechanisms in Africa are under increasing strain (OECD 2007).

Located on the least developed and poorest continent, African economies are still heavily dependent on subsistence agriculture, and average income per capita is now lower than it was at the end of the 1960s. Consequently, the region contains a growing share of the world's poor. In addition, reductions in fertility and child mortality have meant that, despite the huge impact of the HIV/AIDS epidemic across much of the region, both the absolute size and the proportion of the population age sixty and over have grown and will continue to grow over the next thirty years (Estes, Biggs, and Phillipson 2003).

In Africa, as in other societies such as those in India or China, older people have traditionally been viewed in a positive light, as repositories of information and wisdom. And while African families are generally still intact, development and modernization are closely connected with social and economic changes that can weaken traditional social values and networks that provide care and support in later life. Africa has long carried a high burden of disease, including from malaria and tuberculosis; today it is home to more than 60 percent of all people living with HIV, some 25.8 million in 2005. The vast majority of those affected are still in their prime wage-earning years, at an age when, normally, they would be expected to be the main wage earners and principal sources of financial and material support for older people and children in their families. Many older people have had to deal with the loss of their own support while absorbing the additional responsibilities of caring for their orphaned grandchildren. Increasingly, then, it appears that African societies are being asked to cope with population aging with neither a comprehensive formal social security system nor a well-functioning traditional care system in place (Building Blocks 2004).

The big issue is that majority of the world's population of older people (61 percent or 355 million) live in poorer African countries. This proportion will increase to nearly 70 percent by 2025. For many countries, however, population aging has been accompanied by reductions in per capita income and declining living standards. Epstein (2001) notes that between 1950 and the late 1970s, life expectancy increased by least 10 percent in every developing country in the world, or on average by about fifteen years. However, at the beginning of the twenty- first century, life expectancy has remained below fifty in more than ten developing countries, and since 1970 has actually fallen, or has barely risen in a number of African countries (Phillipson 1998). The AIDS epidemic is certainly a major factor here, but development loans requiring the privatization of health care have also had an impact. Epstein (2001) reports, for example, that by the mid-1990s the African continent was transferring four times more in debt repayment than it spent on health or education. More generally, Help Age International (2000, 8) argues that "older people's poverty is still not a core concern in the social, economic and ethical debates of our time. Their right to development is routinely denied, with aging seen as a minority interest or case for special pleading. Poverty and social exclusion remain the main stumbling blocks to the realisation of the human rights of older people worldwide."

The Challenges and Consequences of Global Aging

While global aging represents a triumph of medical, social, and economic advances, it also presents tremendous challenges. Population aging strains social insurance and pension systems and challenges existing models of social support. It affects economic growth, trade, migration, disease patterns and prevalence, and fundamental assumptions about growing older.

Older people's living arrangements reflect their need for family, community, or institutional support. Living arrangements also indicate sociocultural preferences—for example, some choose to live in nuclear households while others prefer extended families (Estes, Biggs, and Phillipson 2003). The number, and often the percentage, of older people living alone is rising in most countries. In some European countries, more than 40 percent of women age sixty-five and older live alone (Walker and Naegele 2000). Even in societies with strong traditions of older parents living with children, such as in Japan, traditional living arrangements are becoming less common. In the past, living alone in older age often was equated with social isolation or family abandonment. However, research in many cultural settings illustrates that older people, even those living alone, prefer to be in their own homes and local communities (Gilleard and Higgs 2001). This preference is reinforced by greater longevity, expanded social benefits, increased home ownership, elder-friendly housing, and an emphasis in many nations on community care.

Global aging will have dramatic effects on local, regional, and global econo-mies. Most significantly, financial expenditures, labor supply, and total savings will be affected. Changes in the age structures of societies also affect total levels of labor force participation in society, because the likelihood that an individual will be in the labor force varies systematically by age. Concurrently, global pop-ulation aging is projected to lead to lower proportions of the population in the labor force in highly industrialized nations, threatening both productivity and the ability to support an aging population (Krug 2002).

Coupled with rapid growth in the young adult population in third world coun-tries, the World Bank (1994) foresees growing "threats" to international stability pitting different demographic-economic regions against one another. The United Nations (2002) views the relationship between aging populations and labor force participation with panic, recognizing important policy challenges, including the need to reverse recent trends toward decreasing labor force participation of workers in late middle and old age despite mandatory retirement in Western countries such as the United Kingdom (Powell 2005). Social welfare provisions and private-sector pension policies influencing retirement income have a major impact on retirement timing. Hence, a major concern for organizations such as the United Nations and World Bank centers on the number of such "dependent" older people in all developing societies.

Some have argued that the rise of globalization exerts unequal and highly stratified effects on the lives of older people (Estes and Associates 2001). In the developed world, the magnitude and absolute size of expenditure on pro-grammes for older people has made these the first to be targeted with financial cuts. In third-world countries, older people (women especially) have been amongst those most affected by the privatization of health care, and the burden of debt repayments to the World Bank and the IMF (Estes and Associates 2001). Additionally, globalization as a process that stimulates population movement and migration may also produce changes that disrupt the lives of older people. And one must not forget either that they may comprise up to one-third of refu-gees in conflict and emergency situations—a figure which was estimated at over 53 million older people worldwide in 2000 (Estes and Associates 2001).

Nation-states with extensive social programs targeted to the older population (principally health care and income support programs) find the costs of these programs escalating as the number of eligible recipients grows and the duration of eligibility lengthens due to global pressures (Bengston and Lowenstein 2003). Further, few countries have fully funded programs; most countries fund these programs on a pay-as-you-go basis or finance them using general revenue streams. Governments may be limited in how much they can reshape social in-surance programs by raising the age of eligibility, increasing contribution rates, and reducing benefits. Consequently, shortfalls may need to be financed using general revenues. Projections of government expenditures in the United States and other OECD countries show increases in the share of gross domestic product devoted to social entitlements for older populations. In some cases, this share more than doubles as a result of population aging (OECD 2007).

Different countries' age groups have different levels of pace of growth. It is possible for the elements of production—labor and capital—to flow across national boundaries and mitigate the impact of population aging. Studies predict that, in the near term, surplus capital will flow from Europe and North America to emerging markets in Asia and Latin America, where the population is younger and supplies of capital relatively low. In another twenty years, when the baby boom generation in the West has mostly retired, capital likely will flow in the opposite direction (May and Powell 2007). Traditionally, labor is viewed as less mobile than capital, although migration could offset partially the effects of population aging. Currently, 22 percent of physicians and 12 percent of nurses in the United States are foreign born, representing primarily African countries, the Caribbean, and Southeast Asia (OECD 2007). The foreign-born workforce also is growing in most OECD countries. Over the next ten years, the European experience will be particularly instructive in terms of the interplay of aging and migration (OECD 2007). Some pressure groups are now suggesting, for instance, that a rich city like London, which benefits from Ghanaian nurses in the National Health Service, has an ethical obligation to Ghana itself, to provide funds to support that country's health training system because the donor country is losing key personnel.

The life-cycle theory of consumption is that households accumulate wealth during working years to maintain consumption in retirement (Gilleard and Higgs 2001). The total of a country's individual life-cycle savings profiles determines whether households in that country are net savers or nonsavers at any point in time. A country with a high proportion of workers will tend to be dominated by savers, placing downward pressure on the rate of return to capital in that economy. Nation-states with older populations will be tapping their savings and driving rates of return higher because of the scarcity of capital (Gilleard and Higgs 2001).

Retirement resources typically include public and private pensions, financial assets, and property. The relative importance of these resources varies across countries. For example, a groundbreaking study revealed that only 3 percent of Spanish households with at least one member age fifty or older own stocks (shares), compared to 38 percent of Swedish households (Walker and Naegele 2000). The largest component of household wealth in many countries is housing value. This value could fall if large numbers of older homeowners try to sell houses to smaller numbers of younger buyers. How successfully this transition is managed around the world could determine the rise and fall of nations and re-shape the global economy in the era of the post-credit crunch. Two key vehicles of growth are increases in the labor force and productivity. If nation-states cannot maintain the size of their labor forces by persuading older workers to retire later then the challenge will be to maintain growth levels. That will be a particular challenge in Europe, where productivity growth has averaged just 1.3 percent since 1995. By 2024, growth in household financial wealth in the United States, Europe, and Japan will slow from a combined 4.5 percent annual reduction now to 1.3 percent. That will translate into $31 trillion less wealth than if the average age were to remain the same (Cook and Powell, 2007).

Most of Europe's state-funded pension systems encourage early retirement. Now, 85.5 percent percent of adults in France retire from employment by age sixty, and only 1.3 percent engage in employment beyond aged sixty five. In Italy, 62 percent of adults retire from full-time work by the age of fifty-five. That compares with 47 percent of people who earn wages or salaries until they are sixty-five in the United States and 55 percent in Japan (Estes and Associates 2001).

Why the sudden attention to a demographic trend of global aging? In part, it is because the future is already dawning that global trends impact on state power. In South Korea and Japan, which have strong cultural aversions to immigration, small factories, construction companies, and health clinics are relying more on temporary workers from the Philippines, Bangladesh, and Vietnam (OECD 2007). In China, state industries are struggling over how to lay off unneeded middle-age workers when there is no social safety net to support them.

What really has pushed aging to the top of the global agenda, though, are increasing fiscal gaps in part, due to the "global credit crunch" in the United States, Europe, Japan, and elsewhere that could worsen as populations reach retirement age. While United States Social Security is projected to remain solvent until at least 2042, the picture is more acute in Europe. Unlike the United States where most citizens also have private savings plans, in much of Europe up to 90 percent of workers rely almost entirely on public pensions (Walker and Naegele 2000). Austria guarantees 93 percent of pay at retirement, for example, and Spain offers 94.7 percent. Pensions and elder-care costs will increase from 14 percent of capitalist nations' gross domestic product to 18 percent by 2050 (Walker and Naegele 2000).

As people live longer and have fewer children, family structures are also transformed (Bengston and Lowenstein 2004). This has important implications in terms of providing care to older people. Most older people today have children, and many have grandchildren and siblings. However, in countries with very low birth rates, future generations will have few, if any, siblings. As a result of this trend and the global trend toward having fewer children, people will have less familial care and support as they age (Bengston and Lowenstein 2004). Unless there is a fundamental shift in the views of "Fortress Europe," Japan and other countries towards immigrants, and an overcoming of entrenched racial or racist attitudes towards migrants, some parts of the globe will be "elderly heavy" while others will be "elderly light." Were migrants made more welcome in richer societies, then one could envisage a space of carer flows, with more interactions and movements in either direction to the heavy or light end. Or, for example, one could have elderly relocation in the same way as Japanese elderly are relocating into Thailand into new forms of transnational households, in order to seek cheaper care systems for their retirement (Powell 2005).

As a consequence of the global demographics of aging, the changing societies of the post millennium are being confronted with quite profound issues relating to illness and health care, access to housing and economic resources including pension provision. The past several years has witnessed an unprecedented stretching of the human life span. This aging of the global population is without parallel in human history. If these demographic trends continue to escalate, by 2050 the number of older people globally will exceed the number of young for the first time since formal records began raising questions of the power of the nation state in the context of global aging raising further global questions of distribution of power and scarcity of resources to an aging population.

Chapter 10

Conclusion: Reconstructions of Aging

Throughout this book we have critically questioned taken-for-granted assumptions about aging and old age. The book aimed to provide a critical reflection to ideas and concepts of social theory and relevance to aging studies so as to facilitate understanding of modernist perspectives through to postmodern dimensions of human aging.

The discussion began with an assessment of the modern constructions of aging. In chapter two we outlined the historical origins of the biomedical model as a precursor to chapter three, where we analyzed the master narratives of aging into old age, with a focus on biomedical conceptualizations of mind/body "in decline" (Cassel 1991). As was illuminated, in Occidental culture in particular, the aging body is the baseline, subject to relentless forces of negative decline (Powell 2001d). Insofar as there is a history of aging, there is also a history of efforts to control and regulate older people (Powell and Biggs 2000). The master narrative of natural decline of aging bodies hides the location of complex intersections of negative ideas that comprise an aging culture (Biggs and Powell 2000; Longino and Powell 2004). We revealed how a key contribution of social theory as a broad discipline has been to highlight how individual lives and behavior, once thought to be determined solely by biology and psychology (Powell 2001a; Cassel 1991), are, in fact, heavily influenced by social environments in which people live and hence are socially constructed.

In chapter 3 we traced how the adverse quality of life experienced by many older people was caused by the effects of modern capitalism that impinge on the retirement process (Phillipson 1998), particularly gender oppression through materiality and patriarchy (Arber and Ginn 1995). For functionalist gerontology, however, the social situation of older people should be one whereby the person either stays "active" or "disengages." Such theories that highlight modernist narratives have held intellectual respectability in terms of cause and effect for example, "you retire and then you disengage" (cf. Cumming and Henry 1961), the master disengagement epistemic narrative.

The second part of the book used a critical approach to denote ways of thinking to continually challenge the taken-for-grantedness of modernity and open up the possibility for understanding aging through alternative yet postmodern deconstructions of aging. For Seidman (1994, 317) to ignore a shift toward a postmodernism would be "a grave mistake." In assessing the implications of postmodernism for social theory and aging studies, it is important to give postmodernism the credit it deserves and take note of both the epistemological and ontological possibilities it allows for sociological theorizing at localistic levels in everyday life (Seidman 1994). For example, we looked at three areas of postmodern deconstructions of aging: (1) understanding aging body and culture; (2) power/knowledge relations between older people and professional experts; (3) aging in the risk society.

The contemporary cultural, political, economic, and scientific representations of aging within Western culture are, as a result of these deconstructions, becoming increasingly important in social discourses on aging, both in the disciplines of social theory and social gerontology and in the policies and practices of institutions that attempt to define later life (Phillipson 1998).

In chapter 4, the discussion turned to how the intrasubjective aging body has been positioned in postmodern popular culture through biotechnological reconstruction. The postmodern analysis of the aging body is important in restoring the body to interconnected disciplines such as social theory and social gerontology. However, the emphasis on body gender has ebbed and flowed in the sociological imaginary as "female corporeality" and "male embodiment." In a parallel discourse, the book maintains that emergent constructions of aging are becoming increasingly fluid (Gilleard and Higgs 2000), in the process eroding many of the modernist "decline" meanings traditionally associated with old age, but it has also left aging people rootless and prone to increasing uncertainty and "risk."

Alongside this, chapters 5 and 6 highlighted how "social welfare" is a key example of where social discourses on aging have become situated that impinge on the intersubjective dimensions of historical and contemporary everyday life between professional experts and older people based on "power/knowledge," "governmentality," and "technologies of self" (Foucault 1988) and risk (Giddens 1991; Beck 1992). We assessed the discourse of "social welfare" as a key example of a medium used to legitimize and position the identities that older people adopt in contemporary Western societies. It contains recurrently variable technologies that function to reconcile relations between older people and the state. Medico-technical and "case management" neoliberal discourses have been presented as adding choice and reducing boundaries associated with adult aging.

However, as discussed in chapter 5, they also represent an amplification of professional control that can be coerced on lifestyles in older age. As Schrag (1980, 252) points out:

> It is a subtle, erosive process. Almost every agency of education, social welfare and mental health talks the seductive language of prevention, diagnosis and treatment; and almost every client is a hostage to an exchange which trades momentary comfort and institutional peace for an indefinite future of maintenance and control.

At the same time, aging appears to be moving from its traditional concern with "public issues" to the question of how aging is individualized in neoliberal Western societies through governmentality and postmodern culture (Katz 2000). This is particularly apparent in a move toward social discourses of consumerism, which appears to indicate a shift of attention from responding to discrete macro-problems (cf. Townsend 1981) to an attempt to problematize what constitutes the "aging body" and wider questions of embodiment, corporeality, and reflexivity (Biggs and Powell 2001; Powell and Longino 2002). This postmodern trend has the potential to intensely reconstruct both formal expectations and personal aging itself (Calasanti 1996). Chapter 7 explored the notion of risk society and its relationship to aging identities. The change to constructing, deconstructing, and reconstructing an aging identity is partially due to the erosion of values and assumptions of modernity and to the move toward the "risk society" (Beck 1992). Here, aging identities have traditionally depended upon policy discourses within and between professions and institutions of the state in Western culture (Donzelot 1979, 1988). The chapter made the case for a reflexive gerontology that is aware of risk and its impingement on older people as welfare subjects. Chapter 8 explored an underdeveloped theme in social gerontology on narrative. The chapter explicated how narrative can be used as a policy and conceptual tool to interrogate the dynamics of aging experiences. Whilst, that chapter focused on the small scale narratives of policies for older people, what was omitted in the chapter was coverage of macro issues. Hence, chapter 9 explored the macrophysics of power in the guise of global aging. This chapter suggests that to have a fuller understanding of aging, we need to appreciate and situate it within its global context. The chapter revealed case study approaches to Asia, Americas, Europe and Africa.

The pertinent question to raise is: Has all of this been theorized adequately: The answer is that the relationship between social theory and the study of aging has become closely entwined, leading critical gerontologists such as Estes, Biggs, and Phillipson (2003) to question the "commonsense assumptions" that may be held there.

We could argue that the experience of the welfare state has been ambivalent, insofar as it often provides people with what they need but in ways that erode a positive sense of self. However, a perceived oxidization of these structures has led to an interiorization of the position upon which a feasible aging identity can be built. This is reflected in a postmodern interest in the use of "masking" of aging performativity (Featherstone and Hepworth 1993). This has been accompanied by a deconstruction of biomedical discourses of "decline" and "withdrawal" and the promotion of models of "consumer aging" (Estes, Biggs, and Phillipson 2003). Indeed, part of the seductive array of discourses in consumer culture centers on self-subjectification lifestyles. These discourses, which impinge on aging, have thereby taken on a "normative" dimension, which mediates a daily understanding of what it is to age through the life-course.

At the same time, we are alerted to the narrow-minded nature of the discourses supplied by biomedical systems of knowledge and political processes, which affect perceptions of aging. Both biomedical and political developments are uneven, ambivalent, and subject to elision, which means that it is quite possible for different medical and political discourses of aging to coexist in different parts of the postmodern social system.

Each generates a discourse that can legitimate the lives of older people in particular ways, and as their influence accumulates, create the potential of entering into diverse discursive streams (Powell 2001a; Powell and Edwards 2002). Medical and political discourses contribute to a subterranean coherence, which may help to explain their coexistence. Each offers a view of aging while downloading "risk" and uploading "responsibility" onto aging subjects (Biggs and Powell 2001; Powell 2001d).

A further critical reflection centers on the extent of subjectivity afforded to people in later life. It can be suggested that this includes at least two factors key to the process of aging: (1) the creation of spaces in which to perform "consumer" roles and be recognized as consumers, as well as to have intervention when "risk" can be "seen"; (2) the supply of material with which "technologies of self" can flourish without being dominated by biomedical knowledge and professional power (Powell 2001e; Powell and Edwards 2002). Indeed, it can be argued that a modernist narrative of "decline" through postmodern "consumer aging" could coexist, with one emphasizing biomedical surveillance of objects of knowledge while the other highlights self-subjectification, and self-actualization.

Aging is a site upon which power is distributed and "power/knowledge" (cf. Powell 2001a) relations are played out, mainly through narratives engaged at the interpersonal level between subjects/objects of knowledge and professional experts. It is suggested, then, that:

> narratives of aging are personal insofar as we apply techniques to ourselves, while the technologies and the ground on which they are told imply particular distributions of power that will determine the way and the what of the storyline. (Biggs and Powell 2001, 113)

Discourses of aging therefore provide narrative prototypes within which certain categories of persons or groups are encouraged to live out their lives. This performativity may differ significantly from an individual's or group's everyday experience and requires a critical understanding of the postmodern with emphasis on analyses of embodiment, subjectivity, and risk.

Bibliography

Achenbaum, A. W. 1978. Old Age in the New Land. Baltimore: John Hopkins University Press.

Age Concern England. 1997. Age Matters: Report on a National Gallup Survey. London: ACE.

Alcock, P. 1996. Social Policy in Britain: Themes and Issues. Basingstoke: Macmillan.

Allen, J. P. 2010 Middle Egyptian: An Introduction to the Language and Culture of Hieroglyphs Cambridge: Cambridge University Press

Alley, D. E., Putney, N. M, Rice, M., (2009) 'The Increasing Use of Theory in Social Gerontology': 1990-2004 Journals of Gerontology Series B Psychological Sciences and Social Sciences 65 (5): 583–90

Arber, S., and J. Ginn. 1991. Gender and Later Life: A Sociological Analysis of Resources and Constraints. London: Sage.

Arber, S., and J. Ginn, eds. 1995. Connecting Gender and Ageing: A Sociological Approach. Milton Keynes, U.K.: Oxford University Press.

Armstrong, D. 1983. The Political Anatomy of the Body. Cambridge: Cambridge University Press.

Armstrong, D. 1995. Outline of Sociology as Applied to Medicine London: Arnold Publishers

Atkinson, P. 1981. The Clinical Experience: The Construction and Reconstruction of Medical Reality Farnborough: Gower

Baltes, B., and M. F. Baltes. 1990. Successful Aging: Perspectives from the Behavioural Sciences. New York: Cambridge University Press.

Baltes, M., and L. Carstersen. 1996. "The Process of Successful Ageing." Ageing and Society 16: 397–422.

Bauman, Z. 1992. Imitations of Postmodernity. London: Routledge.

———. 2001. The Individualized Society. Cambridge: Polity.

Beck, U. 1986. Risikogesellschaft. Auf dem Weg in eine andere Moderne. Frankfurt am Main: Suhrkamp.

———. 1992. Risk Society: Towards a New Modernity. London: Sage.

———. 1994. "The Reinvention of Politics: Towards a Theory of Reflexive Modernization." In Reflexive Modernization: Politics, Tradition and Aesthetics in the Modern Social Order, edited by U. Beck, A. Giddens, and S. Lash, 1–55. Stanford, Calif.: Stanford University Press.

————. 1998. Democracy Without Enemies, Polity: Cambridge, U.K..

————. 2005. Power and Countervailing Power in the Global Age. Cambridge: Polity.

Becker, H. S., Geer, B, Hughes, E. C. and Strauss, A. L. 1961. Boys in White: Student Culture in Medical School Chicago and London: University of Chicago Press

Bengtson, V. L. and Achenbaum, W. 1993. The Changing Contract Across Generations, Aldine De Gruyter: New York.

Bengston, V. E., Burgess, and T. Parrot. 1997. "Theory, Explanation and a Third Generation of Theoretical Development in Social Gerontology." Journal of Gerontology: Social Sciences 52 (B): 72–88.

Bengtson, V., and R. Schaie. 1999. Handbook of Theories in Gerontology. New York: Springer.

Bengtson V. L., Gans D., Putney N. M., Silverstein M., 2009 Handbook of theories of aging. New York: Springer

Bengtson, V. L., Giarrusso, R., Silverstein, M., and Wang, H. (2000), Families and Intergenerational Relationships in Aging Societies, Hallym International Journal of Aging, Vol. 2, No. 1, pp. 3–10.

Best, F. 1980. Flexible Life Scheduling. New York: Praeger.

BGOP, Better Government of Older People (2000), Better Government for Older People, BGOP: Wolverhampton, U.K..

Biggs, S. 1993. Understanding Ageing. Milton Keynes, U.K.: Oxford University Press.

————. 1996. "A Family Concern: Elder Abuse in British Social Policy." Critical Social Policy 16 (2): 63–88.

————. 1999. The Mature Imagination. Milton Keynes, U.K.: Oxford University Press.

————. 2001, Toward Critical Narrativity: Stories of Aging in Contemporary Social Policy, Journal of Aging Studies, Vol. 15, pp. 1–14.

Biggs, S., and J. L. Powell. 2000. "Surveillance and Elder Abuse: The Rationalities and Technologies of Community Care." Journal of Contemporary Health 4 (1): 43–49.

————. 2001. "A Foucauldian Analysis of Old Age and the Power of Social Welfare." Journal of Aging & Social Policy 12 (2): 93–111.

————. 2002. "Older People and Family Policy: A Critical Narrative." In International Perspectives on the Family, edited by V. Bengston and A. Lowenstein. Thousand Oaks, Calif.: Pine Forge Press.

Biggs, S., Phillipson, C., and Kingston, P. 1995, Elder Abuse in Perspective, Open University Press: Buckingham, U.K..

Biggs, S., Estes, C., and Phillipson, C. 2003, Social Theory, Social Policy and Ageing, Open University Press: Buckingham, U.K..

BJF, Beth Johnson Foundation 1999, Intergenerational Programmes, BJF: Stoke, U.K..

Blair, T. 1996, New Britain: My Vision of a Young Country, Fourth Estate: London.

Blaikie, A. 1999. Ageing and Popular Culture. Cambridge: Cambridge University Press.

Boaz, A., Hayden, C., and Bernard, M. 1999, Attitudes and Aspirations of Older People. DSS Research Report, No. 101, CDS: London.

Bond, J., and P. Coleman. 1990. Ageing in Society. London: Sage.

Bone, M. 1996. Trends in Dependency among Older People in England. London: Office of Population and Census Statistics.

Boneham, M., and K. Blakemore. 1994. Age, Race and Ethnicity. Buckingham: Oxford University Press.

Bornat, J., et al., eds. 1993. Community Care: A Reader. Milton Keynes, U.K.: Oxford University Press.

Bornat, J., Dimmock, B., Jones, D., and Peace, S. (1999), Stepfamilies and Older People, Ageing and Society, Vol. 19, No. 2, pp. 239–62.

Bowl, R. 1986. "Social Work with Old People." In Ageing and Social Policy, edited by C. Phillipson and A. Walker. London: Gower.

Braidotti, R. 1994. Nomadic Subjects. Embodiment and Sexual Difference in Contemporary Feminist Theory. New York: Columbia University Press.

Burchell, G. 1993. "Liberal Government and the Techniques of the Self." Economy and Society 22 (3): 267–82.

Burchell, G., et al. 1991. The Foucault Effect: Studies in Governmentality. Hemel Hempstead: Harvester Wheatsheaf.

Bury, M. 1995. "Ageing, Gender and Sociological Theory." In Connecting Gender and Ageing: A Sociological Approach, edited by S. Arber and J. Ginn. Milton Keynes, U.K.: Oxford University Press.

Butler, J. 1987. Bodies that Matter on the Discursive Limits of "Sex." Oxford: Clarendon.

Bytheway, B. 1993. "Ageing and Biography: The Letters of Bernard and Mary Berenson." Sociology 27 (1): 153–65.

Bytheway, B., and J. Johnson. 1998. "The Sight of Age." In The Body in Everyday Life, edited by S. Nettleton and J. Watson, 62–85.

Bytheway, W. 1995. Ageism. Milton Keynes, U.K.: Oxford University Press.

Cabinet Office U.K.. 1998. Better Government for Older People. London: H.M.S.O.

Calasanti, T. M. 1996. "Incorporating Diversity: Meaning, Levels of Research, and Implications for Theory." The Gerontologist 36 (2): 147–56.

Carmel, S., Morse, C. A., and Torres-Gil, F. M. 2007. Lessons on Aging from Three Nations, Baywood: New York.

Carr-Saunders, A. M., and Wilson, P. A. 1933. The Professions London: The Clarendon Press.

Carter, K. C. 1991. The development of Pasteur's concept of disease: causation and the emergence of specific causes in nineteenth century medicine Bulletin of the History of Medicine 2: 528–48.

Cassel, E. J. 1991. The Nature of Suffering and the Goals of Medicine. New York: Oxford University Press.

Castel, R. 1991. "From Dangerousness to Risk." In The Foucault Effect: Studies in Governmentality, edited by G. Burchell, C. Gordon, and P. Miller. London: Harvester Wheatsheaf: 281–98.

Chadwick, J. and Mann, W. N. 1950. *The Medical Works of Hippocrates* Oxford: Blackwell.

Chamberlayne, P. and King, A. 2000. Cultures of Care, Policy Press: London.

Chambre, S. M. 1993. Volunteerism by Elders: Past Traditions and Future Prospects, The Gerontologist, Vol. 33, pp. 221–28.

Chau, W. F. 1995. "Experts, Networks and Inscriptions in the Fabrication of Accounting Images." Accounting Organisations and Society 20 (2/3): 111–45.

Christian, B. 1996. "The Race for Theory." In Radically Speaking: Feminism Reclaimed, edited by D. Bell and R. Klein. London: Zed Books.

Chudacoff, H. 1989. How Old Are You? Princeton, N.J.: Princeton University Press.

Cloke, P., Johnsen, S., and May, J. 2006. Ethical citizenship? Volunteers and the ethics of providing services for homeless people Geoforum 38(6): 1089-1101.

Clough, R. 1988. Practice, Politics and Power in Social Service Departments. Aldershot, U.K.: Gower.

Clough, R., and C. Hadley. 1996. Care in Chaos. London: Cassel.

Cohen, S. 1985. Visions of Social Control. Cambridge: Polity.

Cole, T., D. Van Tassel, and R. Kastenbaum. 1992. Handbook of the Humanities and Aging. New York: Springer.

Connor, S. 1989. Postmodernist Culture. Oxford: Basil Blackwell.

Conrad, S. 1992. "Old Age in the Modern and Postmodern Western World." In Handbook of the Humanities and Aging, edited by T. Cole. New York: Springer Publishing Company.

Cook, I. G. 2001. A Human Geography of China. London: Curzon.

Cook, I. G., and G. Murray. 2000. China's Third Revolution: Tensions in the Transition to Post-Communism. London: Curzon.

Cook, I. G., and J. L. Powell. 2003. "Active Aging in China." Journal of Social Sciences and Humanities 26 (2): 1–10.

Copeman, W. S. C. 1960. Doctors and Disease in Tudor Times London: Dawson and Sons.

Cousins, M., and A. Hussain. 1984. Michel Foucault. London: Macmillan.

Cumming, E., and W. Henry. 1961. Growing Old: The Process of Disengagement. New York: Basic Books.

Dalley, G. 1988. Ideologies of Caring. London: Macmillan.

Davidson, A. 1986. "Archaeology, Genealogy, Ethics." In Foucault: A Critical Reader, edited by D. Hoy. Oxford: Basil Blackwell.

Deakin, N. 1996. "The Devil's in the Detail: Some Reflections on Contracting for Social Care." Social Policy and Administration 30 (1): 20–38.

De Beauvoir, S. 1979. Old Age. Penguin: London.

Delanty, G. 1999. Social Science: Beyond Constructivism. London: Sage.

Derrida, J. 1978. Writing and Difference. Chicago: University of Chicago Press.

Donzelot, J. 1979. The Policing of Families. London: Hutchinson.

———. 1988. "The Promotion of the Social." Economy and Society 17 (3): 395–427.

Douglas, M. 1985. Risk Acceptability According to the Social Sciences. New York: Sage.

Dreyfus, H., and P. Rabinow. 1983. Michel Foucault: Beyond Hermeneutics, London: Tavistock.

DSS, Department of Social Security 1998, Building a Better Britain for Older People, HMSO: London.

Duckworth, L. 2001, Grandparents Who Bring Up Children Need More Help, Independent, September 13.

Du Gay, P. 1996. Consumption and Identity. London: Sage.

Du, P., and P. Tu. 2000. "Population Ageing and Old Age Security." In The Changing Population of China, edited by X. Peng and Z. Guo, 77–90. Oxford: Blackwell.

Elder, G. 1977. The Alienated: Growing Old Today. London: Writers and Readers Publishing Co-operative.

Erikson, E. 1980. Identity and the Life Cycle: A Re-issue. New York: W. W. Norton.

Estes, C. 1979. The Aging Enterprise. San Francisco: Jossey-Bass.

Estes, C., J. Swan, and L. Gerard. 1982. "Dominant and Competing Paradigms in Gerontology: Towards a Political Economy of Ageing." Ageing and Society 12: 151–64.

Estes, C., and E. A. Binney. 1989. "The Biomedicalization of Aging: Dangers and Dilemmas." The Gerontologist 29 (5): 587–96.

Estes, C., and Associates. 2001. Social Policy and Aging. Thousand Oaks, Calif.: Sage.

Estes, C., S. Biggs, and C. Phillipson. 2003. Social Theory, Social Policy and Ageing. Milton Keynes, U.K.: Oxford University Press.

Ewald, F. 1993. "Two Infinities of Risk." In The Politics of Everyday Fear, edited by B. Massumi. Minneapolis: University of Minnesota Press.

Fattah, E. A., and V. F. Sacco. 1989. Crime and Victimisation of the Elderly. New York: Springer.

Featherstone, M., and M. Hepworth. 1993. "Images in Ageing." In Ageing in Society, edited by J. Bond, P. Coleman, and S. Peace. London: Sage.

Featherstone, M., and A. Wernick. 1995. Images of Ageing. London: Routledge.

Fennell, G., et al. 1988. Sociology of Age. Buckingham: Oxford University Press.

Finch, J. 1986. "Age." In Key Variables in Social Investigation, edited by R. Burgess. London: Routledge & Kegan Paul.

Finch, J. and Mason, J. 1993, Negotiating Family Responsibilities, Routledge: London.

Flynn, R. 1992. Structures of Control in Health Management. London: Routledge.

———. 2002. "Clinical Governance and Governmentality." Health, Risk & Society 4 (2): 155–73.

Fortes, M. 1984. "Age, Generation and Social Structure." In Age and Anthropological Theory, edited by D. Kertzer and J. Keith. London: Cornell University Press.

Foucault, M. 1967. Madness and Civilisation. London: Tavistock.

———. 1972. The Archaeology of Knowledge. London: Tavistock.

———. 1973. The Birth of the Clinic. London: Routledge.

———. 1976. The History of Sexuality. Harmondsworth: Penguin.

———. 1977. Discipline and Punish. London: Tavistock.

———. 1978. "Governmentality." In The Foucault Effect, edited by G. Burchell, C. Gordon, and P. Miller 1991.

———. 1980. Power/Knowledge: Selected Interviews and Other Writings, 1972–1977. New York: Pantheon.

———. 1982. "The Subject of Power." In Michel Foucault: Beyond Structuralism and Hermeneutics, edited by H. Dreyfus and P. Rabinow. Brighton, U.K.: Harvester.

———. 1988. "Technologies of the Self." In Technologies of the Self, edited by L. H. Martin, et al. London: Tavistock.

Frank, A. W. 1990. "Bringing Bodies Back In: A Decade Review." Theory, Culture & Society 7 (1): 131–62.

———. 1991. "For a Sociology of the Body: An Analytical Review." In The Body Social Processes and Cultural Theory, edited by M. Featherstone, M. Hepworth, and B. Turner. London: Sage.

———. 1996. The Wounded Storyteller: Body, Illness and Ethics. Chicago: University of Chicago Press.

Fraser, N. 1987. "Women, Welfare and the Politics of Need Interpretation." Hytapia: A Journal of Feminist Philosophy 2: 102–21.

Friedan, B. 1993. The Fountain of Age. London: Cape Books.

Freidenberg, J. 2000, Growing Old in EL Barrio, New York University Press: New York.

Freund, P. 1988. "Bringing Society into the Body: Understanding Socialized Human Nature." Theory and Society 17: 839–64.

Fullmer, E. M. 1995. "Challenging Biases against Families of Older Gays and Lesbians." In Strengthening Aging Families: Diversity in Practice and Policy, edited by G. C. Smith, S. S. Tobin, et al., 99–119. Thousand Oaks, Calif.: Sage.

Garland, D. 1985. Punishment and Welfare. Aldershot, U.K.: Gower.

George, L. 1995. "The Last Half-Century of Aging Research—and Thoughts for the Future." Journal of Gerontology: Social Sciences 50 (B) (1): 1–3.

Giddens, A. 1987. Social Theory and Modern Sociology. Cambridge: Polity.

———. 1990. The Consequences of Modernity. Cambridge: Polity.

———. 1991. Modernity and Self-Identity: Self and Society in the Late Modern Age. Cambridge: Polity.

———. 1998. The Third Way, Polity: Cambridge.

Gilleard, C., and P. Higgs. 2000. Cultures of Ageing. London: Prentice-Hall.

Girrard, I. and Ogg, J. (1998), Grand-parenting in France and England, paper presented to the British Society of Gerntology, Sheffield, U.K..

Gittens, C. 1997. The Pursuit of Beauty. London: NPG.

Gordon, C. 1991. "Governmental Rationality: An Introduction." In The Foucault Effect, edited by G. Burchell, C. Gordon, and P. Miller, 1–51. Chicago: Chicago University Press.

Granovetter, M. 1985. "Economic Action and Social Structure—The Problem of Embeddedness." American Journal of Sociology 91 (3): 481–510.

———. 1992. "Economic Institutions as Social Constructions," Acta Sociologica 25 (3): 3–11.

Gray, J. 1995. Enlightenment's Wake, Routledge: London.

Greenblatt, S. 1980. Renaissance Self-Fashioning: From More to Shakespeare. Chicago: Chicago University Press.

Grosz, E. 1994. Volitile Bodies. Bloomington: Indiana University Press.

Guardian-ICM Poll 2001, Grandparenting and Retirement Activities, ICM: London.

Gubrium, J. F. (1992), Out of Control: Family Therapy and Domestic Disorder, Sage: Thousand Oaks, CA.

Gutting, G., ed. 1994. The Cambridge Companion to Foucault. Cambridge: Cambridge University Press.

Habermas, J. 1981. The Theory of Communicative Action. London: Beacon Press.

———. 1984. The Philosophical Discourse of Modernity. Cambridge: Polity.

———. 1992. Postmetaphysical Thinking. Cambridge: Polity.

Hacking, I. 1990. The Taming of Chance. Cambridge: Cambridge University Press.

Hall, S., ed. 1992. Modernity and Its Futures. Cambridge: Polity.

Hallam, E., J. Hockey, and G. Howarth. 1999. Beyond the Body: Death and Social Identity. London: Routledge.

Haraway, D. 1991. Simians, Cyborgs and Women. London: Free Association Books.

Hardill, I. and Baines, S. 2007. Volunteering for all? Explaining patterns of volunteering and identifying strategies to promote it, Policy and Politics. 35 (3): 395-412.

Hargrave, T. and Anderson, W. 1992. Finishing Well: Aging and Reparation in the Intergenerational Family, Brunner and Mazel: New York.

Harper, S., and G. Laws. 1995. "Rethinking the Geography of Ageing." Progress in Human Geography 19 (2): 199–221.

Harper, S. 1997. "Constructing Later Life/Constructing the Body: Some Thoughts from Feminist Theory." In Critical Approaches to Ageing and Later Life, edited by A. Jamieson, S. Harper, and C. Victor, 160–71. Buckingham: Open University Press.

Hayden, C., Boaz, A., and Taylor, F. 1999. Attitudes and Aspirations of Older People: A Qualitative Study, DSS Research Report, No. 102, CDS, London.

Hewitt, M. 1983. "Bio-politics and Social Policy: Foucault's Account of Welfare." Theory, Culture and Society 2 (1): 67–84.

Hirst, P. 1981. "The Genesis of the Social." Politics and Power 3: 67–82.

Hockey, J. and A. James. 1993. Growing Up and Growing Old: Ageing and Dependency in the Life Course, London: Sage.

Holstein, J. and Gubrium, J. 2000, The Self We Live By, Oxford University Press: Oxford, U.K..

Holloway, T. 1966. The Apothecaries Act, 1815: A Reinterpretation (part 1) Medical History 10 July 1966, 107–29.

Howe, D. 1992. "Child Abuse and the Bureacratization of Social Work." Sociological Review 40 (3): 491–505.

Howe, A. 1994. Punish and Critique: Towards a Feminist Analysis of Penality. London: Routledge.

Hughes, B. 1995. Older People and Community Care: Critical Theory and Practice. Milton Keynes, U.K.: Oxford University Press.

Ignatieff, M. 1978. A Just Measure of Pain. London: Macmillan.

Ingleby, D. 1985. "Professionals as Socialisers: The 'Psy' Complex." In Research in Law, Deviance and Social Control, edited by A. Scully and S. Spitzer, 7.

Irvine, E. 1954. "Research into Problem Families." British Journal of Psychiatric Social Work 9 (Spring).

Isay, R. A. 1996. Becoming Gay: The Journey to Self-acceptance. New York: Pantheon Books.

Itzin, C. 1986. "Ageism Awareness Training: A Model for Group Work." In Dependency and Interdependency in Old Age: Theoretical Perspectives and Policy Alternatives, edited by C. Phillipson, M. Bernard, and P. Strang. London: Croom Helm.

Izuhara, M. 2000, Family Change and Housing in Postwar Japanese Society, Ashgate: Aldershot, U.K..

Jameson, F. 1991. Postmodernism, or, the Cultural Logic of Late Capitalism. London: Verso.

Jefferys, M., and P. Thane. 1989. "An Ageing Society and Ageing People." In Growing Old in the Twentieth Century, edited by M. Jefferys. London: Routledge.

Jewson, N. D. 1974 Medical Knowledge and the Patronage System in Eighteenth Century England Sociology 8: 369–85.

Jewson, N. D. 1976 The Disappearance of the Sick-Man from the Medical Cosmology Sociology, 10: 225–44.

Johnson, T. J. 1972. Professions and Power MacMillian Press Ltd

Johnson, T. J. 1977. Professions in the Cass Structure in Scase, R (editor) Class Cleavage and Control Allen and Unwin

Johnson, T. 1995. "Governmentality and the Institutionalisation of Expertise." In
Health Professions and the State in Europe, edited by G. Larkin, et al.
London: Routledge.

Jones, C. 1983. State Social Work and the Working Class. London: Macmillan.

Kalish, R. 1979. "The New Ageism and the Failure Models: A Polemic." The Gerontologist 19 (4).

Katz, S. 1996. Disciplining Old Age: The Formation of Gerontological Knowledge, Charlottesville: University Press of Virginia.

————. 1999. "Lifecourse, Lifestyle and Postmodern Culture: Corporate Representations of Later Life," paper presented at Restructuring Work and the Lifecourse: An International Symposium, Institute of Human Development, University of Toronto.

————. 1999. Busy Bodies: Activity, Aging, and the Management of Everyday Life, Journal of Aging Studies, Vol. 14, No. 2, pp. 135–52.

————. 2000. "Busy Bodies: Activity, Aging and the Management of Everyday Life." Journal of Aging Studies 14 (2): 135–52.

Kastenbaum, R. 1993. "Encrusted Elders." In Voices & Visions of Aging, edited by T. Cole. New York: Springer.

Kennedy, G. 1990, College Students Expectations of Grandparent and Grandchild Role Behaviours, The Gerontologist, Vol. 30, No. 1, pp. 43-48.

Kenyon, G., Ruth, J., and Mader, W. 1999, Elements of a Narrative Gerontology, in V. Bengtson and K. Schaie (eds.), Handbook of Theories of Ageing, Springer: New York.

King, H. 2001. Greek and Roman Medicine. London: Bristol Classical Press.

Kivnick, H. 1988. Grandparenthood, Life Review and Psychosocial Development, Journal of Gerontological Social Work, Vol. 12, No. 3, pp. 63–82.

Krug, E. G. 2002. World Report on Violence and Health. Geneva: World Health Organization.

Kunkel, S., and L. Morgan. 1999. Aging: The Social Context. New York: Pine Forge.

Land, H. 1999. The Changing Worlds of Work and Families, Open University Press: Buckingham, U.K..

Lane, J. 1985 The Role of Apprenticeship in Eighteenth Century Medial Education in England. in Bynum W. F. and Porter, R. (1985, editors) William Hunter and the Eighteenth Century Medical World Cambridge University Press

Lindeman, M. 1999. Medicine and Society in Early Modern Europe Cambridge: Cambridge University Press.

Leonard, P. 1997. Postmodern Welfare. London: Sage.

Longino, C. F. 1994. "Pressure from Our Aging Population Will Broaden Our Understanding of Medicine." Academic Medicine 72 (10): 841–47.

Longino, C. F., and J. L. Powell. 2004. "Embodiment and the Study of Aging." In The Body in Human Inquiry: Interdisciplinary Explorations of Embodiment, edited by V. Berdayes. New York: Hampton Press.

Lubove, R. 1966. "Social Work and the Life of the Poor." The Nation, 23 May, 609–11.

Luhmann, N. 1993. Risk: A Sociological Theory. Berlin: Walter de Gruyter.

Lupton, D. 1999. Risk. New York: Routledge.

Lyotard, J. F. 1984. The Postmodern Condition: A Report on Knowledge. Manchester, U.K.: Manchester University Press.

Massumi, B., ed. 1993. The Politics of Everyday Fear. Minneapolis: University of Minnesota Press.

May, T. 1996. Situating Social Theory. Milton Keynes, U.K.: Oxford University Press.

McAdams, D. 1993. The Stories We Live By. New York: Morrow.

McLeod, J. 1997. Narrative and Psychotherapy, Sage: London.

McLennan, G. 1992. "The Enlightenment Project Revisited." In Modernity and Its Futures, edited by S. Hall, D. Held, and T. McGrew. Cambridge: Polity.

Miller, J. 1993. The Passion of Michel Foucault. New York: Simon & Schuster.

Mills, C. W. 1959. The Sociological Imagination. London: Penguin.

Mills, T. 1999, When Grandchildren Grow Up, Journal of Aging Studies, Vol. 13, No. 2, pp. 219–39.

Minkler, M. 1999. Intergenerational Households Headed by Grandparents: Contexts, Realities and Implications for Policy, Journal of Aging Studies, Vol. 13, No. 2, pp. 199–218.

Minkler, M., and C. Estes, eds. 1998. Critical Gerontology: Perspectives from Political and Moral Economy. New York: Baywood.

Mölling, G. 2001. "The Nature of Trust: From George Simmel to a Theory of Expectation, Interpretation and Suspension." Sociology 35 (2): 403–20.

Moody, H. 1998. Aging, Concepts and Controversies. Thousand Oaks, Calif.: Pine Forge Press, Sage.

Morris, D. B. 1991. The Culture of Pain. London: University of California Press.

————. 1998. Illness and Culture in the Postmodern Age. London: University of California Press.

Mouzelis, N. 1991. Back to Sociological Theory. London: Macmillan.

Muirhead-Little, E. (1932) The History of the British Medical Association: 1832 to 1932. London: BMA Publishing.

Murphy, J. W., and C. F. Longino Jr. 1997. "Reason, the Lifeworld, and Appropriate Intervention." Journal of Applied Gerontology 16 (2): 149–51.

Neugarten, B. L. 1974. "Age Groups in American Society and the Rise of the Young-old." Annals of the American Academy of Political and Social Sciences 415: 187–98.

Neugarten, D., ed. 1996. The Meanings of Age. Chicago: University of Chicago Press.

Oberg, P., and L. Tornstam. 1999. "Body Images among Men and Women of Different Ages." Ageing and Society 19: 645–58.

O'Malley, C.D. 1970 The History of Medical Education Berkley and Los Angeles

Pain, R. 2003. "Old Age and Victimisation." In Victimisation, Theory, Research and Policy, edited by P. Davis, et al. London: Macmillan.

Parry, N and Parry, J. 1976 The Rise of The Medical Profession: A Study of Collective Social Mobility New York: Croom Helm Ltd

Patel, N. 1990. A Race against Time. London: Runnymede Trust.

Phillipson, C. 1982. Capitalism and the Construction of Old Age. London: Macmillan.

————. 1988. "Challenging Dependency: Towards a New Social Work with Older People." In Radical Social Work Today, edited by M. Langan and P. Lee. London: Unwin Hyman.

————. 1998. Reconstructing Old Age. London: Sage.

Phillipson, C., and A. Walker, eds. 1986. Ageing and Social Policy: A Critical Assessment. Aldershot, U.K.: Gower.

Phillipson, C., and S. Biggs. 1998. "Modernity and Identity: Themes and Perspectives in the Study of Older Adults." Journal of Aging and Identity 3 (1): 11–23.

Phillipson, C., Bernard, M., Phillips, J., and Ogg, J. (2000), The Family and Community Life of Older People, Routledge: London.

Phillipson, C., and J. L. Powell. 2004. "Risk, Social Welfare and Old Age." In Old Age and Human Agency, edited by E. Tulle. Hauppauge, N.Y.: Nova Science Publishers.

Pillemer, K. and Wolf, R. 1986. Elder Abuse: Conflict in the Family, Auburn House: Westport, CT.

Porter, R. 1995 Medicine in the Enlightenment Amsterdam and Atlanta

Porter, R. 1997 The Greatest Benefit to Mankind: A Medical History of Humanity from Antiquity to the Present London McMillan

Powell, JL and Gilbert, T 2010 Power and Social Work in the U.K.', *Journal of Social Work*, Vol 8, 1, 321–43

Powell, J. L. 1998. "The "Us" and the "Them": Connecting Political Economy and Foucauldian Insights into Ageing Bodies." 1–25, paper presented to the British Sociological Association Annual Conference, University of Edinburgh.

———. 1999. Review of S. Katz (1996), "Disciplining Old Age: The Formation of Gerontological Knowledge." Canadian Journal of Sociology 55 (3): 45–48.

———. 2000. "The Importance of a 'Critical' Sociology of Old Age." Social Science Paper Publisher 3 (1): 1–5.

———. 2001a. "The NHS and Community Care Act 1990 in the United Kingdom: A Critical Review between the Years 1981 to 1996." Sincronia: Journal of Social Sciences and Humanities 4 (4): 1–10.

———. 2001b. "Social Theory and the Aging Body." International Journal of Language, Society and Culture 8 (2): 1–10.

———. 2001c. "Aging and Social Theory: A Sociological Review." Social Science Paper Publisher 4 (2): 1–12.

———. 2001d. "Theorizing Gerontology: The Case of Old Age, Professional Power and Social Policy in the United Kingdom." Journal of Aging & Identity 6 (3): 117–35.

———. 2001e. "Rethinking Structure and Agency: Bio-ethics, Aging and Technologies of the Self." Sincronia: Journal of Social Sciences and Humanities 4 (4): 1–10.

———. 2001f. "Women in British Special Hospitals: A Sociological Approach." Sincronia: Journal of Social Sciences and Humanities 4 (4): 1–14.

———. 2002. "Archaeology and Genealogy: Developments in Foucauldian Gerontology." Sincronia: Journal of Social Sciences and Humanities 5 (1): 1–10.

Powell, J. L., and S. Biggs. 2000. "Managing Old Age: The Disciplinary Web of Power, Surveillance and Normalisation." Journal of Aging and Identity 5 (1): 3–13.

———. 2003. "Foucauldian Gerontology." Electronic Journal of Sociology 7 (3): 1–11.

———. 2004. "Aging, Technologies of Self, and Bio-Medicine: A Foucauldian Excursion." International Journal of Sociology and Social Policy 23 (13): 96–115.

Powell, J. L., and I. Cook. 2000. "'A Tiger Behind and Coming Up Fast': Governmentality and the Politics of Population Control in China." Journal of Aging & Identity 5 (2): 79–90.

———. 2001. "Understanding Foucauldian Philosophy: The Case of the Chinese State and the Surveillance of Older People." International Journal of Language, Society and Culture 8 (1): 1–9.

Powell, J. L., and J. L. Edwards. 2002. "Policy Narratives of Aging: The Right Way, the Third Way or the Wrong Way?" Electronic Journal of Sociology 6 (1): 1–9.

Powell, J. L., and C. F. Longino. 2001. "Towards the Postmodernization of Aging: the Body and Social Theory." Journal of Aging & Identity 6 (4): 20–34.

———. 2002. "Modernism v. Postmodernism: Rethinking Theoretical Tensions in Social Gerontology." Journal of Aging Studies 7 (4): 115–25.

Powell, J. L., and M. M. Edwards. 2003. "Risk and Youth: A Critical Sociological Narrative." International Journal of Sociology and Social Policy 23 (12): 81–95.

Powell, J. L., and A. Wahidin. 2003. "Re-configuring Old Bodies: From the Bio-medical Model to a Critical Epistemology." Journal of Social Sciences and Humanities 26 (2): 1–10.

———. 2004. "Corporate Crime, Aging and Pensions in Great Britain." Journal of Societal and Social Policy 3 (1): 37–55.

Powell, J. and Owen, T. 2007, Reconstructing Postmodernism: Critical Debates, Nova Science: New York.

Qualls, S. 1999, Realising Power in Intergenerational Hierachies, in M. Duffy (ed.), Handbook of Counselling and Psychotherapy with Older Adults, Wiley: New York.

Rabinow, P., ed. 1984. The Foucault Reader. London: Peregrine.

Reddy, S. 1996. "Claims to Expert Knowledge and the Subversion of Democracy: The Triumph of Risk over Uncertainty." Economy and Society 25 (2): 222–54.

Riska, E. 2001 Medical Careers and Feminist Agendas: American, Scandinavian and Russian Women Physicians London: Sage.

Roberto, K. 1990, Grandparent and Grand-child Relationships, in T.H. Brubaker (ed.), Family Relationships in Later Life, Sage: London.

Rose, N. 1993. "Government, Authority, and Expertise in Advanced Liberalism." Economy and Society 22 (3): 283–99.

———. 1996. "The Death of the Social? Refiguring the Territory of Government." Economy and Society 25 (3): 237–56.

Rose, N., and P. Miller. 1992. "Political Power Beyond the State: Problematics of Government." British Journal of Sociology 43 (2): 172–205.

Ryff, C. and Seltzer, M. 1996. The Parental Experience in Midlife, Chicago University Press: Chicago, IL.

Saraga, E., ed. 1998. Embodying the Social: Constructions of Difference. London: Routledge.

Satyamurti, C. 1974. "Women's Occupation and Social Change: The Case of Social Work." Paper presented to 1974 British Sociological Association's Annual Conference.

Scarfe, G. 1993. Scarface. London: Sinclaire-Stevenson.

Scharf, T. and Wenger, G. 1995, International Perspectives on Community Care for Older People, Avebury: Al-dershot, U.K..

Schreck, H. 2000, Community and Caring, UPA: New York.

Schrag, P. 1980. Mind Control. New York: Marion Bowyars.

Seidman, S. 1994. Contested Knowledge: Social Theory in the Postmodern Era. Oxford: Blackwell.

Shilling, C. 1993. The Body & Social Theory. London: Sage.

Shumway, D. 1989. Michel Foucault. Charlottesville: University Press of Virginia.

Silverstein, M. and Bengtson, V.L. 1997, Intergenerational Solidarity and the Structure of Adult Child-Parent Relationships in American Families, American Journal of Sociology, Vol. 103, No. 2, pp. 429–60.

Sinclair, S. 1997 Making Doctors: An Institutional Apprenticeship London: Berg

Sim, J., et al., eds. 1987. Law, Order and the Authoritarian State. Milton Keynes,

U.K.: Oxford University Press.

Siraisis, N. 1990 Medieval and Early Renaissance Medicine: An Introduction to Knowledge and Practice Chicago: Chicago University Press

Smart, B. 1985. Michel Foucault. London: Routledge.

———. 1993. Postmodernity. London: Routledge.

Sontag, S. 1978. "The Double Standard of Ageing." In An Ageing Population, edited by V. Carver and P. Liddiard.M. ilton Keynes, U.K.: Oxford University Press.

———. 1991. Illness as Metaphor and AIDS and Its Metaphors. London: Penguin.

Steuerman, E. 1992. "Habermas vs. Lyotard: Modernity vs. Postmodernity?" In Judging Lyotard, edited by A. Benjamin. London: Routledge.

Stott, M. 1981. Ageing for Beginners. Oxford: Blackwell.

Temkin, O. 1973 Galenism: Rise and Decline of a Medical Philosophy Ithaca, NY: Cornell University Press.

Thompson, E. P. 1967. "Time, Work—Discipline and Industrial Capitalism." Past and Present 38: 56–97.

Thompson, K. 1992. "Social Pluralism and Postmodernity." In Modernity and Its Futures, edited by S. Hall, D. Held, and T. McGrew. Cambridge: Polity.

Thompson, P. 1999, The Role of Grandparents When Parents Part or Die: Some Reflections on the Mythical Decline of the Extended Family, Ageing and Society, Vol. 19, No. 4, pp. 471–503.

Thomson, E. and Minkler, M. 2001, American Grandparents Providing Extensive Childcare to Their Grand-children: Prevalence and Profile, The Gerontologist, Vol. 41, No. 2, pp. 201–9.

Timiras, P., ed. 1997. Physiological Basis of Aging and Geriatrics. 2nd ed. Paris: Masson.

Tinker, A. 1997. Older People in Modern Society. London: Longman.

Townsend, P. 1981. "The Structured Dependency of the Elderly: A Creation of Social Policy in the Twentieth Century." Ageing and Society 1 (1): 5–28.

Townsend, P., and D. Wedderburn. 1965. The Aged in the Welfare State. London: Bell.

Tulle-Winton, E. 1999. "Growing Old and Resistance: Towards a New Cultural Economy of Old Age?" Ageing and Society 19: 281–99.

Tulloch, J., and D. Lupton. 2003. Risk and Everyday Life. London: Sage.

Turner, B. S. 1989. "Ageing, Status Politics and Sociological Theory." British Journal of Sociology 40: 588–606.

Turner, B. S. 1995 Medical Power and Social Knowledge London: Sage Publications

———. 1995. "Ageing and Identity." In Images of Ageing, edited by M. Featherstone and A. Wernick. London: Routledge.

Twigg, J. 2000. "Social Policy and the Body." In Rethinking Social Policy, edited by G. Lewis, S. Gewirtz, and J. Clarke. London: Sage.

U.K.G, U.K. Government. 1981. Growing Older, HMSO: London.

U.K.G, U.K. Government. 1989. Community Care: An Agenda for Action, HMSO: London.

U.K.G, U.K. Government. 1990. NHS and Community Care Act, HMSO: London.

U.K.G, U.K. Government. 1993. No Longer Afraid: The Safeguard of Older People in Domestic Settings, HMSO: London.

U.K.G, U.K. Government. 2000a. Winning the Generation Game, www.cabinetoffice.gov.uk.

U.K.G, U.K. Government. 2000b. Supporting Families, HMSO: London.

Veyne, P. 1980. Foucault revolutionne l'histoire. Paris: Éditions Seuil.

Victor, C. 1987. Old Age in Modern Society. London: Croom Helm.

Vincent, J. 1996. Inequality and Old Age. London: University College London Press.

Vincent, J. 1999. Politics, Power and Old Age. Buckingham: Open University Press.

Virilio, P. 1983. Pure War. New York: Semiotext.

Visker, R. 1995. Michel Foucault. Verso: London.

Wahidin, A., and J. L. Powell. 2001. "The Loss of Aging Identity: Social Theory, Old Age and the Power of Special Hospitals." Journal of Aging & Identity 6 (1): 31–49.

———. 2003. "Reconfiguring Old Bodies: From the Biomedical Model to a Critical Epistemology." Journal of Social Sciences and Humanities 26 (2): 1–10.

Waldrop, D., Weber, J., Herald, S., Pruett, J., Cooper, K., and Jouzapavicius, K. 1999. Wisdom and Life Experience: How Grandfathers Mentor Their Grandchildren, Journal of Aging and Identity, Vol. 4, No. 1, pp. 33–46.

Walker, A. 1981. "Towards a Political Economy of Old Age." Ageing and Society 1: 73–94.

———. 1985. The Care Gap: How Can Local Authorities Meet the Needs of the Elderly? London: Local Government Information Unit.

———. 1987. "The Social Construction of Dependency in Old Age." In The State or the Market? edited by M. Loney, 41–57. London: Sage.

———. 1990. "Poverty and Inequality in Old Age." In Ageing and Society, edited by J. Bond and P. Coleman. London: Sage.

Walker, A. 2002, A Strategy for Active Ageing, International Social Security Review, Vol. 55, No. 1, pp. 121–39.

Walker, A. and Aspalter, C. 2008, Securing the Future for Old Age in Europe, Casa Verde: Hong Kong.

Walker, A., and G. Naegele. 1999. The Politics of Old Age in Europe. Milton Keynes, U.K.: Oxford University Press.

Warnes, A., ed. 1996. Human Ageing and Later Life. London: Edward Arnold.

Wenger, C. 1984, Support Networks for Older People, CSPRD: Bangor, U.K..

Wilkinson, I. 2001. "Social Theories of Risk Perception: At Once Indispensable and Insufficient." Current Sociology 49 (1): 1–22.

Williams, F. 1994. Social Policy: A Critical Introduction, 2nd ed. Oxford: Blackwell.

Wynne, B. 1987. Risk Management and Hazardous Waste. Berlin: Springer.

Index

abuse: of elderly population, 59, 98, 119, 125; familial, 126
accidents, 114
Achenbaum, Andrew, 39
activity theory, 50–51
adoption, 59
Africa, 145–47
African Americans, 132–33
age-based identities, 128
ageism, 12, 34–35, 38–39, 127; disengagement theory and, 50; institutional, 52; stereotypes of, 37, 44, 52, 54, 138
Age of Reason, 25
age prejudice, 8
aging: biological, 14, 28–33; biomedical sciences and, 25–29; construction of problems in, 33–38; culture of, 5, 35, 153; demographic construction of, 40–44; feminism and, 55–57; Foucault and, 78, 104–7; gender and, 55–57, 61; global, 82, 137–51; interpretation of, 3, 13, 47–48, 139; modern theories of, 8–9; narrative and, 123–35, 157; political economy of, 51–55, 63, 105; postmodern theories of, 8–9, 63–65, 81; problematization of, 7–8, 69, 86–87, 155; psychological, 14, 28–33; race and, 57–59; reconstructions of, 137–39, 153–57; sexuality and, 59–60, 109; social constructions of, 14, 45–48, 153; social context of, 38–40; theoretical framework of, 1–5

aging body: biotechnology and, 79–81; gender issues and, 75–79; popular culture and, 74–75; theorizing, 69–73
AIDS/HIV, 133, 146–47
alliances, intergenerational, 130
Alzheimer's disease, 30, 34
Americas, 137, 140–42
appropriation, limits of, 106
Arber, S., 55–56
The Archaeology of Knowledge (Foucault), 88
Armstrong, D., 22
Asia, 142–44
Atkinson, P., 23
autonomization, 101–2, 114; self-autonomization, 119–20

baby boom generation, 41, 140, 144, 149
Bacon, Francis, 74
Baltes, B., 32
Baltes, M. R., 32–33
Barthes, Roland, 87
Bartky, Sandra, 71
Baudrillard, Jean, 65, 68
Bauman, Zygmunt, 2, 73, 82
Beck, U., 108, 115–18, 121, 127
Becker, H., 23
Beckett, Samuel, 74
Bengtson, Vern L., 3, 6, 126
Beth Johnson Foundation, 132
Beveridge, William, 51

About the Authors

John Martyn Chamberlain is lecturer in criminology and social policy at Loughborough University. His academic research interests include criminological and sociological theory as well as risk, governance, and surveillance studies. At a practical policy level he is particularly interested in the relationships that exist between health policy formation, professional governance frameworks and contemporary shifts in criminal justice policy and practice

Jason L. Powell is divisional head of social sciences at University of Central Lancashire. His research interests are focused on aging, social theory, globalization, power, and risk. He has published extensively on issues affecting older people in the United Kingdom, the United States, and China. His most recent work explores relationship of global aging and social theory.

Made in the USA
San Bernardino, CA
08 October 2013